The Instructional Design Knowled

The Instructional Design Knowledge Base: Theory, Research, and Practice provides ID professionals and students at all levels with a comprehensive exploration of the theories and research that serve as a foundation for current and emerging ID practice. This book offers both current and classic interpretations of theory from a range of disciplines and approaches. It encompasses general systems, communication, learning, early instructional, media, conditions-based, constructivist design, and performance improvement theories.

Features include:

- Rich representations of the ID literature;
- Concise theory summaries;
- Specific examples of how theory is applied to practice;
- Recommendations for future research;
- A glossary of related terms; and
- A comprehensive list of references.

A perfect resource for instructional design and technology doctoral, masters, and educational specialist certificate programs, *The Instructional Design Knowledge Base* provides students and scholars with a comprehensive background for ID practice and a foundation for future ID thinking.

Rita C. Richey is Professor Emeritus of Instructional Technology at Wayne State University.

James D. Klein is Professor of Educational Technology at Arizona State University.

Monica W. Tracey is Associate Professor of Instructional Technology at Wayne State University.

The Instructional Design Knowledge Base

Theory, Research, and Practice

Rita C. Richey
James D. Klein
Monica W. Tracey

 Routledge
Taylor & Francis Group

NEW YORK AND LONDON

First published 2011
by Routledge
711 Third Avenue, New York, NY 10017

Simultaneously published in the UK
by Routledge
2 Park Square, Milton Park, Abingdon, Oxon OX14 4RN

Routledge is an imprint of the Taylor & Francis Group, an informa business

© 2011 Taylor & Francis

The right of Rita C. Richey, James D. Klein, and Monica W. Tracey to be identified as authors of this work has been asserted by them in accordance with sections 77 and 78 of the Copyright, Designs and Patents Act 1988.

Typeset in Minion by Swales & Willis Ltd, Exeter, Devon

Library of Congress Cataloging in Publication Data
Richey, Rita.
  The instructional design knowledge base : theory, research, and practice / Rita C. Richey, James D. Klein,
  Monica W. Tracey.
  p. cm.
  Includes bibliographical references and index.
  1. Teaching. 2. Instructional systems—Design. 3. Continuing education. 4. Occupational training.
  5. Human information processing. I. Klein, James D. II. Tracey, Monica W. III. Title.
  LC5219.R495 2011
  371.3—dc22
  2010016006

ISBN13: 978–0–415–80200–0 (hbk)
ISBN13: 978–0–415–80201–7 (pbk)
ISBN13: 978–0–203–84098–6 (ebk)

For the next wonderful generation:
Madeline, Lily, and Mason

For Bob:
Without him, the field would still be a mystery to me

For my family:
Andrew, my rock, my joy, and my forever
And our daughters Carly and Caitlin,
May your lives be filled with as much joy as you have given us

CONTENTS

LIST OF TABLES

LIST OF FIGURES

PREFACE

This book is a product of passion for the field and a lot of hard work. The process of writing it has left us once again in awe of the breadth and complexity of the field of instructional design (ID). We have attempted to describe in some detail the ID knowledge base, reviewing its broad theory base, the research that supports this theory (noting the lack of research in some instances), and how all of this translates into ID practice. We anticipate that it will be read and used primarily by ID scholars and advanced graduate students. At the same time, we hope that practitioners will be able to use this book as a basis for making and justifying the many decisions they face in the course of an ID project.

KEY ELEMENTS OF THE BOOK

We define the ID theory base quite broadly. As such, we address the foundational theories from other disciplines, as well as those which have been constructed by ID scholars. We present a range of theoretical positions including time-honored and modern interpretations of theory long recognized as instrumental in shaping ID practice. For example, communication theory has always been considered important, but what is communication from a constructivist point of view? We also discuss theory that is not always thought of as foundational to ID, such as social learning theory.

This book was also written with the assumption that a theory stems not only from research and theorizing, but also from the philosophical orientations of its community of advocates. Therefore, we have also explored the underlying philosophical positions of each theory cluster. For example, we explain how some early theorists considered general systems theory a philosophy of nonlinear thinking.

Research is also critical to the theory discussions in this book. We recognize the basic empirical support from which a theory was formed, and explore in more detail the studies that attempt to validate the ID applications of these theories. Finally, we suggest some new research that we think would contribute to the application of these theories in a variety of design settings.

In addition to this book's emphasis on theory, it is filled with descriptions of ID practice that is rooted in theory. Examples of current and emerging practice are both discussed. For instance, we discuss how social networking tools are used in constructivist ID.

Finally, we have attempted not to simply describe and explain the theoretical foundations of ID in this book, but to synthesize the information from each of these theories into an instructional design knowledge base. This knowledge base takes the form of a multifaceted taxonomy that we hope will serve as a guide to understanding ID practice while guiding future ID research and theory development.

This book is based upon an extensive review of the literature. At the end of each chapter we provide a concise summary of each theory base and its elements that contribute to the knowledge base. In addition, there is a full glossary of terms to further aid your understanding of these many complex concepts.

OVERVIEW OF THE BOOK

This book consists of an introductory chapter, a discussion of eight theory bases, and a description of the final knowledge base. Below we describe the ten chapters that comprise the main body of the book.

Chapter 1, "The Dimensions of an Instructional Design Knowledge Base", explores the nature and scope of instructional design, as well as the characteristics of knowledge bases in general. It examines the role of theory and models in a knowledge base, and introduces the six major domains of the ID knowledge base.

Chapter 2, "General Systems Theory", discusses one of the foundational ID theory bases through an examination of the major elements of systems theory and the systems approach, its most common application in the field of ID. In addition, this chapter identifies and describes new trends in systems analysis and systems synthesis.

Chapter 3, "Communication Theory", presents the evolution of communication models from the classic work of Shannon and Weaver to current constructivist views of the communication process. The impact of communication theory on ID is explored in terms of the role of language, the communication channel, and the attention-getting properties of messages. The unique role of mediated communication and culture are also explored.

Chapter 4, "Learning Theory", examines the classical views of behavioral and cognitive learning, as well as social learning theory. Not only are the basic tenets of each of these theory clusters described, but examples of the many ways learning theory impacts ID are also discussed. This discussion includes recent applications of learning theory, such as contextual analysis.

Chapter 5, "Early Instructional Theory", focuses on the contributions of the early scholars of curriculum and instruction (e.g., Ralph Tyler), individualized instruction (e.g., Benjamin Bloom), and cognitive approaches to instruction (e.g., Jerome Bruner). Such work has had an enormous impact on ID, including identifying and sequencing behavioral objectives, and the management of instruction.

Chapter 6, "Media Theory", provides an overview of the role of media in the learning process—how it represents reality, provides structure, and creates entire learning environments. This chapter also includes a full discussion of the various approaches to media selection and media use.

Chapter 7, "Conditions-Based Theory", highlights the key principles that distinguish conditions-based theory and it emphasizes the work of the theory's major scholars, Robert Gagné and David Merrill. This chapter also addresses the ways in which conditions-based theory is currently being refined and developed, such as through the design of instruction for complex learning and problem solving.

Chapter 8, "Constructivist Design Theory", explores the ways in which constructivist philosophy influences instructional design by examining its three key principles. Then we discuss the manner in which these principles impact the various facets of the ID process. This discussion also includes an exploration of how constructivist thinking has reshaped ID processes and models.

Chapter 9, "Performance Improvement Theory", centers on the issues facing designers who focus on enhancing individual and organizational performance. Five basic performance improvement models and three approaches to evaluation are described. The performance improvement orientation to ID is explored in terms of competency development, analysis, intervention strategies, transfer of training, and evaluation.

Chapter 10, "A Taxonomy of the Instructional Design Knowledge Base", concludes this book. We first discuss the general nature of taxonomies and then describe how we consolidated the vast array of information presented throughout this book into a taxonomy of ID. Finally, we present taxonomies for the six domains of the field and discuss how they can be used by practitioners and researchers.

In this book we have tried to describe the very complex intellectual base of instructional design, and at the same time describe the diverse approaches to ID practice that reflect this foundation. The theory-research-practice interactions are included throughout. In addition, we are making a call for continued empirical work to support these and future applications of ID theory. Perhaps you will be encouraged to undertake such research or perhaps the formation of new theory that others may write about.

Rita C. Richey   James D. Klein
Monica W. Tracey   Tempe, Arizona
Detroit, Michigan

ACKNOWLEDGMENTS

We have stood on the shoulders of many scholars while writing this book. Two of the people whose insightful work have shaped our thinking and in turn this book are Pat Smith and Tim Ragan. As we go to press, the ID field has been saddened by the passing of our good friend Tim. We want to thank Pat and Tim for their contributions to ID and to this book. Their influence goes on.

There are other "giants of the field" whose presence is felt in this book as well, and we thank them for their years of dedicated work. (If we started a specific list, we would invariably leave someone out. So, the better part of valor is to be mercifully general.)

We also owe our great appreciation to others who have helped bring this project to fruition, including the students who "tested" chapters in their classes, and Sara Kacin and Kelly Unger who were involved in literature searches. Family members often provided more than moral support; Jayne Klein and Leslie Klein lent their time and computing skills to many tables and figures, and Charles Elder provided frequent solicited and unsolicited opinions. Finally, James Quinn used portions of the book in his teaching and provided very important input. This book is much richer due to all of you.

As usual, the staffs at Routledge and Taylor & Francis have been of invaluable help during the course of this project. Special thanks to Sarah Burrows, who helped bring this project into existence, and to Alexandra Sharp and Alex Masulis, who have helped us end it. We also thank the reviewers who gave generously of their time, and whose work, while masked in anonymity, did so much to shape the final product.

1

THE DIMENSIONS OF AN INSTRUCTIONAL DESIGN KNOWLEDGE BASE

Instructional design (ID) today is an established profession, as well as an area of study. As a profession, it consists of a series of well-defined competencies, and an active group of practitioners who work in increasingly complex and sophisticated environments. As an area of study, it has a rich and growing foundation of research and theory viewed from increasingly diverse points of view. Both the practice and the study of ID can be seen in two ways: as strategies for creating particular products and as the implementation and management of the overall design process. In either of these orientations ID is a planning process. As such, it is distinguished from development processes, the actual production of instructional materials.

The immediate precursors of this field were research and development of training materials produced during World War II and the programmed instruction movement (Reiser, 2007a). However, the ID field did not emerge in a formal sense until the 1960s in higher education settings, even though the term "instructional design" was not typically used until the 1970s. Instead many designers thought of themselves as educational psychologists, media specialists, or perhaps training designers (Dick, 1987). Since the 1980s, the preponderance of ID practice has occurred in the private sector, primarily in business and industrial settings. However, designers also work in government and military settings, health care, P–12 schools, and even in nonprofit and community settings. Correspondingly, there are hundreds of academic programs that educate and train these professionals.

Designers work with all types of instruction, including employee training workshops, online and web-based instruction, and train-the-trainer programs. Moreover, in the current milieu, instructional designers also deal with noninstructional interventions created to solve workplace problems for which training is not the appropriate solution.

This book is not about how to design instruction, but rather it explores the intellectual foundations of the ID field, its knowledge base. We will consider the wide range of ID theoretical and conceptual foundations that currently shape the field. In doing so, we will examine eight clusters of theories, the underlying philosophical orientations of each, the evolution of such thinking, and the research which supports these theories. In addition, we will explore the traditional and emerging applications of each theory to ID. Before we begin this task, however, we will discuss:

- The dimensions of ID; and
- The nature of disciplinary knowledge bases, including the role of theories and models.

INSTRUCTIONAL DESIGN: AN OVERVIEW

ID, even though it is an established field, is at times viewed from various perspectives. In this section we will first examine alternative definitions of ID and then present the one that we are using here. In addition we will explore the scope of the field and its major areas of concern.

The Definition of Instructional Design

ID has been defined over the years in a variety of ways. Most of the definitions high-light process. Smith and Ragan's (2005) definition fits into this genre, although theirs is quite generalized. To them, ID is "the systematic and reflective process of translating principles of learning and instruction into plans for instructional materials, activities, information resources, and evaluation" (p. 4). This definition emphasizes ID's scientific foundations and the range of products emanating from ID projects. The vast majority of process-oriented definitions, however, are closely tied to the traditional instructional systems design (ISD) process (i.e., analysis, design, development, implementation, and evaluation). Dick, Carey, and Carey (2009) simply say that ID is ISD. While others may not be as direct, in essence they are agreeing with this approach (see Morrison, Ross, & Kemp, 2007; Piskurich, 2006; Seels & Glasgow, 1998 for example).

One exception would be Reigeluth (1983), who interprets ID as a facet of instruction, "the process of deciding what methods of instruction are best for bringing about desired changes in student knowledge and skills for a specific course content and a specific student population" (p. 7). Reigeluth's orientation accentuates strategy selection and de-emphasizes the analysis phase; it is also less compatible with the current emphasis on non-instructional interventions. Nonetheless, here too design is viewed as a planning activity.

Some ID definitions stress function more than process. Gustafson and Branch (2007) say that "Instructional design (ID) is a systematic process that is employed to develop education and training programs in a consistent and reliable fashion" (p. 11). Piskurich (2006) posits that "Instructional design stripped to its basics is simply a process for helping you to create effective training in an efficient manner" (p. 1). Another function-oriented interpretation of ID is presented by Reigeluth (1983). He describes ID as "a body of knowledge that prescribes instructional actions to optimize desired outcomes, such as achievement and affect" (p. 5).

In spite of the alternative emphases of these various definitions, we believe that there would likely be little fundamental disagreement among these scholars as to the essential nature of ID. We presume that most would agree with Smith and Ragan's (2005) position that "Design is distinguished from other forms of instructional planning by the level of precision, care and expertise that is employed in the planning, development, and evaluation process" (p. 6). In keeping with this position, we think:

ID is the science and art of creating detailed specifications for the development, evaluation, and maintenance of situations which facilitate learning and performance.

The Scope of Instructional Design

ID encompasses a broad range of activity from analysis through evaluation. It includes the initial planning steps in a project and often works through the creation of procedures that ensure the continued operation of the intervention. At times, design tasks are blurred with development tasks. Some designers write materials such as trainer's guides, work sheets, or job aids. While they typically make media selection decisions, they seldom produce the final piece of mediated instruction. Even though many view evaluation as a separate activity, designers typically write test items and collect performance data. They also often conduct evaluations of existing products. While designers are intimately concerned with the delivery of instruction, they are not necessarily teachers or trainers.

To many designers, ID processes are almost synonymous with the various design phases. But ID knowledge (and consequently the entire knowledge base) addresses more than the procedural steps in these phases. ID knowledge relates to a wide variety of topics that impact many parts of the design process. We picture the ID knowledge base as relating to the following six content domains:

- Learners and Learning Processes;
- Learning and Performance Contexts;
- Content Structure and Sequence;
- Instructional and Noninstructional Strategies;
- Media and Delivery Systems; and
- Designers and Design Processes.

These topics cover the most critical ID concepts, processes, and research.[1] Design is intimately involved with learning and with learners. The arrays of instructional and noninstructional strategies are often dependent upon our understanding of how people learn and perform and how their backgrounds impact learning and performance. Design processes are also dependent upon the nature of the content, the type of learning environment, and the many media and delivery options that can be incorporated into a particular design. Moreover, design processes are impacted to some extent by the characteristics of the designers themselves.

These domains encompass a broad array of specific elements that play a role in ID. Learning contexts, for example, refer to instructional settings as well as organizational climates. Each domain impacts the traditional design phases in multiple ways. These domains, however, are not distinct unto themselves, and in many cases they overlap. Figure 1.1 portrays a view of the major domains of the ID knowledge base.

---

1 While evaluation is usually considered a part of the instructional design process, we are viewing the general field of evaluation as a separate area of research and practice, one upon which designers draw as they do their work. We discuss evaluation topics at various points in this book, but do not view it as a distinct ID domain.

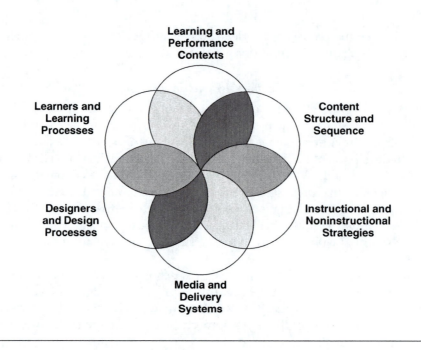

Figure 1.1 The Domains of the Instructional Design Knowledge Base.

Throughout this book, we will build on this framework as we explore the ID knowledge base in detail. We will identify the many elements of ID and thereby expand these domains through an investigation of the major sources of ID knowledge.

THE CHARACTERISTICS OF A KNOWLEDGE BASE

In this section we will discuss knowledge bases in general, beginning with an examination of what a knowledge base is from our point of view. Theory is a principle component of any disciplinary knowledge base, and we will describe the various types of theory and their uses. However, in the ID field many types of models also dominate thinking. Consequently, we also explore the nature of models here.

The Nature of Disciplinary Knowledge

In the simplest interpretation, a knowledge base is what a field has learned about itself over time. As such, a knowledge base is always growing and is never static; there is an evolutionary quality to it. A knowledge base is dependent upon the collective ingenuity of those who have worked or studied in a field. Knowledge bases can also be influenced by the advancements in other related disciplines and professions, since fields are seldom isolated entities. Finally, knowledge bases are infused with the problems and issues that have defined a field throughout its history, and by the various positions taken with respect to these issues.

The Components of a Knowledge Base

In simpler and more concrete terms, Lundvall and Johnson (1994) see knowledge bases as consisting of four components:

- Know-what;
- Know-why;
- Know-how; and
- Know-who.

This view can be applied to ID knowledge. Design consists of factual knowledge relating to many topics, such as the definitions of a mental model or a learning hierarchy. The knowledge base also consists of scientific knowledge, such as information processing theory or findings from current brain research and their implications for formal learning. The knowledge gained from research provides the rationale for solving design problems in a given way. Designers, of course, have skills—how to perform the many tasks that are part of ID. For example, they need to know how to conduct a task analysis or how to construct a design document. Finally, designers (especially those with academic training) know of the people who have contributed to the ID field, and in turn to its knowledge base. For example, they would know of Robert Gagné's contributions to the field.

The components of the ID knowledge base can be viewed in two ways: as theoretical knowledge and as practical knowledge. Wallace (1979) distinguishes these two concepts in this way: "Theoretical knowledge has for its end the attainment of truth and that alone, whereas practical knowledge seeks truth as a means to an end, so as to order it to practice or operation" (p. 263). In other words, knowledge can be an end in itself, or the end can be exemplary practice. These orientations, however, are not mutually exclusive. Theories can be practical and applied as well as abstract, and practical knowledge can be based upon theoretical knowledge. Wallace (1979) calls disciplines that are both theoretical and practical the practice sciences. This is similar to John Dewey's very early discussion of "linking sciences"—those which connect learning theory and educational practice (Reigeluth, 1983, 1997).

In many respects, ID falls into the category of a practice or a linking science. It seeks ultimately to improve practice, and as such its knowledge base is shaped by practitioner experience, as well as by theory and its foundational research. At times it seems there are conflicts between experience and theory, and these discrepancies have challenged many designers. One way of dealing with such discrepancies is to heed Kaplan's (1964) insight that we learn *from* experience rather than *by* experience. Experience plus reflection then creates the lessons that become part of the ID knowledge base.

Alternative Views of Knowledge

This knowledge base discussion thus far addresses what kind of knowledge is appropriate, but one can also examine knowledge bases in terms of the way such information is synthesized. Diesing (1991) suggests that there are three types of knowledge:

(1) systems of laws which describe interconnected regularities of society; (2) descriptions, from the inside, of a way of life, community, person, belief system, or scientific community's beliefs; (3) structural models, mathematical or verbal, of dynamic processes exemplified in particular cases. (p. 325)

These three orientations to knowledge imply various methods of inquiry: traditional quantitative research and theorizing, qualitative research and participant observations, and model building. All of these methodologies are seen in the ID literature. These alternative approaches to inquiry also reflect alternative views of the nature of knowledge and truth that have dominated the philosophy of science over the years.

In the first half of the twentieth century there was a common adherence to the tenets of logical empiricism or logical positivism. This thinking relied upon the value of sensory data as a means of determining truth. It eschewed descriptions of the external world that emphasized "the essence of things" (Deising, 1991, p. 4); it avoided any study of reality that was not based upon empirical observation and verification. The ideal products of such inquiry were universal generalizations. However, because such thinking discounted the impact of culture, history, and individual characteristics, it ultimately lost general support. Post-positivists recognized the role of these factors, but they still valued the power of empirical observation and conditional generalizations. Diesing's emphasis on systems of laws describing societal norms is consistent with this latter orientation.

On the other hand, the hermeneutic approach to science "does not require detachment or neutrality of the scientist. It required involvement, even participation in the culture of the author" (Diesing, 1991, p. 122). This orientation views knowledge as specific to an individual rather than generalized to a large population. Knowledge is a function of what the individual already knows. Inquiry then involves a study of actions in context. Researchers determine meaning through dialogue with "informants". This leads to Diesing's second type of knowledge: inside descriptions of particular beliefs. The hermeneutic scholar is "skeptical of aggregate data; he observes that quantitative measurement is based on a preunderstanding of shared meanings" (Diesing, 1991, p. 145). Ultimately, the concern with "shared meanings" can lead to doubts in the value of any generalization. This position continues to create controversy.

The emphasis on models (Diesing's third view of knowledge) evolved out of pragmatic approaches to problem solving and operations research. It also reflected the applied science orientation to knowledge. Knowledge should be configured in such as a way so that it is useful in solving daily problems. It also reflects approaching complex situations by breaking them into small parts and describing one part at a time. Again, this approach emphasizes quantification (Diesing, 1991).

All of these ways of viewing and presenting knowledge are evident in the ID literature. Over time, some views have been more dominant than others, but the ID knowledge base reflects all interpretations of the meaning of truth. It includes a wide variety of theories based upon multiple types of research and many models. Since many scholars have argued that the existence of multiple approaches to research and multiple views of the world are essential to the growth of science, ID is in good stead.

The Nature of Theory

A theory, according to Hoover and Donovan (1995) is "a set of related propositions that attempts to explain, and sometimes to predict, a set of events" (p. 69). However, Kaplan (1964) provides a valuable insight: "the formation of theories is not just the discovery of a hidden fact; the theory is a way of looking at the facts, or organizing and representing them" (p. 309). It involves more than observation; it "calls for the exercise of creative imagination" (p. 308).

Types of Theory

The Hoover and Donovan definition implies a theory with a formal, rather narrative style. There is much in the literature called "theory" that is not written in proposition form. This is especially true of current ID theory. Many scholars and philosophers of science recognize varying types and levels of theory. Snow (1973), for example, identifies six levels of theories progressing from formative hypotheses to a formal axiomatic theory. The goal of each is an empirically-based explanation of events that clearly identifies all relevant variables and their relationships.

A common view, however, is to categorize theories as being either inductive or deductive, reflecting the way in which they were constructed. Inductive theories consist of general verbal statements that ideally describe and explain the critical phenomena. These statements are made after examination of a series of particulars, usually data about the way a small group of individuals behave.

For example, assume you are going to construct a proposition related to the effects of mediated instruction. You would review the literature for research results relating to this topic. Perhaps you would find results relating to the use of online instruction, older computer-assisted instruction, or a variety of other media. You would conduct your own research to address gaps in the literature. A general proposition would be constructed by integrating the findings from the various studies. This one proposition might become part of a more comprehensive inductive theory concerning media effects.

The ideas that inspire the hypotheses of underlying research frequently come from other theories. This has been especially true with ID. In addition, hypotheses are based upon theoretical concepts which are not yet organized into theoretical frameworks but are prominent in the thinking and research of the discipline. Once tested, these confirmed hypotheses also contribute to an inductive theory. This theory would then require extended verification and testing using new sets of data, followed by replication.

Deductive theories, on the other hand, are constructed using deductive logic. Deductive thinking involves the development of additional propositions by logically deriving them from a series of general assumptions. Typically, these assumptions are grounded in empirical data and have been confirmed through a testing and validation process. The deductive phase involves movement from general to specific thinking. Blalock (1969) is one of many who caution that all theory, inductive or deductive,

> . . . must be grounded in empirical data. It would be highly misleading to suggest that theories are first arrived at by a deductive process and *then* tested. The actual process is much more fluid than this and undoubtedly always involves an inductive effort. (p. 8; emphasis in the original)

Zhao (1996) notes the popularity of theory and theory construction in the late 1960s and 1970s and then the subsequent movement from searching for general *laws* to a search for the *conditions* under which phenomena occurred. This coincided with recognition of methodological pluralism in theory construction. Many approaches to theory building are now acceptable, as long as the concepts and the relationships between them are clearly defined, and the propositions are testable. However, empirical testing was and still is the critical factor since "the difference between a good hunch and a good theory lies in the fact that while the former is based on intuition, the latter on empirical evidence" (Zhao, 1996, p. 316).

Functions of Theory

Theories, regardless of their form, serve a variety of functions. Again Hoover and Donovan (1995) have described these succinctly. They cite four major uses of theory in social scientific thinking:

1. Theory provides *patterns* for the interpretation of data.
2. Theory *links* one study with another.
3. Theories supply frameworks within which concepts and variables acquire *special significance.*
4. Theory allows us to interpret the *larger meaning* of our findings for ourselves and others. (p. 40; emphasis in the original)

Thus, theories are useful. They provide the structure through which one's interpretation of complex activities can be verified. Littlejohn (1989) concisely describes the use of theories: "The first function of theory is to organize and summarize knowledge" (p. 21). This is important to a field such as ID which encompasses such a broad spectrum of study and is applied to many diverse settings.

Hoover and Donovan's general definition of "theory" speaks to an overall explanatory role. The basis, however, of such explanation is description. Often the research which forms the foundations for construction of propositions is of a descriptive nature. Dubin (1969) asserts that "the more profound the descriptive knowledge, the better the theory is likely to be" (p. 237). Thus, descriptive research is critical to a knowledge base. It can lead to descriptive and explanatory theory.

For many scholars, the ultimate role of theory is that of a predictor of events. This, however, requires a sophisticated level of development which is difficult to achieve for theories related to human behavior where there is typically a high degree of uncertainty. Moreover, there are those who question whether prediction is even possible in areas related to human learning which are governed by social factors and individual differences (Jonassen, Hennon, Ondrusek, Samouilova, Spaulding, Yueh et al., 1997). Others welcome these complexities in the effort to improve existing theory and devise new predictive theory at the same time.

The Nature of Models

Models have been equated with theories in some literature, but we are separating the two concepts here. Various types of models are used in ID practice, and they can serve an important role in theory construction as well. In all cases, however, the term "model" implies a representation of reality presented with a degree of structure and order, and models are typically idealized and simplified views of reality.

Harre (1960) identified two kinds of models: micromorphs and paramorphs. Micromorphs are physical, visual replicas, such as a computer simulation or a scale model of a large object. Paramorphs, on the other hand, are symbolic models, typically using verbal descriptions. As Harre (1960) notes, the simplest example of a paramorph is the verbal analogy. The more common paramorphs can be categorized as either:

- Conceptual models;
- Procedural models; or
- Mathematical models.

A conceptual model is the type most likely to be confused with theory, as it is a general, verbal description of a particular view of reality. Conceptual models are usually more abstract than theories that deal with more specific concepts and propositions (Fawcett, 1989). Typically, they are not truly explanatory, but the relevant components are presented and fully defined. A conceptual model is a product of synthesizing related research; it is more likely to be supported by experience, or only limited amounts of data. Conceptual models are analytic in nature. They typically describe the relevant events based upon deductive processes of logic and analysis, as well as inferences from observations. Conceptual models, like theories, are usually general and context-free.

Taxonomies are conceptual models. Another example from the ID field would be Dale's (1946) Cone of Experience. (See Chapter 6.) This is a diagram which portrays the relationships between various media in terms of their proximity to reality and as a continuum from concrete to abstract. However, conceptual models can be totally narrative, and at times are called "conceptual frameworks". These models can facilitate research, and can serve as the intellectual framework for theory development. Moreover, Fawcett (1989) suggests that all theory is dependent upon preexisting conceptual models.

Procedural models are more straightforward. They describe how to perform a task. In ID such steps are usually based upon the knowledge of what creates a successful product. This knowledge is usually either experience-based or it is derived from another related theory or model. Procedural models often serve as guides to the solution of specific problems. While most procedural models are verbal, they may be visual as well. A process flowchart would be a good example of a visual procedural model. The most common procedural models in ID, however, are the instructional systems design models that prescribe the steps that should be followed in a design project. Ideally, procedural models would be based upon a confirmed theory or at least evaluation data, rather than totally upon experience-based knowledge.

Mathematical models are equations which describe the relationships between various components of a situation. By applying data from new situations to a mathematical model, one can simulate the results. To devise a precise formula, one must have a great deal of data from similar situations, so that the exact relationships can be determined. Mathematical models can play several roles. The typical function is to reflect the tenets of a theory in a quantitative fashion. Thus, mathematical models become highly abstract, even as they are highly precise. They are always dependent, however, upon a narrative description for full explanation. There are few mathematical models currently relating to ID, although mathematical modeling is an important method of theory construction in other social sciences, such as economics and political science.

FOUNDATIONS OF THE INSTRUCTIONAL DESIGN KNOWLEDGE BASE

The six ID domains provide the structure for the ID knowledge base. These domains can be fully defined and explicated by the theoretical foundations of the field. ID relies upon theories and models from other disciplines as well as those which have evolved from its own history to complete these definitions. As such, the ID knowledge base is multidisciplinary in nature. The theories from other disciplines that are most critical to this field are:

- General Systems Theory;
- Communication Theory;
- Learning Theory; and
- Early Instructional Theory.

For the most part, these theories were formed prior to the emergence of ID as a separate field of study and as a profession, and most serve as ID's intellectual ancestors.

Since ID became established in its own right, it has been developing its own theory base. The most critical contributors to the ID knowledge base emanating from our own scholars are:

- Media Theory;
- Conditions-Based Theory;
- Constructivist Design Theory; and
- Performance Improvement Theory.

We will explore each of these eight theory bases. In Chapter 2, we begin with an examination of general systems theory.

2

GENERAL SYSTEMS THEORY

General systems theory (GST) is a key part of the theoretical family tree of instructional design (ID). Traditionally, GST principles have shaped the direction and orientation of most ID procedures. Conscious (or unconscious) adherence to this theory spawns systemic and systematic thinking, both of which provide a basis for understanding and solving a wide range of design problems.

The term "general systems theory" refers to one way of viewing our environment. There are no formal statements of law, but rather a series of concepts and orientations which have been used by many disciplines to organize and show the relationships between the various parts of the empirical world. GST has an interdisciplinary orientation.

GST was rooted originally in Viennese biological research and studies of the philosophy of science. Weiss's first descriptions of biological system theory were made in the 1920s after his butterfly research led him to question whether studying isolated parts of a complex organism was a reasonable approach to learning about the organism as a whole (Drack & Apfalter, 2007). At approximately the same time through the study of philosophy, Bertalanffy was making a case for an "organismic biology" and the theory of open systems and steady states (Drack & Apfalter, 2007). This early thinking led to what we know today as GST.

The summary of GST which follows is, in effect, an explanation of what a system is (in general) and how it operates. These general concepts can then be applied to a wide range of disciplines, including ID.

THE NATURE OF GENERAL SYSTEMS THEORY
Definitions and Types of Systems

There are many definitions of the term "system". Although there are some variations in emphasis, the definition proposed by Hall and Fagen (1975) is still useful: "A system is a set of objects together with relationships between the objects and between their attributes" (p. 52). In other words, the human body is a system because it consists of many parts which relate to one another (i.e., they are connected). A political party is also a system because it has many parts which work together (even though its operation is at times considerably less organized than the human body). A pile of leaves is not a system since there are no connections between the individual leaves other than the fact that they happen to have been swept into the same pile. They do not perform a function together.

The concept of a system has been amplified further through the notions of open and closed systems. A closed system is one which is isolated from its environment, while an open system is one which can interact with its environment (Bertalanffy, 1968). If a member of Congress were to make voting decisions based entirely upon his or her own notions without reading, without listening to the opinions of others, without talking to constituents, this would be an example of a closed system. Once these many interactions occur, the system would be opened.

Churchman (1964) proposes that the truly *general* system is closed and has "ultimate stability" (p. 174); it can resist all changes in the environment and therefore keep its original value. The system designer can enlarge (i.e., generalize) the system to accommodate any likely changes in the environment that can have detrimental effects on the performance of the system. If it were possible to predict all possible changes in the environment the designer would have created a general system that is permanently closed. He suggests, however, that this event is not likely to occur.

Open systems operate in such a manner that they demonstrate a phenomena called the principle of equifinality. The principle of equifinality states that an open system can reach its final state, or final goals, in a number of different ways, because it can interact with its surroundings. Contrasting to this is a closed system in which the final state is absolutely determined by the initial conditions. Thus, there would be no way to make alterations in the system, to react to error. This reemphasizes the importance of establishing processes in contrived systems in which interaction is established with the surrounding environment, or the elements of the related suprasystem.

Figure 2.1 provides an overview of a general system, its structure, and some of the key processes that are inherent in systems principles. It graphically shows the various parts of a system and the relationships between these parts. Below, we describe the components and processes found in a general system.

The Environment of a System

Hall and Fagen (1975) have described the environment of a system as "the set of all objects, a change in whose attributes affect the system and also those objects whose attributes are changes by the behavior of the system" (p. 56). Miller (1978) expanded this definition, differentiating between the immediate environment and the total environment of a system. Inherent in this distinction is the notion of a system also functioning as a part of a larger system, referred to as the suprasystem. The entire environment would include not only the immediate environment, and the suprasystem (minus the target system under consideration), but also all the larger systems at all higher levels. Furthermore, Miller (1978) states:

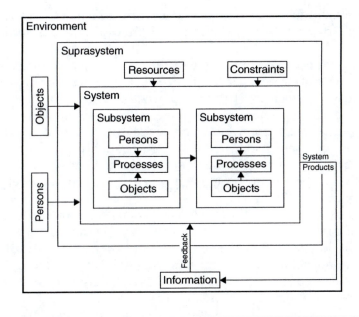

Figure 2.1 An Overview of a General System.

The relationship between a system and its environment is important. In order to survive, the system must interact with and adjust to its environment, the other parts of the supra-system. These processes alter both the system and its environment. It is not surprising that characteristically living systems adapt to their environment and, in return, mold it. The result is that, after some period of interaction, each in some sense becomes a mirror of the other . . . (pp. 29–30)

The relationship and interaction between a system and its environment can be generally described. There is a flow both inward and outward from the system into its environment.

First, the environment provides the persons and objects which enter the system. The quality of these elements will to a great extent determine the quality of the operation of the system.

Second, the environment and the suprasystem establish the constraints upon the system. An example would be an education or training system which relies upon an outside source for funding. Clearly, the extent to which this occurs constrains or facilitates the system's activities.

Third, the suprasystem receives the products of an open system. These products then become a functioning part of the environment. They can thus influence the operation of the suprasystem.

The Structure of a System

The structure within the system itself is also important. One can identify subsystems within the target system. These are organized structures with identifiable, but more limited purposes and functions than the target system itself. Nevertheless, these subsystems have clearly identifiable parts and there are clear relationships between these parts.

Miller (1978) has elaborated upon the distinctions between actual subsystems and discrete components of a system. He emphasizes that mere structure does not characterize a subsystem. Rather, there must also be a process or role associated with the structure to be categorized as a subsystem. For example, within a specific instructional system one might have a self-instructional learning device, such as a web-based instructional program. This is a component of the system. However, if this system also had a function in which web-based instructional programs were designed, developed, and evaluated, then this facet would become not only a component, but also a subsystem of the larger instructional system.

Thus, a system is, by nature, hierarchical (Laszlo, 1972). An understanding of the complexities of a system and of those forces which affect the operation of a system is dependent upon clear delineation of not only the target system, but also of an identification of the environment, the related suprasystems, and the subsystems. This is the case for both natural and most contrived systems. A hierarchical system reflects the emphasis on order in systems thinking, even amid diverse structures.

Cortes, Przeworski, and Sprague (1974) have described the role of a system's structure. Structure, they say, is "an ordered set of interconnected operations performed by the elements of a system" (p. 8). It is the structure itself which dictates the function of the system.

This definition of structure is based upon an inherent assumption that a system is composed of a series of related subsystems. That is, related operations are both components and processes, and therefore subsystems. So to extend the definition, the ultimate function of a system is necessarily determined by the component processes operating within the target system. Thus, when analyzing a given system, one must be particularly careful not only to identify all component subsystems accurately, but to relate these operations to the overall functioning of the system as a whole. For example, an instructional designer analyzing a performance problem should examine the human and nonhuman elements of the organization to identify how they relate to the causes of the problem. While the specific elements of a system may vary, the overall organization or structure of the system cannot vary without changing the fundamental purpose and nature of that system (Cortes et al., 1974).

The Adjusting Properties of a System

Laszlo (1972) viewed the principles of self-stabilization and self-organization as part of the basic systems constructs. Inherent in all open systems is the capacity to adjust themselves to their environments. The primary manner systems stabilize themselves is through the use of feedback. Feedback is information about the products of a system which has been collected from the environment. Typically, the information relates either to the strengths and weakness of these products, or to sources of error created by the system. Feedback can be both positive and negative, although positive feedback is not always desirable and negative feedback should not always be avoided. The terms simply describe the varying functions of feedback.

Negative feedback allows the system to function in a homeostatic fashion. It keeps the system on course, and attempts to maintain a constant product. Furthermore, negative feedback attempts to maintain the same quality of response of the system to its environment as was originally planned. For example, if an instructional system was designed to teach children to read up to the fifth grade level, processes built into the plan would provide remediation for those who were not at that level to assure that the system's goal would be reached. (Conceivably the systems would not have been designed to facilitate progress beyond the fifth grade level in keeping with the system's goals.) The processes and procedures built into the system design to maintain a constant output are examples of negative feedback.

Positive feedback, on the other hand, creates the mechanisms through which an open system can be changed by interacting with its environment. This change can constitute growth in the system, or it could destroy the system altogether. Here, Laszlo's concept of self-organization emerges. The system does more than adjust processes to maintain a product of the same caliber as originally conceived. It actually reorganizes itself and develops a new response to the environment. This is an example of how systems and their environments can grow to complement one another.

An example of positive feedback can be seen by looking again at the instructional system designed to bring children to the fifth grade reading level. Let us assume that the neighborhood around this school changes, and because of organized preschool experiences many children have more advanced reading skills when they enter school than had previously been the case. Positive feedback procedures in the system would allow the curriculum to change. Certain sections of content would perhaps receive less emphasis and new content would be added; the system's goal would change to direct children to a seventh grade reading level, for example. It is no longer exactly the same instructional system.

These types of system changes can be either good or bad; they can lead to progress, or to self-destruction. Evaluating system changes often becomes a matter of values. In anticipation of such dilemmas, some systems build mechanisms into the original design which allow for conscious examination of questions, such as:

- Has the system outlived its usefulness?
- Should one attempt to maintain the original purpose, in spite of changes in the environment?
- Should another system be designed which attempts to modify the environment?

Systems, although ordered, can still be dynamic. They can be continually responsive to the evolution of organizations and societies.

The Philosophical Orientations of General Systems Theory

The study of GST and its specific applications is based upon a belief that much of our world is ordered and rational. Typically, the natural parts of our universe follow this pattern. The human body, the stars, the planets—each of these is an example of the ordered world. In many cases we do not fully understand the order, or the exact nature of the processes which are operating, but we know that these are not random structures. However, when we examine many human organizations—businesses, governments, rules which control societies—at times we may perceive chaos rather than order. The GST adherent would seek order and rationality even in contrived systems.

The study of systems seems to be an extension of a basic belief in the value of order, and in the value of planning to create order in our lives. This is not to say that the pursuit of order is an attempt to mechanize our lives. In fact, GST was originally an attempt to refute the mechanistic doctrines of science that prevailed in the early twentieth century (Hammond, 2002). GST is an orientation toward understanding relationships and the effects of a given process, attitude, or object upon other people and other events. GST, especially those principles espoused by Bertalanffy, is "based on the concept of the open system and emphasizes creativity, spontaneity and the progressive emergence of increasingly complex self-organizing systems" (Hammond, 2002, p. 434). There have been conflicting messages from systems theorists and systems-oriented practitioners. One is of free will, interdisciplinarity, and multiple points of view. The other is of order and control, determinism, and technical management.

There are other philosophical tensions inherent in GST. For example, Churchman (1965/1996) viewed systems thinking as an extension of two opposing philosophical orientations, both of which have a rational foundation. One philosophy suggests that the process of building any whole entity must begin with an emphasis of its parts. The other philosophy suggests that the whole must be conceptualized before the parts can be apparent. In a sense, this is an analysis-synthesis conflict. The proper approach was not clear to Churchman and there are still proponents on both sides of the question. Empiricists would look to a data-based approach for resolving the argument, but many feel that this is too simple an answer.

Boulding (1964), one of the early GST leaders, had a somewhat unique view. He saw general systems as a "point of view rather than a body of doctrine" (p. 25). Thus, he thought of GST as more of a philosophical orientation as opposed to being a formal theory. This perspective, Boulding argues, is dependent upon the values of its adherents. While the most dominant GST values are a predisposition towards order, quantification, and empirical referents, Churchman sees them as the "enemies within" that shape the way humans define and deal with their problems (McIntyre, 2003, p. 490). Such an orientation, according to Churchman, can constrain systems design and decision making (McIntyre, 2003).

Boulding (1964) interpreted GST as encompassing the goal of building a general system, as well as constructing a general theory of systems. This general system would have to exist together with specific disciplinary systems. The dangers of a general system, however, could be ambiguity, superficiality, and a failure to recognize true randomness.

For many GST advocates, systems philosophy contrasts sharply with that of classical science. This was the view of Bertalanffy, considered by most to be the father of GST. He saw systems theory (and its extension, systems inquiry) as reordering the prevailing scientific thought. This GST view of science reflected an "expansionist, nonlinear dynamic, and synthetic mode of thinking" (Banathy, 1996, p. 74). This is consistent with the GST position that synthesis is the culminating activity of inquiry. However, it contrasted with the orientation of traditional science which was then almost exclusively analytical (Banathy, 1996), and in many ways it contrasts with the current common misconception of systems theory as being interwoven with technology, flowcharts, and linearity.

GENERAL SYSTEMS THEORY AND INSTRUCTIONAL DESIGN

The principles of GST have had a profound influence upon the general orientation of most ID projects today. They serve as the underlying theoretical foundation for most procedural models of ID. Over the years, the application of GST principles to ID occurred in roughly a two-step progression. First, the systems approach was conceptualized. Second, the systems approach was proceduralized into what we now know as instructional systems design (ISD) models.

The Systems Approach

The use of GST in many disciplines initially was known as the systems approach. Putnam (1964) viewed the systems approach as basically a process of building and testing (via simulation) discrete models in various fields. However, Ryan (1975), speaking in reference to learning systems, had one of the most comprehensive definitions of the systems approach:

> A systems approach is an operational concept, referring to a scientific, systematic, and rational procedure for optimizing outcomes of an organization or structure, by implementing a set of related operations to study an existing system, solve problems, and develop new or modify existing systems. (p. 121)

Thus, the systems approach reflects the basic notions of order and of planning. It can be used to draw meaning out of existing structures, as well as to create new structures and solve problems.

The early systems approach literature identified the various steps or stages attributed to this process as it is applied in a variety of contexts. Table 2.1 summarizes stages of the systems approach from some of this literature.

Table 2.1 A Comparison of the Stages in the Systems Approach: Excerpts from the Early Literature 1968–1981

Reference	Stages Identified
Banathy (1968)	• Analysis of Systems • Solution of Problems • Development of Systems
Kaufman (1970)	• Systems Analysis (Identifying the Problem, Determining Alternatives) • System Synthesis (Choosing a Solution Strategy, Implementing the Solution Strategy, and Determining Effectiveness)
Silvern (1972)	• Analysis • Synthesis • Modeling • Simulation
Ryan (1975)	• Study Existing System • Solve Problems • Design System
Romiszowski (1981)	• Define Problem • Analyze Problem • Design/Develop Solution • Implement • Control/Evaluate

There are many similarities among these views of the systems approach with the common thread being reliance upon the traditional scientific method of problem solving.

A closer inspection of this literature shows that the basic elements of GST are still incorporated in these various interpretations of the systems approach. They each include:

- A consistent definition of system;
- The notion of purpose within a system;
- An emphasis upon structure; and
- The concept of self-regulation.

The sense of purpose inherent in the systems approach is demonstrated by the movement among the stages to the creation of a new system designed to solve an existing problem. The analysis stage in the systems approach tends to emphasize the system's structure, and the concept of self-regulation is the basis of the evaluation components.

Another way to understand the concept of the systems approach is to understand what it is *not*. Krippendorf (1975) cites an example of a nonsystems approach: the analysis of a single variable or event. Such tactics ignore the fact that a system emphasizes the relationships between its various parts. Analysis of single units as isolated elements (without identifying the interactions of those elements with the other parts of the system, subsystem, or suprasystem) ignores the hierarchical structure of systems and the recognized interdependencies among components.

The systems approach, as summarized by Kaufman (1970), can be condensed into two processes: analysis and synthesis. Silvern (1972) described analysis as a process which emphasizes two distinct phases: (1) the identification of component parts and (2) the identification of the relationships between the parts and the whole system. This is a cognitive skill fundamental to the understanding of systems theory and the application of the systems approach.

Identifying the parts of a system can be a detailed process. Those parts can include components, such as:

- Persons;
- Objects;
- Processes;
- External constraints; and
- Resources available.

The relationships among these parts can also take several forms, including:

- A chronological sequence among processes;
- A flow of data or information between parts; or
- The raw materials (persons or objects) which enter or exit from a system.

These relationships, or connections, between parts of a system can exist within a subsystem, between subsystems, or between the system and its environment.

Analysis is repeated in many ways when using the systems approach. (See Table 2.1.) For example, analysis is critical to:

- Studying existing systems (Ryan);
- Defining and analyzing problems (Romiszowski); and
- Identifying problems and determining alternatives (Kaufman).

Synthesis is the second major stage in each of the systems approach descriptions in Table 2.1. Following analysis, it involves the design of a new system so that the identified problem can be solved. This can occur by either:

- Establishing new relationships between existing parts; or
- Identifying new parts and creating relationships between them.

This phase of the systems approach is purely creative. In the alternative descriptions, synthesis is not only referred to overtly, but it is implied in the stage of designing or developing systems (Banathy, Romiszowski, and Ryan) and as choosing a solution strategy (Kaufman).

Instructional Systems Design Models

Building upon the explorations of the systems approach, fairly straightforward models of ID procedures were developed beginning in the late 1960s. These models as a group were known as instructional systems design models. They were constructed to "visually communicate their associated processes to stakeholders by illustrating the procedures that make it possible to produce instruction" (Gustafson & Branch, 2002, p. 2). These procedures are known collectively as the ADDIE model to emphasize the five core elements of the ISD process: analyze, design, develop, implement, and evaluate. Figure 2.2 visually captures the intent of the ADDIE model.

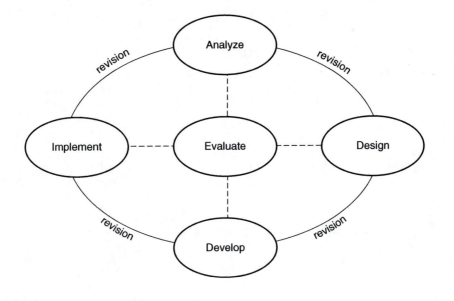

Figure 2.2 The ADDIE Model.

Note: From *Survey of Instructional Development Models* (4th ed.) by K.L. Gustafson and R.M. Branch, 2002, p. 3. Public Domain, 2002, ERIC Clearinghouse on Information & Technology.

Many ISD models have been devised over the years.[1] These models tend to emphasize the unique conditions of various instructional settings, as well as alternative orientations to the ID process itself. Some are visually represented to appear as linear, step-by-step procedures (see, for example, Dick, Carey, & Carey 2009), while others emphasize fluidity and the iterative nature of the process (see, for example, Morrison, Ross, & Kemp, 2007). Some are more appropriate for novice designers (see Brown & Green, 2006), while others demand the competencies of expert instructional designers (see Jones & Richey, 2000). Some combine both novice and expert elements (see Cennamo & Kalk, 2005). However, they all tend to reflect the basic ADDIE elements. These elements are general enough to be applicable to overall program design, as well as the design of instructional materials which may be directed to only a single objective. They can be used with any particular type of content or delivery approach. Table 2.2 provides an overview of a representative sample of these models.

Table 2.2 An Overview of Representative Instructional Systems Design Models

Model	Primary Setting	Unique Emphases
Branson (1975)	Military	• Large-Scale ID Projects • Learner Differences • Content Analysis • Management, Implementation, and Control
Edwards (1982)	Community Health Agencies • Staff Development • Patient Education	• Program Administration • Evaluation, Installation, and Program Maintenance • Program Marketing
Diamond (1989)	Higher Education • Comprehensive Curriculum • Course Development	• Institutional Priorities and Concerns • Design Support Team • Faculty Ownership
Seels & Glasgow (1998)	General Product Development	• Project Management • Diffusion of Results • Interactive and Concurrent Steps in Design Phase • Products Designed for Use by Others
Smith & Ragan (2005)	ID in All Settings	• Cognitive Psychology • Instructional Strategy Selection and Development • Systematic Problem Solving
Smaldino, Lowther, & Russell (2008)	K–12 Education Classrooms	• Learner Characteristics • Media Selection • Technology Integration • Modification of Existing Materials

1 For a more complete review and discussion of ISD models, see Gustafson and Branch (2002) or Molenda and Boling (2008). In addition, many proprietary models have been developed by individual organizations that are not available in the general literature.

Andrews and Goodson (1980) examined the details of 40 ID models. In doing so, they summarized the ISD process in its many variations with 14 common tasks. These tasks serve as a starting point when describing the essence of current ISD models. We have built upon their explanation by adding a final evaluation element (one that would encompass both summative and confirmative evaluation), updating language, and expanding design tasks to reflect current practice. Table 2.3 presents this new view of the common tasks and relates them to the components of the more general ADDIE model.

These ISD common tasks reflect the influence not only of the systems approach, but of the principles of GST itself. The connections between the tasks common to most ISD models and GST principles are shown in Table 2.4. Here you can see one of the key theoretical rationales that support the various steps in which designers typically engage.

ISD models have been used for a variety of purposes. Fundamentally, however, they establish the criteria for design practice that meets commonly held quality standards. They have other roles, however. The key purpose of the Dick and Carey model (1978), the first widely published and used ISD model, was to serve as a teaching tool, a vehicle for training new instructional designers. In addition, many models serve as a project management and organization tool. Lead designers often use them to structure and plan the activities of large and small-scale design projects. As such, the model then becomes a way of visualizing and explaining project plans to design teams and clients as well. This is especially true of proprietary models.

Table 2.3 A Comparison of the ADDIE Model Components and Instructional Systems Design Common Tasks

ADDIE Element	ISD Common Tasks
Analyze	• Assessment of need, problem identification, job tasks, competence, context, or training requirements • Determination of whether solution should be instructional and/or noninstructional • Formulation of system, environmental, and organizational descriptions and identification of resources and constraints • Characterization of learner population • Analysis of goals and objectives for types of skills/learning required
Design	• Formulation of broad goals and detailed objectives stated in observable terms • Sequencing of goals and objectives to facilitate learning and performance • Planning for assessment and evaluation of learning and performance • Consideration of alternative solutions • Formulation of instructional and noninstructional strategies to match content, individual, and organizational requirements • Selection of media to implement strategies
Develop	• Author and produce interventions based on design plan
Implement	• Development of materials and procedures for installing, maintaining, and periodically repairing the instructional program • Costing instructional programs
Evaluate	• Development of assessment items that match goals and objectives • Empirical try-out of courseware with learner population, diagnosis of learning and courseware failures, and revision of courseware based on diagnosis • Evaluate after full-scale implementation

Table 2.4 A Comparison of Instructional Systems Design Common Tasks and General Systems Theory Principles

ISD Common Tasks	Related GST Principle
ANALYZE • Assessment of need, problem identification, occupational analysis, competence, or training requirements • Formulation of system and environmental descriptions and identification of constraints • Characterization of learner population • Analysis of goals and subgoals for types of skills/learning required	• Systems are ordered and are complete wholes • Environments determine quality and establish constraints in open systems • Relationships among system elements and attributes of elements • Systems are hierarchical
DESIGN • Formulation of broad goals and detailed subgoals stated in observable terms • Sequencing of goals and subgoals to facilitate learning • Consideration of alternative solutions to instruction • Formulation of instructional strategy to match subject-matter and learner requirements • Selection of media to implement strategies	• Systems have a common purpose • Systems consist of components and processes • Systems are ordered • Structure determines function • Systems components and process are related
DEVELOP • Development of courseware based on strategies	• Structure determines function
IMPLEMENT • Development of materials and procedures for installing, maintaining, and periodically repairing the instructional program • Costing instructional programs	• Environment determines quality and establishes constraints in open systems
EVALUATE • Development of pretest and post-test matching goals and subgoals • Empirical try-out of courseware with learner population, diagnosis of learning and courseware failures, and courseware revision • Evaluate after full-scale implementation	• Use of feedback to stabilize or reorganize in an open system

Originally, ISD models were not typically empirically validated. Their advancement was based to a great extent upon the credibility of unchallenged tradition and practitioner support (Richey & Klein, 2007). The proliferation of ISD models, however, even without scientific support, speaks to the manner in which the models have successfully addressed specific organizational concerns and the needs of specific user groups.

In spite of the widespread use of ISD models, presently there is an undercurrent of dissatisfaction in some quarters. This tends to reflect concerns such as:

• The amount of time required to complete the process faithfully given workplace constraints and demands;
• The discrepancies between the linearity implied by many ISD models and the realities of ID practices in natural work environments;
• The heavy reliance upon analytic techniques which can produce fragmented content; and

- The tendency for some designers to produce boring, noncreative instruction when following regularized, systematic ID procedures.

These concerns have in some cases led to alternative orientations to the entire ID process (see Willis, 2000). They have also prompted research into ways of addressing such problems, and in many cases, new and enhanced ISD models have been developed. Nonetheless, instructional systems design is still the dominant orientation of designers in most workplace environments.

TRENDS IN SYSTEMATIC INSTRUCTIONAL DESIGN

Today, the principles of GST are still providing the impetus for much of what we do in ID. There are still ISD models in use, although many modifications and entirely new models have been constructed to meet new and emerging ID problems. These models and procedures reflect new interpretations of traditional GST principles relating to analysis and synthesis.

New Approaches to Analysis

Analysis in early ISD models was primarily directed toward instructional content and the learner's previous knowledge of this content. For example, in Briggs's (1970) model the only analysis task concerned determining the structure and sequence of the objectives. While military models put a greater emphasis on analysis, they also concentrated on content. The Inter-Service ISD Model by Branson (1975) spoke to the analysis of jobs and existing courses, and the Navy model addressed job analysis and job task analysis (Department of the Navy, 1980). The original Dick and Carey model (1978) had two analysis phases—instructional analysis and the identification of learner entry behaviors—both of which were content-related analysis phases. Instructional analysis involved breaking the content into its subordinate and superordinate skills, and behavioral analysis sought to identify which of these skills learners already possessed prior to instruction.

The early Air Force ISD procedures were among the very few that reflected a more modern approach to analysis (Department of the Air Force, 1979). In this model the analysis of system requirements included:

- An identification of the nature and scope of humans in the system;
- A detailed collection of data regarding the system and its operation, including information on purpose, function, major subsystems, equipment needed, operation policies, environmental constraints, and human-system interface;
- An identification of specific duties and tasks required for each job performance; and
- A determination of whether training is necessary.

Although this approach to analysis implies a great deal of control, hierarchy, and structure, it does branch out beyond the traditional analytic emphasis on instructional content.

Contemporary instructional designers employ content analysis procedures, many of which are the same as used in the early ISD models. However, they also routinely analyze organizational problems, contexts impacting the instructional process, and a wide range of learner characteristics.

Analyzing Problems

Typically, the product of early ISD efforts was an instructional product—a course, a self-instructional activity, or perhaps an entire program. As the ID field became more sophisticated, there was a realization that the product was only an intermediate step; learning was seen as the ultimate goal. Then even learning was seen as a transition; transfer of training or application of what was learned was viewed as the critical objective. Today, even this is not sufficient. The products of designer efforts should be linked to not only performance changes, but to organizational improvement. The instructional products should help solve organizational problems. Consequently, the analysis aspect of ISD must initially focus on these problems. This corresponds with Swanson's (1999) observation that to improve system performance, one must "focus the analysis for improving performance at the appropriate system frames" (p. 7).

Problem analysis is inherent in a number of "front-end analysis" terms. Gordon (1994) includes it in her organizational analysis. Piskurich (2006) speaks of it as an organizational needs assessment, and Smith and Ragan (2005) characterize this type of analysis as a needs assessment that uses the problem model. They identify four steps to this process:

- Determine whether there really is a problem.
- Determine whether the cause of the problem is related to employees' performance in training environments or to learners' achievement in educational environments.
- Determine whether the solution to the achievement/performance problem is learning.
- Determine whether instruction for these learning goals is currently offered. (p. 45)

This problem analysis orientation implicitly recognizes that instruction may not be the way to solve all problems, and thus narrows the scope of problems that the instructional designer should tackle. It also reflects the thinking behind the 1979 Air Force ISD model.

Focusing on organizational problems (as opposed to only stressing content) plays a part in many current approaches to ISD. It reflects both the systemic and the systematic facets of ISD. It recognizes the manner in which resources and constraints can impact an open system's operation. Moreover, it clarifies the basic purpose of an instructional system.

Analyzing Context

In addition to content concerns, designers today often place an equal emphasis on context. There is no longer the implication that all ID interventions are environmentally neutral and applicable to any setting. This is a direct application of those GST principles related to the importance of environment on system functioning. In many cases, it is easy to see the notion of environment and the suprasystem in today's emphasis on context.

Context has been defined broadly by Tessmer and Richey (1997) who suggest that there are three different contexts that impact ID: an orienting context, an instructional context, and a transfer context. (See Chapter 4 for a more complete description.) Many ISD models now incorporate contextual analysis procedures. Dick et al. (2009) suggest that a contextual analysis of the performance (i.e., transfer) setting should address managerial or supervisor support, social and physical aspects of the site where the skills will be applied, and relevance of the skills to the workplace. They also recommend a contextual analysis of the learning environment that considers the compatibility between the instructional site and the instructional requirements, the ability of the site to simulate the workplace and to accommodate or constrain a variety of instructional strategies.

Smith and Ragan (2005) also move beyond traditional content analysis to analyzing the learning context. They consider context to be not only a physical place, but also to include "the temporal and social environment" (p. 43). Their interpretation of context includes not only the many aspects of the teaching environment, but also the philosophies or restrictions of the organization in which the instruction takes place.

Morrison et al. (2007) use the Tessmer-Richey contextual scheme in their ISD model. They incorporate contextual analyses directed toward the orienting, instructional, and transfer environments. They provide examples of how this analysis can be conducted in a variety of settings: schools, corporations, higher education. Adapting to the environment has become a standard part of the designer's task.

Analyzing Learner Characteristics

For the most part, learner analysis in early ISD models was a matter of measuring prerequisite skills and devising instructional prescriptions in keeping with the learner's ability and skill level. This is not to say that instructional issues such as motivation were unimportant, but predesign analysis did not typically address such factors. Today, a wider variety of learner characteristics are also addressed in the analysis phase. These include:

- Demographic characteristics and individual differences that may influence the selection of one instructional strategy over another;
- Beliefs and attitudes that may impact learning, transfer, and motivation; and
- Mental models that may influence the selection of instructional methods.

Critical demographic characteristics such as age, work experience, and educational level have proven to impact learner attitudes and performance in education and training programs (Richey, 1992). These characteristics can play an increasingly important role as the learner ages. For example, while using complex technology may be routine for children, it can pose learning barriers for older adults. With respect to employee training, extensive work experience in a given field can counteract the lack of a formal education. Designers are now far more conscious of the role of demographics in knowledge acquisition and transfer.

Individual differences, such as the expectancies and values held by learners, also play an important role in ID (Keller, 1983). For example, a learner with a high need for affiliation may prefer to work with others but will also exhibit off-task behaviors when placed in collaborative learning settings (Klein & Schnackenberg, 2000).

Attitudes are important predictors not only of motivation towards learning, but also of how much is learned and the extent to which the material is transferred to other settings. For example, a learner's attitudes towards the delivery system used in instruction can directly predict the amount learned. Knowledge transfer is not directly attributed only to the amount learned, but rather to the attitudes one has toward that which was learned (Richey, 1992).

The learners' mental models of the task domain influence how they will understand the domain of knowledge (van Merriënboer & Kirschner, 2007). As such, designers are now beginning to take steps to determine the typical mental models of learners and to select a mental model of the task domain to guide the instruction. If the object of the instruction is for learners to acquire the mental model of an expert in the field, this may involve moving through a series of mental models: from a novice's mental model, to that of an intermediate performer, and finally to that of an expert (Gordon, 1994).

Much of the new types of learner analyses are dependent upon recent research. However, they also reflect the fundamental GST predisposition towards analyzing the relationships between the various system components and the attributes of these components.

New Approaches to Synthesis

Synthesis occurs at the design and develop phases of the ADDIE model. It includes identifying goals and objectives, sequencing content, making strategy and media decision, and developing the courseware. Even though technology has changed dramatically over the years and design is now often a team project rather than an individual enterprise, has the fundamental approach to creating the product changed? In many ways the answer is "no", but in some fundamental ways the synthesis phase has changed. To a great extent these changes are the result of pressures to complete the design task in a shorter period of time. However, the two changes that we will discuss here—rapid prototyping and the use of learning objects—reflect the influence of GST and systemic thinking.

Rapid Prototyping

Rapid prototyping involves "the development of a working model of an instructional product that is used early in a project to assist in the analysis, design, development, and evaluation of an instructional innovation" (Jones & Richey, 2000, p. 63). There are many different types of prototypes. Some are workable versions of the final project, while others are shells that simply demonstrate the appearance of the final product. All approaches to rapid prototyping typically involve the designers and the clients working as a team throughout the course of the project.

Cennamo and Kalk's (2005) ID model combines the typical ISD phases with "the iterative cycles found in rapid prototyping models" (p. 6). This model presents ID as an evolving process in which designers continually revisit five key elements—learners, outcomes, activities, assessment, and evaluation—even as they proceed through the traditional ISD phases. This design process is very fluid; it incorporates the use of prototypes throughout the course of the project. Paper and working prototypes are developed and reviewed by the entire design team, learners, and typically clients as well.

Most ID projects using such rapid prototyping techniques and other fluid approaches have many of the design tasks being completed by teams with individuals working concurrently in a nonlinear fashion. The systemic orientation, however, is not lost. All team members work together toward one defined goal. The use of prototypes highlights the goal in each design phase, and ensures that all team members (including clients) continue to agree on the goal throughout the project. Prototypes ensure that all parts of the instruction—the activities, the assessment, and the supporting materials—are directed toward the same goal, pictured in the same way by all parties. Feedback from the environment—design team members, learners, and clients—is gathered on a regular, almost continuing, basis to stabilize the system. Efforts are made to ensure that the new instruction will function well within the larger system in which it will operate.

These aims are not unusual for most ISD projects. However, rapid prototyping is an advancement that incorporates specific procedures that make them more likely to be achieved. Moreover, they can be achieved in less time than is typical of projects conducted in a more traditional fashion.

Learning Objects

With the growing interest in learning objects, there have been a growing number of definitions of this term. We will use Churchill's (2007) definition: "A learning object is a representation designed to afford uses in different educational contexts" (p. 484). The implications of this definition is that learning objects are "digital, utilizing different media modalities . . . and . . . they are designed to afford educational reuse" (p. 484). These small sections of digital material are typically stored in a database, available for incorporation into a wide range of delivery media (Barritt & Alderman, 2004). They can be used for a variety of purposes: content presentation, drill and practice with feedback, simulation, concept representation, information display, and context illustrations (Churchill, 2007). Learning objects, by design, are intended to be used in multiple contexts with a variety of types of students even though they address a single objective.

Learning objects are ID elements originating out of the age of technology-based instruction. They are ingenious solutions for those pressed to build a large number of related (but separate) instructional materials in short periods of time. They have also been suggested as one way of meeting the challenges of globalized educational efforts (Laverde, Cifuentes, & Rodríguez, 2007). One can simply reuse instructional segments over and over again in multiple learning contexts. This involves an expansion of the traditional ADDIE model. Barritt and Alderman (2004) provide one example of this expanded process involving reusable learning objects (RLOs). They view design as "Design and Mine", and this new design process has six components:

- Determine learning architecture;
- Create learning objectives;
- Design learning activities;
- Determine delivery options;
- Create a high-level design document; and
- Mine database to reuse or repurpose existing RLOs. (p. 134)

Clearly, identifying the learning object itself involves an analytic process, but here we would like to stress the new approach to synthesis. Synthesis is one innovative aspect of ISD, but it is also one of the most difficult phases if the object is creative, exciting, and effective learning experiences. Learning objects help designers and developers use their time efficiently and avoid reinventing the wheel.

The use of learning objects also reflects the tenets of GST. Even though learning objects are small units of instruction, their effectiveness is dependent upon the extent to which the ultimate instructional setting is viewed as whole (i.e., systemically). Nurmi and Jaakkola (2006) studied the effects of learning objects in classrooms and concluded:

LOs, and the instructional arrangements within learning environments, are interacting together to stimulate certain kinds of student learning activities, behaviours and outcomes. LOs should therefore only be understood as one part of the larger learning environment, not as a self-contained instructional solution. (p. 245)

Thus, once again, it is the relationships among the various system elements that are critical, and it is the environment that determines ultimate quality. Designers using learning objects effectively are creating not just an isolated piece of instruction, but a total teaching-learning system.

RESEARCH, GENERAL SYSTEMS THEORY, AND INSTRUCTIONAL DESIGN

While there have been many applications of GST to the field of ID, the question arises as to the extent to which these practical applications have been tested and empirically validated over time. This is a question that we will address with each of the theoretical foundations of ID covered in this book. Here we will discuss ID research which confirms the applicability of GST principles, and recommend new research that would speak to the continuing viability of these ideas.

Empirical Support of General Systems Theory Applications in Instructional Design

Instructional systems design models are the primary way in which systems thinking has been applied to ID. Initially these models had little empirical support; tradition, academic recommendations and practitioner advocacy sustained their use. Today, empirical validation of new ID models is beginning to occur. For example, Higgins and Reiser's (1985) research involved the controlled testing of a media selection model. Taylor and Ellis (1991) evaluated classroom training to determine how effective the ISD model was as applied in programs of the U.S. Navy. Tracey (2009) validated an ISD model enhanced with a consideration of multiple intelligences.

New research methodologies are being devised to study and test design strategies, many of which are rooted in GST. Design and development research (Richey & Klein, 2007), design-based research (Design-Based Research Collective, 2003), and formative research (Reigeluth & Frick, 1999) are the principle types of inquiry used now for these purposes. Nonetheless (to quote the perennial tagline in dissertations), additional research is needed.

Recommendations for Research on Systemic Instructional Design

A systemic orientation is one which recognizes the role and impact of many elements in a given environment. ID research with a GST foundation would explore the impact of the various elements of a design environment and of the learning and performance environments. Such research would confirm which elements were critical and what the relationships among these elements were. This can be done from a quantitative point of view such as a study by Quiñones, Ford, Sego, and Smith (1995/1996). They examined the relationships between individual characteristics, transfer environment characteristics, and the opportunity to perform, and as a result produced a conceptual model of variable relationships. Research of this type could be conducted measuring factors such as design team attitudes, resources, and time-on-task to determine their impact on project success.

An interpretive orientation to research could also be useful. This "tends to emphasize the subjectivist, communicational, cultural, political, ethical and esthetic—that is the qualitative and discursive aspects" (Schwaninger, 2006, p. 587). There are many possible studies of this type that could address the environmental factors involved in designer decision making. How do designers deal with time pressures (e.g., a study of the role of resources)? How do designers deal with client misunderstandings of the real problem in the organization (e.g., a study of environmental constraints)? When and how do designers incorporate such analysis into their projects (e.g., a study of processes and their related factors)?

One of the fundamental tenets of a general view of instructional systems design is that the processes are applicable to all types of content and all workplace settings. This principle is essentially unsupported empirically. While some research has addressed the use of ISD in K–12 educational settings (see Reiser, 1994 and Young, Reiser, & Dick, 1998), there has not been a systematic examination of the extent to which ISD procedures easily apply to varying work settings. This, and other general ID principles, should be formally studied.

SUMMARY

GST is a central part of the ID knowledge base. This chapter presented the basic tenets of GST, explored its philosophical and empirical underpinnings, and examined the way in which it has been applied in our field, as well as the current trends in its use. Table 2.5 is a précis of this material.

Table 2.5 An Overview of General Systems Theory and Instructional Design

1. **Key Principles:**
   - A system is ordered, a complete whole, open or closed, natural or contrived.
   - A system consists of components and processes.
   - There is a defined relationship between the various elements of a system and between the attributes of these elements.
   - A system is hierarchical, existing within an environment, typically called a suprasystem, and containing smaller units called subsystems.
   - The structure of the system determines its function.
   - Within an open system, the environment can determine the quality of the products of the system by establishing constraints upon the system, and provide feedback that can either stabilize or reorganize the system.

2. **Philosophical Emphases:** Order, rationality, planning, and quantification; Progressive self-organization; Multiple and interdisciplinary points of view; Nonlinear and synthesis thinking.

3. **Basic Research Support:** Early biological research to identify interrelated system effects.

4. **Early Contributors:** GST: Ludwig von Bertalanffy, Kenneth Boulding, C. West Churchman, and Paul Weiss; ISD: Bela Banathy, Walter Dick, Roger Kaufman, and Leonard Silvern.

5. **ID Applications:**
   - ISD Models

6. **Supporting ID Research:**
   - Some Identification of Performance Environment Elements (e.g., Taylor & Ellis, 1991)
   - Some Model Validation Research (e.g., Higgins & Reiser, 1985; Tracey, 2008)

7. **Related Concepts:**
   - ADDIE
   - Equifinality
   - Learning Objects
   - Rapid Prototyping
   - System Analysis and Synthesis
   - Systems Approach

In Chapter 1 we identified the six major content domains of the ID knowledge base:

- Learners and Learning Processes;
- Learning and Performance Contexts;
- Content Structure and Sequence:
- Instructional and Noninstructional Strategies;
- Media and Delivery Systems; and
- Designers and Design Processes.

Here we will begin filling in the details of this view of the field and its knowledge base. GST has relevance for five of these six domains. Table 2.6 shows these domains and the various design elements that stem from our discussion of GST.

Table 2.6 Instructional Design Domains and Elements Related to General Systems Theory

Learners and Learning Processes
- Learner Characteristics (Demographics, Individual Differences, Beliefs and Attitudes, Mental Models)

Learning and Performance Contexts
- Climate (External Influences and Constraints, Organizational Climate, Physical Resources)
- Environment (Orienting Context, Instructional Context, Transfer Context)
- Setting (K–12 Schools, Higher Education, Business/Industry, Health Care, Community, Government)

Content Structure and Sequence
- Instructional Sequences (Job Task Order, Learning Difficulty Order)

Instructional and Noninstructional Strategies
- Feedback

Designers and Design Processes
- Analysis (Content, Context, Cost, Job, Learner, Problem, Organization)
- Design and Development (Goals and Objectives, Strategy and Media Selection, Rapid Prototyping, Learning Objects)
- Designer Characteristics (Expertise)
- Evaluation (Formative, Summative, Confirmative)
- ISD processes (ADDIE)

In essence, Tables 2.5 and 2.6 present the core of the ID knowledge base as it pertains to GST. As we discuss each of the other theoretical foundations of ID, we will expand upon this ID domain framework and continue to provide concise summaries of the theories.

Chapter 3 deals with communication theory. While this is an entirely separate genre of thought, you will find that many communication theorists were also influenced by systems thinking.

3

COMMUNICATION THEORY

Communication is one of the most basic activities of human beings and is "one of the perspectives that gives us the most insight into human nature" (Heath & Bryant, 2000, p. 2). Thus, it is not surprising that the study of the communication process has impacted many disciplines, including journalism, psychology, management sciences, information technology, political science, and education. Its wide range of applications speaks to the scope of communication theory, and to the complexity of communication as a human activity. It involves the use of biological systems, cognitive systems, and social-psychological systems. Communication encompasses more than private interactions between individuals. It also includes interactions (most often public) between groups and large masses of people. Instructional designers are concerned with communication in many forms: oral, written, and mediated. Designers also are concerned with both instant and delayed communication.

There is a variety of conceptual models and theories relating to particular aspects of the communication process. There are theories of linguistics and models of human language development. Persuasion and its applications are distinct areas of study, and the field of mass media has its own models and theories. We are concerned with communication as it impacts the design and delivery of instruction. However, even with this limitation, communication and its related theory cover a wide array of topics and points of view. We will explore this theory base by describing:

- Representative definitions, models, and orientations to communication;
- Traditional and emerging applications of communication theory in instructional design (ID); and
- The empirical foundations of communication theory as a part of the ID knowledge base.

ALTERNATIVE VIEWS OF COMMUNICATION

Given the complexity of the communication process, it is not surprising that its definition (and its theory) has changed over the years. Littlejohn (1989) characterized these

31

various points of view as four alternative perspectives: the transmissional perspective, the behavioral perspective, the interactional perspective, and the transactional perspective. While other scholars present somewhat different configurations, all agree that there are fundamental differences in the way communication has been defined and in the models which stem from these varying definitions. Here we will use the Littlejohn structure to examine the alternative definitions and their related models of communication.

The Transmission Emphasis

In 1951 Miller said "Communication means that information is passed from one place to another" (p. 6), and the theory stemming from this definition explained the process of transmitting such information. This orientation was based for the most part on the seminal work of Shannon and Weaver (1949). Here Shannon devised a mathematical theory of communication which he saw primarily as a digital process, and Weaver provided a detailed introduction which described how the theory could apply to a wider audience of people interested in human communication. The original Shannon-Weaver model is shown in Figure 3.1.

This model was presented as a communication system, reflecting the interest in general systems theory (GST) at that time. The fundamental process involves a source (a person or a person's brain, to be precise) selecting a message, changing the message into a signal, and then sending these signals over a particular communication channel. In the process of such a transmission, there can be interference from noise which can distort the message before the signal is finally received and transferred to the ultimate destination (i.e., the receiver's brain) to determine the message's meaning.

Richey (1986) presents a message transmission model that is more applicable to instructional designers. This is shown in Figure 3.2.

The source could be many things—a teacher, a textbook, or a website, for example. In any case, the source should be seen as a combination of culture, experiences, and resulting attitudes and aptitudes. The channel is typically viewed as being either audio

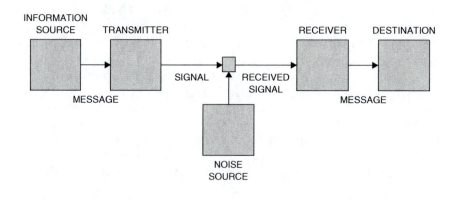

Figure 3.1 The Mathematical Model of Communication.

Note: From *The Mathematical Theory of Communication* by C.E. Shannon & W. Weaver, 1949, p. 7. Copyright 1949 by The University of Illinois Press. Used with permission.

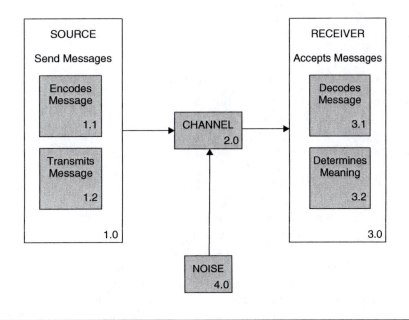

Figure 3.2 A Model of the Transmission of Messages.

Note: From *The Theoretical and Conceptual Bases of Instructional Design* by R. Richey, 1986, p. 44. Copyright 1986 by Rita C. Richey. Used with permission.

or visual. Designers generally think of the channel as the vehicle, or medium, of message transmission. Noise is anything that interferes with the message—sound, confusing images, or even differing values relating to the topic. Noise can be several people talking at once, or the use of ambiguous words. Noise need not always be auditory; it can be visual or even cultural.

The transmission process is, on the surface, simple. It is a linear process, one in which interaction is portrayed by senders and receivers changing roles. Once a message is received and understood (presumably as it was originally intended), the receiver can then become a sender and transmit another message back to the original source. It is a process, however, which Weaver saw as applying to all types of communication— written, oral, musical, visual, and even the arts. This orientation reflects Weaver's view of communication as "all of the procedures by which one mind may affect another" (Shannon & Weaver, 1949, p. 2).

Weaver, however, saw three major and often overlapping problems that should be addressed: (1) There was a technical problem concerning how accurately the symbols transmitted the message; (2) There was a semantic problem relating to how precisely words convey the essence of the original message; and (3) There was an effectiveness problem relating to whether the message had the intended effect on conduct. These were the concerns of the supporting theory.

Others saw more problems with the basic linearity of the model and the assumption that communication is effective only when the received message is identical to the message sent. Heath and Bryant (2000) describe the process this way: "the source 'injects' information and other influence into the receiver's mind . . . a message is a 'lump' of meaning—like a bullet—that transports and inserts an idea into the receiver's brain" (pp. 46–47). This reaction to transmission models led to the development of other definitions and models of communication.

The Behavioral Emphasis

The first substitute suggested for the transmission model of communication was the behavioral model. In many respects the behavioral orientation to communication was very close to the transmission viewpoint. Behavioral views portrayed communication as basically a stimulus-response (S-R) situation, with the sender stimulating a "meaning" (i.e., the response) in the receiver (Heath & Bryant, 2000). The behavioral model most closely allied to education was that of Berlo (1960), the Sender-Message-Channel-Receiver Model (S-M-C-R), as summarized in Table 3.1.

The S-M-C-R Model is reminiscent of the Shannon-Weaver transmission model, but here the message and the words of the message become the stimulus rather than the sender per se. The message is the central part of the process. To educators and instructional designers, messages include not only oral messages, but also written and visual messages embedded in instructional interventions. The response is "anything that the individual does as a result of perceiving the stimulus" (Berlo, 1960, p. 75). Both the sender and the receiver are viewed broadly in terms of their background, skills, and attitudes.

As with the ID perspective of the transmission model, the channels in the behavioral model are the vehicles, or media of message transmission. The channel was critical to the S-M-C-R Model, but Berlo interpreted it differently from Shannon and Weaver, who saw the channel primarily as a physical transmitter. To Berlo "the channel was no longer considered an object, but was seen in light of the human sense that would be used to decode the message" (Januszewski, 2001, p. 30).

Feedback is an essential concept of the behavioral orientation, differing from the transmission approach. In the Berlo S-M-C-R Model, feedback from the receiver clarifies how the message was understood. Berlo saw learning as a stimulus-response process, one that included interpreting the stimulus as well as the consequences of the response (i.e., whether it was rewarding or not).

Another behaviorally-influenced communications model is that of Westley and MacLean (1955). Their challenge was to develop a communications research model that would address situations in which the communicator (i.e., the sender) was not physically present. This is the typical mass communication situation. Educators are often concerned with mass communications models because instructional messages are

Table 3.1 An Overview of the Berlo Model of Communication

Major Communication Elements and Their Components			
Source	Message	Channel	Receiver
• Communication Skills	• Content Elements	• Seeing	• Communication Skills
• Attitudes	• Treatment Elements	• Hearing	• Attitudes
• Knowledge	• Code Structure	• Touching	• Knowledge
• Social System		• Smelling	• Social System
• Culture		• Tasting	• Culture

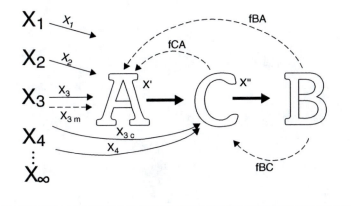

Figure 3.3 The Westley and MacLean S-R Communication Model.

Note: From "A Conceptual Model for Communications Research" by B. H. Westley and M. S. MacLean, 1955, *Audio Visual Communications Review*, 3(1), p. 9. Copyright 1955 by the Association for Educational Communications and Technology. Used with permission.

delivered not only by a primary communicator (i.e., the teacher), but also by information gatekeepers (i.e., the textbook, or another type of instructional material). While Westley and MacLean actually developed four versions of their S-R communication model, Figure 3.3 portrays the most complex of these models.

This model can also be understood from a designer's perspective. Messages (x' and x") are transmitted about particular objects or events $(X_1 - X_\infty)$ to B, the receiver (or the learner). The events could represent the underlying instructional content. These messages may come from A, the basic communicator (e.g., a teacher or an author of instructional materials), or they may come from C, a secondary source of information (e.g., a type of instructional material, mediated or nonmediated). The receiver can give feedback to the original communicator (fBA) or to the information gatekeeper (fBC) or there may be feedback from the information source back to the original communicator (fCA).

These behavioral communication models appear to be more process-oriented and less linear than transmissions models of communication. However, they are not truly interactive. They are still what have been called direct effects models, and they do not describe a truly interactive communication process.

The Interactive Emphasis

George Gerbner was a communication scholar originally trained as an instructional technologist. He viewed communication as "interaction through messages" (Gerbner as cited in Heath & Bryant, 2000, p. 47). With this interpretation the message still has a dominant role in the process, but the emphasis is no longer on simply passing information from one place to the other. Here communication is seen as a social process. This contrasts to the perceptions many had of the transmission models and the behavioral models as being mechanical processes.

One of the first interactive models of communication was that of Schramm (1954). Schramm's model stems from seeing communication as an effort "to establish a

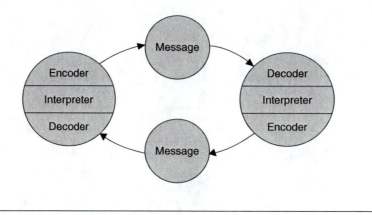

Figure 3.4 The Schramm Interactive Model of Communication.

Note: From *Human Communication Theory and Research: Concepts, Contexts, and Challenges* (2nd ed.) by R. L. J. Heath & Bryant, 2000, p. 66. Copyright 2000 by Lawrence Erlbaum Associates, Publishers. Used with permission.

'commonness' with someone . . . to share information, an idea, or an attitude" (p. 3). While many of the elements in the Schramm model are similar to those we have previously described (i.e., source, message, destination), in his model communication is not only an interactive process, but one in which senders and receivers are actually operating at the same time. This model is shown in Figure 3.4.

From this perspective, communication is not linear, nor does it have an S-R orientation. It can even be more than reciprocal reactions between two parties. Communication is a constant and dynamic process, one that occurs in the midst of another process: feedback. Schramm's model implies that messages are interpreted by individuals based upon their own backgrounds and understandings of the particular situation. Feedback, of course, comes from the receiver of the message. This feedback can take many forms, such as verbal or facial expressions or actions. However, senders may get feedback from the message itself when the words are heard, for example. Often this can result in on-the-spot revisions to the message.

When communication is seen as a process with parallel messages being sent at once, it typically involves multiple, rather than single, channels of communication. For example, messages may be sent at the same time through sounds, size of print, and connotation of words.

Finally, messages are not simply decoded; they are interpreted. Thus, the Schramm model implies that messages are understood by individuals based upon their own backgrounds and understandings of the particular situation.

The Transaction Emphasis

In spite of the social emphases of the interactional perspective, some scholars now visualize communication as a process in which determining meaning is not seen as an interpretation process, but as a matter of sharing and co-creating meaning among actively engaged participants. This is called the transactional perspective. Communication is even more dependent upon the situation at hand, the cultural backgrounds and previous experiences of those involved than in the alternative perspectives.

Campos (2007) presents a new view of communication that falls in this genre. Campos defines communication as "a biological mechanism that enables the subject to make sense of himself or herself *and* of the outside world" (p. 396). This is a very different orientation than those we have previously examined. Essentially it suggests that communication is creating (not delivering) meaning, a process that like knowledge itself is "contextually situated" (p. 387).

The Campos model is influenced by the work of three major scholars: Jean Piaget, Jean-Blaise Grize, and Jürgen Habermas. Piaget saw communications as a process of exchanging values. Similarly, Grize saw communication as a schematization process which is "a progressive process of construction and reconstruction of meanings in which interlocutors help to interpret each other's and one's own world" (Grize as cited by Campos, 2007, p. 392). Habermas's model of social cooperation completes the theoretical base. This point of view suggests that one must always connect the individual to his or her social system. Communication is not only dependent upon one's subjective experiences, but one's "images of the world" (Campos, 2007, p. 395) are also dependent upon economic and political conditions.

Campos's Ecology of Meanings model presents communication as being intertwined with the mental operations and mental images of the participants. Meaning is configured through a mutual understanding of the world and the social environment. This model is presented in Figure 3.5.

Here communication *partners* jointly construct Habermasian "images of the world" which may be absorbed into an individual's "configurations of meanings". Such configurations would result from the schematization processes as described by Grize. Configurations of meanings are built over a lifetime of experiences and reflect the many dimensions of the environment in which one lives, including the affective and

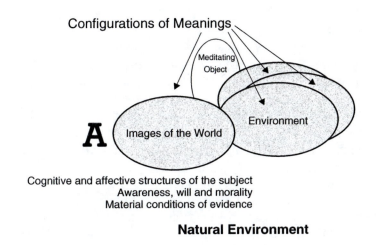

Figure 3.5 The Campos Ecologies of Meaning Model of Communication.

Note: From "Ecology of Meanings: A Critical Constructivist Communication Model" by M. N. Campos, 2007, *Communication Theory*, 17(4), p. 398. Copyright 2007 by Wiley-Blackwell, Inc. Used with permission.

moral values, the political and economic constraints, and the dominant socio-cultural assumptions.

Communication then is a matter of constructing individual and contextualized knowledge in cooperation with others. (This approach is similar to constructivist design theory as discussed in Chapter 8.) This process can occur quite simply through conversation or through mediating objects. Typical objects, from an instructional designer's point of view, might include film, television, websites, or computer-based simulations. However, these mediating objects also reflect the intentions, meanings, and viewpoints of another partner in the communication process.

The Philosophical Orientations of Communications Theory

It has been suggested that one's perspective of the communication process is primarily a function of one's beliefs about the nature of knowledge (Littlejohn, 1989). Thus, the alternative descriptions of communication that we have just examined are in part dependent upon differing basic philosophical orientations. In general, these four approaches to communication can be related to two clusters of philosophical thinking. The transmission and behavioral perspectives can be explained in terms of empiricism and rationalism. Littlejohn (1989) refers to this orientation as "World View I", one which is defined by generalizations supported by data. On the other hand, the interaction and transaction perspectives can be explained in terms of humanism and constructivism. This is Littlejohn's "World View II", a view in which the world is seen as constantly changing to accommodate the contexts in which individuals are interacting. To a great extent, one can see these different philosophies—empiricism, rationalism, humanism, and constructivism—as being on a continuum. They characterize knowledge generation and meaning-making as ranging from being very external processes to being very internal processes. Similarly, these philosophical orientations view truth as ranging somewhere between being seen as universal or pertaining only to individuals.

Empiricism, Rationalism, and Communication

Empiricists view knowledge as being external to the human being. Such knowledge is discovered through experience based in the five senses and objective observation. Knowledge can not be derived from unvalidated assumptions, preconceptions, or biases. In keeping with these beliefs, empiricists rely upon data and controlled research to formulate new knowledge. Reality should be obvious to the trained observer. Most scientific research is conducted in a manner consistent with this positivist point of view.

The issue separating various camps of empiricists is the role (or even the existence) of prior information. Is the mind a blank slate only to become active through an accumulation of experience, or is it an active participant in the experience? The more radical empiricists would take the former position; other empiricists would maintain that the mind is active, but there are no "truths that can be known without recourse to experience" (Brown, 2005, p. 244).

Although often related to empiricism, rationalism emphasizes the role of reasoning (as opposed to sensory experience) in the creation of knowledge. As a consequence, truth can be derived through intellectual activity rather than scientific activity. Such knowledge is not to be confused with opinion, however, which is typically not supported by data (as the empiricists would want) or by carefully worked out logic. Rationalists argue that not all propositions can be tested empirically and their proof is dependent upon reasoning. Einstein's mathematical development of the theory of relativity would be one example of this type of scientific reasoning. He considered this process to be doing "thought experiments".

Similar to the empiricists, rationalists view knowledge as being external to the individual and believe that truth can be universal and verifiable. The empiricist-rationalist distinctions also can become blurred when considering the role of the mind in meaning-making. Moderate empiricists and moderate rationalists could share some beliefs with respect to there being a mind active in meaning-making; however, empiricists would likely say there were no a priori truths. Both of these philosophies can be used to explain the development of knowledge or to justify existing knowledge.

Transmission and behavioral orientations to communication are clearly within the empiricist-rationalist genre. From a knowledge development perspective, the Shannon-Weaver, Berlo, and Westley-MacLean models were developed through scientific reasoning and tested through empirical research. From a knowledge justification perspective, they are all considered receiver theories. In other words, these three models see communication as being dependent upon the message being sensed (i.e., experienced) by the receiver. Moreover, the philosophic assumption of each of these communication models is that truth is dependent upon the extent to which the message was received as intended.

Humanism, Constructivism, and Communication

The interactional and transaction perspectives as exemplified by the Schramm and Campos models have a very different orientation. However, these two models can be viewed on a philosophical continuum with the Schramm model still reflecting some elements of empiricism and rationalism, and the Campos model representing a purer view of humanism and constructivism.

Humanism in general involves an emphasis on individual men and women and issues that concern their welfare and happiness. While historically, humanism implied a split between religion and science, today humanists are more likely to emphasize human emotions and feelings. Humanists rely "on the methods of reason, science and democracy for the solution of human problems" (Lamont, 1984, p. 147). On the surface, this seems similar to the rationalists; however, while humanists are willing to recognize the importance of reasoning, they "do not accept that reason can provide the basis for morality, but may appeal to feelings or emotions instead" (Lacey, 2005, p. 402).

The Schramm communication model is a social model that emphasizes sharing rather than delivering messages; it emphasizes interaction rather than action (Schramm, 1971). Schramm stresses the concurrent actions of all of the human participants and the significance of an individual's interpretation of a message. Knowledge then arises out of interpretation rather than only understanding facts as the empiricists would suggest. The Schramm model also reflects elements of rationalism, especially in terms of its process of development. In terms of knowledge justification, however, it is more humanist in nature. Nonetheless, it also suggests some elements of constructivism.

Constructivism[1] is a philosophical orientation of particular importance to the process of knowledge development. It involves more than simply emphasizing the individual. Rather it is an assumption that knowledge, even though it reflects the outside world, is uniquely shaped (i.e., constructed) by each person. Knowledge (and by extension truth and reality) is internal to the individual. As such, knowledge is by definition situational and highly reflective of one's context; there are no universal truths, no truly shared conceptions of reality (Duffy & Jonassen, 1992).

The degree to which the environment and society influence the knowledge development process is a matter of some debate. The radical constructivist position would suggest that meaning-making is entirely a function of the individual's perspectives and experiences, while the social constructivist position would highlight the importance of context (Fox, 2008). Some view these two perspectives as being complementary (Cobb, 1994). Others see knowledge development primarily as a matter of enculturation even though ultimately it is an individual activity (Driver, Asoko, Leach, Mortimer, & Scott as discussed in Duffy & Cunningham, 1996).

The Campos communication model is a straightforward reflection of constructivist philosophies. It is one which eschews the role of both message reception and message interpretation. Instead meaning (and one's view of reality) is initially constructed both alone and in cooperation with others involved in the communication process. Ultimately, meaning becomes a part of the individual's view of the world. This is a model which stresses a broad array of environmental influences. There is no recognition of many of the traditional components of the communication process: sender, receiver, channel, or noise. Even the mediating objects do not have the same role as conventional delivery systems; they serve as lenses which help shape the meaning (Campos, 2007).

COMMUNICATION THEORY AND INSTRUCTIONAL DESIGN

All instruction is a matter of communication, whether it is delivered orally by a teacher, in writing and visuals in books or other materials, or through various forms of media. Here we will explore ways in which communication theory and models have influenced the design of instruction. The applications of communication theory to ID are most prevalent in what is known as message design, the "planning for the manipulation of the physical form of the message" (Grabowski, 1995, p. 226). Message design techniques and topics have varied over time as a result of the characteristics and capabilities of emerging technologies. This was most obvious with the advent of computer-based and web-based instruction. This section will explore the following basic elements of the communication process in terms of their roles in the design of both mediated and nonmediated instructional messages:

---

1 We are viewing constructivism here as a philosophy. This designation varies across literature. Some education scholars see constructivism as a learning theory; this is sometimes called "cognitive constructivism". Others see it as a teaching methodology or an approach to the teaching-learning process. These points of view are highly inter-related. The confusion is perhaps to be expected given constructivism's epistemological emphasis on knowledge development. Constructivist philosophy, however, is a general set of beliefs that serves as a foundation for work in many disciplines.

- The role and impact of written and visual language on meaning-making;
- The influence of channel on effective instructional communication; and
- The attention-getting properties of a message.

The Role of Language

"Language is fundamental to thinking and learning" (Spector, 2008, p. 24). Language, however, is a multifaceted concept which encompasses far more than the language rooted in words. Pettersson (1989) describes various approaches to categorizing language: (1) as spoken, written, and visual; (2) as verbal and pictorial; (3) as verbal (including spoken, written, and tactile) and nonverbal (including audio, visual, and other). Designers, however, are most often concerned with instructional messages conveyed through written and visual language. Language is a major element of most communication models in their explanations of message encoding, message structure, and message interpretation. It is an inherent part of transmission, behavioral, and interactive approaches to communication, and even the transaction emphasis is dependent upon language.

Written Language

Most instructional messages are encoded and organized using words and sentences. Both the vocabulary and the grammar of a language are viewed today as being culturally induced. Vocabulary is subject to the influence of the culture, personal experiences, and values of the sender of the message. Even grammar has a structure that allows receivers of a message to understand the real content by stripping away the surface noise (Campbell, 1982). The human mind, however, is able to process messages that are well organized more quickly. According to Campbell (1982):

> Information is easier to remember when it is in an orderly state, rich in pattern and structure, highly interconnected, containing a good deal of redundancy. Disorderly information that lacks structure is easy to forget. (p. 214)

Thus, good instructional designers are most always good writers. What this means specifically involves things such as avoiding long sentences with many subordinate clauses, passive voice, abstract expressions, and not including examples (Hartley, 2004).

When written language is printed (as instructional messages typically are), a new array of issues emerge. Hartley (2004) describes the many guidelines that have emerged from text design research that facilitate learner understanding of printed text. These guidelines relate to topics such as page and type size, typeface, use of capitalized and italicized letters, and spacing. Today word processing programs provide designers with a wide array of options with respect to each of these text design decisions, and the choices made greatly impact the communication process. Text design, however, not only deals with the written language, but in many ways it converges on issues relating to the visual aspects of the message.

Visual Language

Images and visual messages also employ a type of language, but this is a language that is rooted in perception and one that "affects us directly and involves instinct and emotion, before the linear logic derived from [written] language can be imposed on it" (Barry, 1997, p. 116). Visual language is presentational in form and simultaneous and connotative in nature (Seels, 1994). Like written language, visual language also has a type of grammar with a set of organizing principles.

These principles for the most part stem from Gestaltian theory. (See Chapter 4 for a detailed discussion.) Here are a few of the most important. We attend to the dominant aspects of the visual and subtleties are frequently lost. We tend to group similar images together in our minds and perceive relationships and patterns among these images. Images that are incomplete typically are perceived as complete, closed, and coherent. We see what we expect based upon our past experiences (Barry, 1997).

Instructional designers rely heavily upon the power of visuals as communication tools and ultimately as learning tools since it is commonly agreed that pictures are more easily remembered than are words. Some visuals are used primarily for cosmetic or entertainment reasons or to orient learners to a particular aspect of the instruction. Most designers, however, use them to convey specific information, and there are a number of elements that impact this process.

For example, the fidelity of the visual has long been considered critical to conveying accurate information. In general, the more realistic visual is more detailed. A photograph, thus, is closer to reality than a simple black and white line drawing. Color, on the other hand does not tend to impact learning other than being an effective way to differentiate ideas or to direct attention to key concepts (Fleming, 1987). Visuals can serve not only as elements of instructional materials, but as the instructional message itself.

The Role of the Communication Channel

The nature of a channel of communication was introduced by Shannon and Weaver (1949). While the views of what communication is have changed over the years, the role of the communication channel has remained important to designers especially as multimedia technology has become more sophisticated. In today's world dominated by the Internet, many senses are typically involved in mediated communication. There are complex visuals, often animated, and always in color. There is sound. There is text. The basic problems confronting designers involve whether learners can accommodate these simultaneous stimuli and if they can, how much and what type of information can be processed in this manner (Moore, Burton, & Myers, 2004).

Single- and Multiple-Channel Communication

With the early interest in audio-visual instruction, researchers have addressed the issue of whether learning was facilitated by providing information via more than one sensory channel. Research has not been definitive. Early scholars tended to believe that humans could only handle a given amount of stimuli and therefore multiple-channel learning is only effective with a small amount of information or if the information comes at a very slow rate of speed. Thus, the single-channel approach is preferable (Travers, 1970). However, Moore, Burton, and Myers's (2004) more recent review of the research leads them to believe that "the human information processing system appears to function as a multiple-channel system until the system capacity overloads . . . (and it) seems to revert to a single-channel system" (p. 998).

This issue has more than academic importance. It is central to the utility of multimedia instruction and to the manner in which the new interactive technologies are employed. It speaks, for example, to the extent to which the instructional stimuli in various modes should be redundant, to the extent to which learners should be able to control the rate and type of instructional presentations, to the effects of screen size and visual clarity, and even to the extent to which the learner's past experiences with technology and various delivery systems impact information processing. It also forces designers to consider the information load of each piece of instruction.

Information Load

Marsh (1979) defined the information load of a message as the product of the number of chunks of information and the saliency or previous experience one has had with the information. Thus, factors such as the number of words or concepts, the complexity of the sentence structure, and the extent to which the content has been well integrated impact information load. Similarly, the number of details in a picture, or the use of color and motion increase the information load carried through the communication channels. Load is also affected by the rate of message delivery, and the amount of redundancy in the message. Too much redundancy or too fast a presentation can lead to an unnecessary number of stimuli through which the human mind must sort and select. Too slow a presentation or too little redundancy can lead to error and misunderstanding.

The information load of a message is related to the more current notion of cognitive load. Information load, however, emphasizes message structure, and cognitive load emphasizes the impact of the message structure on cognitive processing. The literature identifies three types of cognitive load. The first type, intrinsic load, is dependent upon the basic nature and difficulty of the material. The second type, extraneous cognitive load, "depends upon the way the instruction is designed, organized and presented" (Moore et al., 2004, p. 983). The third type, germane cognitive load, pertains to the effort that learners must exert to take the material and construct a mental schema. Each of these factors is important to instructional designers, but the most "appropriate instructional designs decrease extraneous cognitive load but increase germane cognitive load" (Sweller, van Merrienboer, & Paas, 1998, p. 259).

The efficiency of any instructional message is to a great extent a function of the message's load, but when the message is transmitted through both auditory and visual channels, learning can actually be increased because students are using both auditory and visual working memories (Mayer, Heiser, & Lonn, 2001; Mousavi, Low, & Sweller, 1995; Seel, 2008). This may be especially true when related auditory and visual elements of the instructional message are presented contiguously (Seel, 2008).

The Attention-Getting Properties of Messages

Another critical message characteristic relates to those properties that attract the attention of the learner (i.e., the receiver of the message). There are various types of attention. There can be both conscious and nonconscious awareness of a particular part of a message. There can be partial and selective attention, and there can be arousal which is a type of passive attention created by reactions to various conditions (Reed, 1988). Designers must be aware of all types of attention.

Most of the communication models we have discussed recognize the role of noise, those many stimuli that can confuse the receiver or distort a message. Communication theorists and instructional designers alike are concerned with how, in spite of such noise, certain parts of a message are noticed and acted upon and others are missed. These selective attention-getting properties can be a function of the manner in which the text or visual is presented, or they can be a function of the nature of the content.

Cueing Techniques

Designers have traditionally used many techniques to cue the receiver to the important parts of printed messages. Cues which fall into these categories are designed primarily to enhance quick perception. Designers can literally point to the important parts of the text with arrows, or highlight the critical parts with color. They can use bold face or very large type. Duchastel (1982) identified printing and display techniques (e.g., different typefaces, side headings, labeling, and illustrations) which help the reader to focus on critical information. These are typographical cues. However, using white space and headings to highlight critical information is also considered to be typographical cueing (Glynn, Britton, & Tillman, 1985). Winn and Holliday (1982) have identified other cues that help learners interpret diagrams and charts when they make suggestions such as arranging layouts to reflect sequential relationships among concepts, and highlighting major concept categories.

Attention-getting elements of messages delivered in nonprint media have also been investigated. In these materials narrative text is often less important than factors such as sound and animation (Lancaster & Warner, 1985). In multimedia messages, audio can provide verbal cues of importance and loud sound functions much as large print in highlighting critical information. Mediated instruction allows other cueing techniques. For example, Geiger and Reeves (1993) studied the role of cuts as devices to direct television viewers' attention from one scene to another so that they can make sense of the array of visual images. They conclude that in television viewing meaning is dependent not only upon the structure of the message (i.e., the cuts between the scenes), but also on nonvisual elements of the message, especially the extent to which it conforms to viewer past experiences and expectations.

Content-Generated Attention

The past experiences of learners serve as elements of their prior knowledge and understandings. When there are connections between this prior knowledge and the content of the message, learners tend to pay more attention to this familiar material. This is known as the activation of mental schemata. (See Chapter 4.) This procedure makes it easier to process the new information by reducing the cognitive load and minimizing the stress on working memory (Seel, 2008). This is a very different type of attention-getting property from that of using cues, one that approaches the role of arousal and motivation. It suggests the utility of building on the learner's existing frame of reference to enhance selective attention. It is reminiscent of the emphases placed on receiver attitudes, knowledge, social system, and culture in the Berlo model and in the cognitive and the role of the configurations of meaning in the Campos model.

This, however, does not mean that it is wise for instructional designers to purposely include especially interesting and intriguing material that is not directly related to the learning task at hand. Such material has been called seductive details by Garner, Gillingham, and White (1989). Interesting stories, cartoons, or animations can actually disrupt learning by diverting cognitive processing to irrelevant details (Mayer, Griffith, Jurkowitz, & Rothman, 2008). In other words, the "bells and whistles" that are now technologically possible in multimedia instruction can become noise (Mayer et al., 2001).

TRENDS IN COMMUNICATION-RELATED
INSTRUCTIONAL DESIGN

Communication theory continues to influence instructional designers, although today the more common orientation to communication tends to emphasize interaction or transaction, rather than transmission or behavior. Good designers use established message design techniques in print materials as a matter of course. The application of message design principles in multimedia and web-based environments is also common, although there is often more experimentation with the best way to handle multimedia elements. A major concern of current instructional designers deals with how to effectively structure instructional messages delivered in a computer-based format. On a very different note (and in keeping with the dominance of interactive and transactive communication models today), designers are more focused on the experiential backgrounds of the participants in the communication process, both the sender and the receiver. Theorists and practitioners alike are concerned with how these factors impact learning and meaning making.

Designing Mediated Communication

The current emphases on multimedia and use of sophisticated technologies have led to a variety of new message design concerns. These range from facilitating online communication among and between individuals to topics such as the debilitating impact of a learner's attention being split between competing bits of information.

Online Communication

Mediated communication currently covers a wide range of activities: e-mail, instant messaging, chat rooms, live chat, list serves, blogs, social networking vehicles, text messaging, and of course the cell phone. The nature of the communication channel is constantly changing. Moreover, the literature (and most informal reports from parents) shows that young people tend to prefer using the more interactive and synchronous modes as opposed to the less interactive methods, although the preferences tend to depend upon whether students are interacting with peers or relatives. For social communication, instant messaging is dominant (Quan-Haase, 2007).

Not surprisingly, most of these new communication avenues are being incorporated into formal instruction, not only in traditional face-to-face instruction, but also in online programs and other forms of distance education. Designers of online instruction are concerned not only with how these communication strategies can facilitate learning, they are also interested in how these activities can promote learner collaboration and cooperation and how they can aid students through tutoring and coaching.

While the object of many instructors is to use the many new technologies to increase student communication in online settings, the more relevant question often concerns the nature of the communication rather than the quantity of messages. For example, while social interactions abound among students, only the content-related messages impact formal learning. Moreover, communication should be overt; lurking in a discussion does not typically aid the learner. More active involvement helps students do better. Similarly, the quantity of instructor messages to students does not in itself increase student performance. The social role of the instructor is important. Interpersonal messages from instructors are motivational and increase the students' social presence (Gerber, Grundt, & Grote, 2008; Visser, Plomp, Amirault, & Kuiper, 2002). Designers are selecting instructional strategies and media that facilitate communication among learners and promote collaboration and interaction in spite of distance separations.

The Split Attention Dilemma

Split attention became an important concern of teaching and learning scholars as a by-product of the exploration of factors that create a load on cognitive processing. While split attention can occur when learners must integrate information that is in two different places in a piece of instructional material, i.e., some pages removed from each other (Posiak & Morrison, 2008), the most common problem is when instructional information is presented in two different modalities, i.e., auditory or visual (Mayer & Moreno, 1998). In many respects this is simply another way of exploring the issue of single- and multiple-channel learning. Efforts to study the split attention phenomenon, however, lead easily to examining the related question of how redundant information in both the auditory and visual channels impacts learning.

In multimedia instruction redundant information tends to be in one of two forms: (1) animations with explanatory text, or (2) animations with audio explanations. The current wisdom supports the latter approach—always presenting words as spoken text—because the first tactic tends to overload the visual working memory and the learner's visual attention is split between reading the words and analyzing the visuals. In other words, "when they are looking at the words they cannot look at the animation, and when they look at the animation they cannot look at the words" (Mayer, 2008, p. 766). The study of split attention has led to very concrete principles of designing instructional messages in a multimedia format.

Learner Background and Meaning-Making

In today's world, the positivist orientation, one which seeks universal generalizations, has lost its broad base of support because it tends to discount the impact of culture, history, and individual characteristics. Factors that attune instruction to unique learners are more important to current instructional designers. This is now the case in corporate training, K–12 environments, and higher education. Consequently, the culture and distinctive backgrounds of both the senders and receivers of the instructional messages become central to the design task.

The Impact of Culture

Education and training is increasingly an activity with worldwide implications. This phenomenon is exacerbated by reliance upon the Internet as a means of delivering instruction which in turn allows learners to be dispersed throughout the world. Even local student bodies often have a large amount of ethnic diversity. Thus, the learner's culture now plays a critical role in the learning process.

Culture has been defined in many ways, but most generally it is assumed that "culture is a manifestation of ways in which an identifiable group adapts to its changing environment" (Wild & Henderson, 1997, p. 183). To be more specific, culture pertains to factors such as customs, traditional ways of thinking and acting, societal norms and moral standards, and language and speech patterns.

There are two major ways in which instructional designers address culture. They either globalize (or internationalize) the instruction so that the materials are in effect culture-free or they localize the instruction so that the needs of a particular group of learners are directly met and the materials are culture-specific. If the globalization route is taken, then designers must avoid using techniques such as humor, acronyms, collo-quial language, and culture-specific metaphors (Young, 2008). The resulting instruction then becomes cross-cultural in nature.

On the other hand, culture elements can become integral to the instruction. Young (2009) has devised an ID model that integrates cultural considerations into each phase of the ID process. It is a model that requires a culturally sensitive design team, including a cultural expert who represents the targeted learning community. It is a comprehensive model that can be used for custom development of new instructional products or for modifying or evaluating existing products. Many factors are addressed in terms of the particular target audience, including the suitability of the:

- Content, including information that is backgrounded (i.e., assumed and de-emphasized) and that which is foregrounded;
- Visual representations;
- Instructional strategies; and
- Distribution formats.

The target audiences are analyzed in many ways. They are considered in terms of elements such as aesthetics, economy, language and symbolic communication, demo-graphics, history, and beliefs and values. All of these factors impact the manner in which learners process, understand, and interpret instructional messages. They also influence the manner in which the instruction itself is constructed since it may reflect the cultural orientation of the designer.

The Impact of Age

Many feel that generational commonalities create a culture, and generational effects have long influenced communication. These effects can be quite apparent when the communication is through technology. Consequently, current designers are especially conscious of the impact age has on learning with technology. Interestingly, gender effects on technology-based learning, which were once common, are seldom apparent in the younger generation (Dresang, Gross, & Holt, 2007; Wang, Wu, & Wang, 2009).

This new generation is often called the "Net-Generation" to reflect their having been born into and grown up with the Internet. Technology-based communication is a regular part of a typical day. They send text messages, instant messages, and e-mails. It is routine to use the Internet, and simulations and gaming activities are ordinary. This generation has a "novel ability to read multiples texts (e.g., words, images, and video)" (DeGennaro, 2008, p. 1). Moreover, through these processes they use these technologies to socially construct new knowledge (DeGennaro, 2008). They make meaning with each other and with technology. Astute instructional design-ers are building upon these habits by employing many vehicles of mobile-learning (e.g., personal digital assistants, iPods, and wireless computers) to make learning an anytime/anyplace activity.

While older adult learners are less likely to gravitate to mobile-learning (Wang et al., 2009), they can be taught to use computer-based instruction. However, in these situations special attention needs to be given to the cognitive load of the message so that working memories are not over-taxed and pacing decisions should ideally be left to the learner (Van Gerven, Paas, & Tabbers, 2006). We cannot be sure that these more problematic issues will continue to impact older adults and technology use. Czaja et al. (2006) suggest that the technology difficulties of many older adults may be seen as historical idiosyncrasies rather than evidence of age-related decline since these people grew up in the time in which computers were first introduced. If this is true, as today's younger adults age, their behavior patterns and attitudes may well be very different from the previous generation. This is encouraging since technology-based communication is becoming the norm in the workplace.

RESEARCH, COMMUNICATIONS THEORY, AND INSTRUCTIONAL DESIGN

Communications theory has a fairly robust empirical base, and its ID applications have a similarly firm research foundation. This research started early in the history of the field and is continuing today. Here we will provide an overview of representative research that informs ID practitioners of the most important and effective applications of communication theory, and then we will suggest new avenues of research that could provide further support.

Empirical Support of Communication Theory Applications in Instructional Design

The ID field looks to communication theory primarily as a guide to message design. The principles and their supporting research address messages delivered through both text and visuals with an increasing emphasis on multimedia. Some of the richest of these research agendas pertain to:

- Explorations of the impact of the communication channel (see Saettler, 1968; Moore, Burton, & Myers, 1996, 2004);
- Typographical and visual cueing techniques (see Hartley, 1996, 2004); and
- Message structure and its impact on information processing (see Pettersson, 1989; Sweller et al., 1998; Mayer, 2008).

The early approaches to communication were primarily from a GST orientation. However, much of the newer research is now drawing upon advancements in other fields. For example, the new cognitive load literature is intimately involved with psychology and cognitive information processing theory. Voss (2008) has constructed a model of those factors that impact the design of static visual information which integrates research from message design, cognitive psychology, neurology, and information theory. It is likely that others will carry on such interdisciplinary work.

Recommendations for Continuing Research

Given the well-established tradition of research in this area, there is no reason to believe it will not continue. We suspect that much of this new research will focus on the new interactive media and online learning since these delivery formats are so dominant at this time. Not only will the mechanics of the communication process be studied in these environments, but we expect to see that more psychological aspects of mediated communication will be addressed. For example, some have suggested that online and technology-enhanced communication can be more open, and more democratic. There will be many opportunities to study this and other hypotheses given the proliferation of blogs.

Another area of research recommendations relates to the way in which new knowledge is acquired through social communication processes. These projects could explore simultaneous communication activities that may or may not involve technology. Such research may venture into areas such as joint problem solving, teamwork, or distributed cognition. It is also likely that the exploration of the role of learner background in developing or accepting new ideas will continue as education and training become even more globalized.

SUMMARY

Communications theory was one of the earliest parts of the ID knowledge base to be developed, and it continues to be shaped today. This chapter has shown the course of this development first by exploring the evolution of communication models, and by matching these models to a similar philosophical evolution of ways in which we have understood the nature of knowledge and meaning-making. In addition we have described the impact of these various lines of thinking on ID practice, both traditionally and in relation to the new and emerging emphases in education and training. Table 3.2 summarizes all of this material.

Table 3.2 An Overview of Communications Theory and Instructional Design

1. **Key Principles:**
    * The communication process can be viewed as a matter of transmission, behavior, interaction, or transaction.
    * The typical components of the communication process are the information source, the message, channels (auditory and visual), noise, environment, information receiver (including cultural backgrounds and previous experiences), interpretation of meaning, and feedback.

2. **Philosophical Emphases:** The following generalizations can be made:
    * Transmission and behavioral emphases have an empiricist and/or a rationalist view.
    * The interaction emphasis has a humanist view.
    * The transaction emphasis has a constructivist view.

3. **Basic Research Support:** Shannon's early channel and noise research; Gestalt research and theory related to perception.

4. **Early Contributors:** Communication Theory: David Berlo, Malcolm MacLean, Wilbur Schramm, Claude Shannon, Warren Weaver, and Bruce Westley; ID Applications: James Hartley and Robert Travers.

5. **ID Applications:**
    * Culture-Based ID Models
    * Message Design
    * Multimedia Design

Table 3.2 *Continued*

6. **Supporting ID Research:** Studies of:
   • Elements that direct attention in instruction (e.g. Frank Dwyer)
   • Multimedia message design (e.g. Richard Mayer)
   • Single- vs. multiple-channel processing (e.g. Robert Travers, Allan Paivio)
   • Studies of effects of message structure on cognitive processing (e.g. John Sweller and colleagues)

7. **Related Concepts:**
   • Cognitive Load
   • Cueing Techniques
   • Globalized and Localized Education and Training
   • Information Load
   • Single- and Multi-channeled Communication
   • Split Attention
   • Visual Language and Learning

Communication theory adds a great deal to the ID knowledge base, and has implications for each of its major domains. Table 3.3 shows the ID elements that branch out from communication theory and how they fit into the six domains of the ID knowledge base.

Table 3.3 Instructional Design Domains and Elements Related to Communications Theory

Learners and Learning Processes
   • Learner Characteristics (Attitudes, Background, Culture, Demographics, Motivation)

Learning and Performance Contexts
   • Environment (Message Context, Social Systems, Society, Technology-Based)
   • Physical Materials and Arrangements

Content Structure and Sequence
   • Information and Cognitive Load
   • Message Structure (e.g., Vocabulary, Grammar, Visuals, Color)

Instructional and Noninstructional Strategies
   • Eliminating Noise
   • Facilitating Interaction and Social Communication
   • Facilitating Online Communication
   • Giving and Receiving Feedback
   • Securing and Focusing Attention

Media and Delivery Systems
   • Auditory and Visual Delivery Channels
   • New Technologies and Message Transmission

Designers and Design Processes
   • Message Design (e.g., Gaining Attention, Typographical and Visual Cues)
   • Multimedia Design (e.g., Avoiding Split Attention, Information Redundancy, Sound Perception)
   • Text Design (e.g., Page and Type Size, Typeface, Spacing, Capitalization)

When you add these elements to those stemming from GST, you can see how the ID knowledge base is growing. This development will continue in Chapter 4, which relates to learning theory. This is a complex theory base rooted in a long research history, one which is vital to ID.

4

LEARNING THEORY

The primary purpose of instructional design (ID) is to facilitate learning and improve performance. Therefore, theories which explain learning are extremely relevant to designers and the field's knowledge base. Learning theory involves understanding the role of human behavior and mental functions of the mind. It also provides noteworthy explanations of both learning and performance. In this chapter we will explore:

- Several learning theories including behavioral, cognitive, and social learning approaches;
- The application of learning theory to ID; and
- Empirical foundations for learning theory applications to ID.

LEARNING THEORY AND INSTRUCTIONAL DESIGN

Although psychologists have been interested in studying the process of learning since the late 1800s, their views of learning have evolved over the years. Early definitions primarily focus on a change due to certain external conditions as indicated by Hilgard (1956) who states that "learning is the process by which an activity originates or is changed through reacting to an encountered situation . . ." (p. 3). Building on early definitions, Mayer (1982) acknowledges experience as a key ingredient in learning. A central element in current definitions of learning focus on the process of acquiring knowledge and skill (Ni & Branch, 2008) rather than on changes in behavior. Although all of these components in learning are significant, we believe that Mayer's (1982) definition of learning is still relevant today:

> "Learning" is the relatively permanent change in a person's knowledge or behavior due to experience. This definition has three components: (1) the duration of the change is long-term rather than short-term; (2) the locus of the change is the content and structure of knowledge in memory or the behavior of the learner; (3) the cause of the

change is the learner's experience in the environment rather than fatigue, motivation, drugs, physical condition, or psychological intervention. (p. 1040)

While there are definitions of learning that reflect other points of view, in this chapter we will explore behavioral, cognitive, and social learning theories within the framework of the Mayer definition. In addition we will discuss ID applications stemming from each of these theories.

Behavioral Learning Theory

Behavioral psychologists view learning as the ability to perform new behaviors; they focus on a stimulus-response approach to learning. Actions may be established by a researcher or, in applied situations, by a facilitator, teacher, or instructional materials. In these learning situations, there is an effort to create conditions which will enable the learner to demonstrate desired behaviors and perform them over a period of time.

Here we will summarize the major principles of three key behavioral theories and then discuss their importance to ID. These theories are connectionism, classical conditioning, and operant conditioning.

Connectionism

One of the original stimulus-response theories was developed by Edward L. Thorndike. His theory was a type of bond psychology, typically called connectionism. He saw learning as a trial and error process. One learns by making a response, receiving reinforcements if it is correct, and thereby making a connection.

Thorndike's most famous experiments dealt with hungry cats. The cats were placed in a closed box with food outside. The objective was for the cat to discover how to open the door in the box and find the food. At first, the cat's behavior was random and time consuming; however, after accidentally finding the solution, later trials were much shorter (Guthrie, 1960). Results from these studies formed the basis of Thorndike's theory of connectionism.

There are three major laws in this theory: the laws of effect, readiness, and exercise. The law of effect basically indicates that once a connection is made, the strength of that connection is dependent on what follows. A reward will strengthen the behavior, making it habitual, and a punishment will weaken the behavior. Thorndike thought that rewards were much more important than punishments (Mowrer, 1960).

The law of readiness indicates that if an organism is prepared for action, it will behave in a manner that maintains the connection. Thus, making a connection will be satisfying. But if the organism is not ready, the connection will become annoying, and the organism will do things to eliminate it. This is not like reading readiness, because it has nothing to do with having the necessary prerequisite skills or being mature enough. Rather, it is a physical readiness for action (Bower & Hilgard, 1981).

Finally, there is the law of exercise. This relates to strengthening connections through practice and weakening other connections through disuse. The law of exercise has implications for the use of practice and the concept of forgetting. Thorndike emphasized the importance of practice followed by rewards for a correct response. Thus, his laws of effect and exercise are related. Thorndike put no emphasis on the role of meaning or understanding. His work concentrated on ways of increasing the occurrence of certain behaviors, and understanding how they occurred (Bower & Hilgard, 1981).

Classical Conditioning

Ivan Pavlov was one of the first true behaviorists. In studying dogs, he looked for situations in which one could produce a natural response (i.e., salivation) by using an unrelated stimulus (i.e., light). This phenomenon occurred after the unrelated stimulus had been combined for a period of time with food—a more natural elicitor of the desired response. In a normal situation, the natural response (i.e., salivation) is the unconditioned response to the unconditioned stimulus (i.e., food). However, the natural response can become a conditioned response if paired often enough with a conditioned stimulus (i.e., light).

There are many aspects to Pavlov's ideas based on his classical conditioning experiments. Three of them will be discussed here: reinforcement, experimental extinction, and generalization. Reinforcement occurs when the probability of a response (as measured by its frequency or speed) is altered by a stimulus provided by an experimenter. Positive reinforcement is when the provision of a stimulus increases the probability of a desired response. Negative reinforcement, on the other hand, is when the removal of a stimulus decreases the probability of an undesired response.

Experimental extinction occurs when reinforcement is discontinued and the conditioned stimulus is presented alone, without the unconditioned stimulus. In the salivating dog example, experimental extinction is achieved by dropping the unconditioned stimulus (i.e., food) until the conditioned response (i.e., salivating to the light) no longer occurs. A phenomenon which routinely occurs in this situation has been labeled "spontaneous recovery". In other words, the conditioned response can suddenly reappear with no prompting. Extinction is not a case of forgetting. The response is weakened considerably, but can reoccur (Bower & Hilgard, 1981).

Generalization occurs when the eliciting properties of one stimulus are taken on by a similar stimulus. In Pavlov's studies, once a dog learned to salivate in response to hearing a certain sound, it would salivate when a similar sound was presented. Generalization means responding the same way to similar stimuli (Woolfolk, 1998).

Operant Conditioning

B. F. Skinner is considered by many to be one of the most influential psychologists of the twentieth century. He continued the development of theory related to stimulus-response and reinforcement by focusing on operant conditioning—manipulating variables in an effort to identify, predict, and control behavior. The goal of operant conditioning is to strengthen a response by following it with reinforcement.

Some of the most important aspects of Skinner's theory relate to the role of reinforcement in operant conditioning. Similar to Pavlov, Skinner also distinguishes between positive and negative reinforcement. For example, food and water are positive reinforcement for a deprived organism. Providing this type of stimulus will increase the chance that the desired behaviors will recur. A loud noise and extreme heat or cold are examples of aversive stimuli. Removing such an aversive stimulus will likely increase the probability that a desired behavior will occur. Punishment is not negative reinforcement.

Reinforcement of operant behavior is not always consistent over time (Bower & Hilgard, 1981). Casinos are an excellent example. Players know that they will not win every time they put money into a slot machine. However, slot machines are programmed so that the schedule for administering money (i.e., intermittent reinforcement) has an impact upon conditioning and the resulting strength of the response. A player will win money often enough to continue the game. Skinner's principle of time intervals explains this situation. There is a relationship between time intervals which separate the reinforcement (i.e., how often the slot machine gives money) and the resulting behavior (i.e., continuing to play the slot machine). Intermittent reinforcement tends to lead to a continued response.

Extinction ultimately occurs when the reinforcement that has maintained the behavior simply stops (Driscoll, 2005). In the casino example, if the slot machine stops delivering money the player will eventually stop playing. Skinner concluded that if the goal is to eliminate a response completely, punishment is not the most effective technique. In the casino example, yelling at the player to stop playing would be an ineffective way to eliminate the behavior. Eliminating the reinforcement (i.e., the money winnings) is a more effective way to achieve the desired behavior (i.e., the player stops playing the slot machine).

Another important area of Skinner's theory is the notion of shaping (Bower & Hilgard, 1981). In working with animals, Skinner trained some to press and hold down a lever with force. First, he rewarded the animal with food for any lever-press. Then he rewarded only those presses which successively exceeded that force. The result was the extinction of weaker presses and the strengthening of forceful ones, thus shaping the behavior.

Instructional Design Applications of Behavioral Learning Theory

Skinner's conclusions related to operant conditioning, reinforcement, time intervals, extinction, and shaping have been applied to many practical situations and in numerous instructional contexts. According to Driscoll (2007), "The principles . . . that Skinner and his disciples investigated in their research and tried out in instructional applications have had significant impact on the ID field" (p. 38). Here we discuss several applications of behavioral learning theory to ID, including teaching machines and programmed instruction, task analysis, behavioral objectives, practice and feedback, and behavioral fluency.

Teaching Machines and Programmed Instruction

The introduction of Skinner's teaching machines in the 1950s was an early application of the behavioral principle of shaping. Teaching machines require students to work through a series of small frames of instruction that are sequenced in a prescribed order and to compose responses to practice items related to the content (Skinner, 1958). A correct response allows students to go to the next step in the sequence, while an incorrect answer requires them to repeat the frame.

Teaching machines led to the development of programmed instruction. These programmed materials included: (1) content broken into small, carefully designed sequenced steps; (2) active participation where learners compose a response, rather than selecting it from among alternatives; (3) immediate feedback to shape and maintain the learner's behavior; and (4) learner control of the pace of instruction. Skinner called these materials programmed instruction (Reiser, 2007a).

According to Heinich (1970), "Programmed instruction has been credited by some with introducing the systems approach to education" (p. 123). Furthermore, Lumsdaine (1964) indicates that Skinner's work on programmed instruction inspired many psychologists to become interested in the practical problems of instruction. Programmed instruction follows an empirical approach to analyzing instructional problems. This principle is followed today when instructional designers conduct task analysis.

Task Analysis

Behavioral learning theory is applied to ID to analyze the tasks a student undertakes to reach an instructional goal. According to Jonassen and Hannum (1986), "In some contexts, task analysis is limited to developing an inventory of steps routinely performed on a job" (p. 2). Also known as procedural analysis or job analysis, the product of a task analysis is a list of the observable steps and the skills required at each step (Gagné, Briggs, & Wager, 1992). Thus, a task analysis includes the identification and breakdown of tasks that must be learned and the description of the overt behaviors needed to perform those tasks.

Designers use task analysis to deconstruct the steps involved in performing a task. Once the desired task is identified, each step leading to that task must be determined. All of the steps required to perform the desired task are documented and listed in a sequential manner. Following a systems approach to ID, the output of task analysis serves as an input for developing behavioral objectives.

Behavioral Objectives

Behavioral objectives are precise statements written in measurable terms that describe what learners are expected to do after instruction (Mager, 1962). Objectives are statements of learning outcomes that typically include three components (Dick, Carey, & Carey, 2009; Smith & Ragan, 2005). The first part is a description of an observable behavior using an action verb (e.g., interpret, establish, negotiate). The second component is the conditions under which students exhibit the behavior. Conditions often include the tools or information learners will be given when they demonstrate the behavior (e.g., technology, measurement instruments, job aids). The final part is the standard or criterion which describes how well the learner must perform the task (e.g., accuracy, time, number of correct responses). Most instructional designers create objectives following this approach. It stems directly from the behaviorist emphases on observable performance rather than on learning processes.

Practice and Feedback

The law of exercise, which suggests that connections are strengthened through practice and weakened through disuse, has important implications for the design of instruction. Most systematic ID models include the element of practice. As Driscoll (2007) states, ". . . specifying desired behaviors as objectives points out the need to ensure that learners have sufficient opportunities to practice these behaviors as they learn" (p. 38). Dick et al. (2009) suggest that designers can enhance learning by providing practice activities that are directly relevant to objectives. Research consistently shows that practice coupled with feedback has a strong impact on learning. (See Chapter 7.)

Early notions of feedback were influenced heavily by behavioral learning principles suggesting that feedback was essentially the same as reinforcement (Driscoll, 2007). But as Kulvavy and Wager (1993) indicate, "The feedback-as-reinforcer position . . . is basically illogical, supported virtually by no data, and has rarely been directly espoused by Skinner himself" (p. 4). This suggests that using feedback as a reward or motivator during instruction has little impact on learning. However, when feedback is used correctly, it can provide information to learners. From a behaviorist point of view, information feedback provides learners with verification of results (Kulhavy & Stock, 1989).

Behavioral Fluency

To some educators, learning goals encompass more than simply acquiring new behaviors. Instead these behaviors need to be performed at a minimum rate. This is known as behavioral fluency. Behavioral fluency is the combination of accuracy plus speed that characterizes competent performance (Binder, 1996). Fluency-based education strives for automatic or second-nature performance outcomes (Haughton, 1972). Research on behavioral fluency suggests that learners who achieve appropriate frequencies of accurate performance are more likely to retain what they have learned, be resistant to distractions, and be more likely to transfer their learning to other situations (Binder, 1993). The acronym REAPS (retention, endurance, applications, and performance standards) is used to describe the components of behavioral fluency (Binder, 1996). Designers use REAPS principles when the content requires both accuracy and speed as measures of successful performance. These ID principles once again emphasize the importance of practice (Binder, 1993)

Cognitive Learning Theory

Cognitive psychology has a different theoretical orientation than behaviorism. The original purpose of the cognitive revolution was to bring the "mind" back into the human sciences (Bruner, 1990). Thus, the tenets of cognitive psychology are based on how individuals obtain, process, and use information. Cognitive learning theory focuses on explaining the cognitive structures, processes, and representations that mediate instruction and learning (Smith & Ragan, 2005). Cognitive theorists believe the learner's mental processes are the major factor in explaining learning. The ways that learners process and apply information changes one's thoughts and internal mental structures. Here we will examine three cognitive orientations: Gestalt theory (a link between behavioral and true cognitive theory), information processing theory, and schema theory.

Gestalt Theory

One of the early movements to offer alternatives to the stimulus-response approach to learning started in Germany in the first part of the twentieth century. Max Wertheimer, Wolfgang Kohler, Kurt Koffka, and Kurt Lewin were the leaders of what became known as Gestalt theory. Gestalt means "both shape or form and entity or individual . . . Gestalt psychology is the study of how people see and understand the relation of the whole to the parts that make it up" (Winn, 2004, p. 82). Instead of seeing behavior as isolated incidences, Gestalt psychologists believe that an individual always reacts in a total, well-organized response to a situation (Mowrer, 1960). Furthermore, central thinking processes account for more behaviors than simple stimulus-response activities. Thus, Gestalt theory was one of the very early cognitive learning theories, and an important forerunner of information processing theory.

Some of the concepts in Gestalt theory apply directly to learning. These include the laws of similarity, proximity, and closure. These laws explain perceptual principles of organization that describe how learners recognize and remember various aspects of instruction. In addition, they also explain what learners tend not to notice or remember. The law of similarity states that items with similar features (such as similar color or form) tend to be grouped together in our minds. The law of proximity states that elements with close proximity to one another also tend to form perceptual groups. Finally, the law of closure refers to the act of mentally completing a physically incomplete object (Bower & Hilgard, 1981). Since closed figures are more stable, learners tend to remember open figures as instead being closed.

Gestalt principles explain symmetry and perceptual organization as emergent properties similar to the concept of the whole as being greater than the individual parts. A memory trace is one example of symmetry and perceptual organization. It is a change in the memory system resulting from perception and encoding of information (Weiner, 1966). Information stored in memory, such as concepts and words, are represented as bundles with attributes or features called trace elements. Memory traces represent a past event in the present and tend to be reproduced differently from the original. When a learner recalls something from the past, it is retrieved from memory, and the learner may restructure or remember things more organized than originally presented. Learners will systematically and progressively move toward a "good" gestalt. They may make the memory more uniform, sharpen or highlight important details, or normalize the memory into something familiar. A trace is "a 'cognitive blueprint' that specifies the conditions under which the recollection of the event will occur" (Tulving & Watkins, 1975, p. 262).

Information Processing Theory

Information processing theory is based upon the view of the human mind operating in much the same way as a computer: taking in data, then analyzing, storing, and retrieving it. Here we explore learning and how the mind operates from this position.

Memory, according to Seel (2008), "is the mental faculty of retaining and recalling past experiences" (p. 40). From the information processing vantage point, there are at least three different types of memories, each of which serves a different function in the learning process (Atkinson & Shiffrin, 1968). These three memories are shown in Figure 4.1.

Sensory memory is the first stage of information processing (Driscoll, 2005). Information is received here in either a visual or an auditory form. The information that comes into the sensory memory is held for a brief time, just long enough for one's attention mechanisms to determine if the information is relevant, or if it should be ignored.

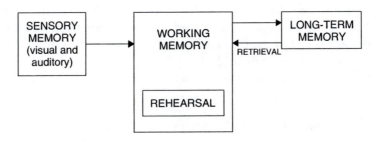

Figure 4.1 The Memory System from an Information Processing Viewpoint.

Note: Adapted from *The Theoretical and Conceptual Bases of Instructional Design* by R. Richey, 1986, p. 68. Copyright 1986 by Rita C. Richey. Used with permission.

If the information is attended to, it moves to the second type of memory: working memory. Here information is organized and held on a short-term basis. The time information is held in working memory is determined by two things: the amount of information being stored and the rehearsal process. Working memory has a limited information capacity. According to long-standing research, only seven, plus or minus two, chunks of information can be retained in working memory at one time (Miller, 1956). Thus, information in working memory can be replaced by new incoming information if the load capacity is exceeded. Information is constantly moving in and out of working memory.

While information is being held in working memory the learner engages in the process of rehearsal. Rehearsal facilitates information storage and recall. It also can create new cognitive structures leading to a more efficient long-term memory (Ericsson & Chase, 1982). If the learning situation demands instant recall, more rehearsal is needed. This includes activities which help process material into active working memory to facilitate deeper processing for recall. Rehearsal readies information for immediate recall, as well as organizes it for transfer to long-term memory—the third type of memory.

The information in long-term memory is commonly considered to be that which has been learned and can be retrieved on demand. Long-term memory can be consciously controlled. The information stored in long-term memory, however, must be meaningful. One of the goals of ID is to create instruction that assists learners in making sense of information so that information can enter and be retained in long-term memory. This process involves the use of mental schema.

Schema Theory

Schema theory focuses on the construction of mental schema or data structures that represent generic concepts (Smith & Ragan, 2005). A schema exists in long-term memory and refers to how our knowledge is organized in memory. The notion of a mental schema is critical to understanding cognitive theory. Through the use of a schema, learners are able to attend to or activate certain parts of memory. A schema aids in comprehension, storage, and retrieval of new knowledge. It also aids perception by facilitating selective attention, comprehension, and recall by facilitating an orderly search of one's memory.

Learners organize existing knowledge into schema structures, and then use these existing structures to assist them in making sense of new information. Piaget suggests that human development is characterized through acquiring and modifying schema (Ginsburg & Opper, 1979). He maintains that schema determines how people react to events and reflect the individual's total knowledge. As new information is stored in previously formed schemata, they are constantly restructuring and redeveloping, changing how learners see and interpret the world.

Information is used to create a new schema or modify existing schema. Rumelhart and Norman (1978) outline three methods to create or modify schemata:

- Accretion—an abstract concept is added to an existing schema connecting to that schema without altering its essence;
- Tuning—an existing schema is modified slightly to better conform to existing experience; and
- Restructuring—the creation of a new schema which substitutes or incorporates old schema.

In ID, the use of extensive practice assists learners in acquiring and altering schemata and allows for their use in subsequent learning.

Instructional Design Applications of Cognitive Learning Theory

Here we discuss the cognitive design strategies that facilitate the storage and retrieval of information, including message design techniques, and instructional strategies such as rehearsal, chunking, mnemonics, and the use of advance organizers. In addition, we discuss the use of cognitive task analysis, a cognitive design process.

Message Design Strategies

Many of the lessons of cognitive learning theory relate to how good instruction can attract attention and facilitate recall. Building upon Gestalt principles, designers will first highlight an inherent order and organization in the lesson. This conceptual structure aids in establishing and preserving accurate memories of the instruction. Moreover, the extent to which this structure is consistent with learner past experiences, the more likely it is to aid learning. However, the structure of instructional materials can also have physical elements that aid perception and then in turn memory. For example, color coding techniques and symmetrical and balanced visuals often serve this purpose. The general appearance of the textbook page or the computer screen often impacts learning more than the individual parts of the presentation.

Rehearsal

One of the goals of rehearsal is to relate learners' prior experiences and knowledge (stored in long-term memory) with new information in working memory. Learners with previous knowledge of a topic can recall many things from long-term memory that can help them process the new information. Learners with little prior knowledge, however, can only make a few of these connections. Instructional designers can incorporate multiple rehearsal strategies in a lesson, such as repeating key points, providing questions and answers, predicting and restating, reviewing, and summarizing. Study skills such as note taking, underlining, and using study guide questions can also facilitate rehearsal.

Chunking

Only a limited amount of information can remain in working memory, but there is a process for increasing this amount: chunking. We have previously cited the classic Miller study (1956) showing that seven (plus or minus two) items are typically held in working memory. While this principle is still appropriate, the amount of information in a single item can be altered by chunking, or grouping, similar information. For example, remembering each individual number of a phone number such as 5513628943 may be difficult. However, if you chunk first the area code numbers (551), then the exchange (362), and finally the last four numbers (8943), it will be easier to hold this number in working memory just long enough to dial the number. Miller (1956) refers to this process as recoding the information.

To promote efficient learning and long-term retention, instructional designers can create materials that incorporate recoding activities which recognize the standard capacity of short-term memories. For example, a designer is creating instruction that teaches how to operate a piece of equipment that requires 15 steps. The designer can chunk the steps into three logically named groups with five steps in each group to assist learners in retrieval.

Mnemonics

Mnemonics are another useful technique for promoting information storage and retrieval. Learning what may appear to be unrelated information will make more sense when connecting it in a memorable fashion. A mnemonic provides a retrieval cue for factual information (Kuo & Hooper, 2004). For example, when given the task of learning the names of the Great Lakes, a learner may use the word "HOMES" (Huron, Ontario, Michigan, Erie, and Superior) to help make the names of the lakes more meaningful. The word "HOMES" is familiar, and makes logical sense to learners, thus allowing them to recall the names of the Great Lakes. Through the use of mnemonics, instructional designers can facilitate the use of cues to retrieve information from the learner's relatively permanent memory storage. Mnemonics provide a substitute for rote memorization.

Advance Organizers

Advance organizers are introductory materials that are presented at a higher level of generalization, simplification, and comprehensiveness than the learning content itself. The advance organizer is presented prior to the material to help bridge the gap between what learners know and what they need to know when learning the material (Ausubel, 1978). The construction of an organizer depends on the nature of the content, the age of the learner, and the learner's prior knowledge of the information. It is an overview or a summary presentation of the principal ideas, omitting the specific details in the learning material itself (Ausubel, 1978).

Cognitive Task Analysis

With the current dominance of cognitivism in ID, the task and learner analysis components of ID models were expanded (Saettler, 1990). Rather than focusing only on observable tasks to be performed, instructional designers began to use techniques for analyzing the nonobservable and mental tasks that will be taught. According to Schraagen, Chipman, and Shalin (2000) cognitive task analysis "is the extension of traditional task analysis techniques to yield information about the knowledge, thought processes, and goal structures that underlie observable task performance" (p. 3).

For example, if a design project focused on employee coaching techniques, the designer would document the steps managers must perform in a coaching session. In addition, the mental tasks the manager would perform while coaching the employee would also be documented. These tasks could include on-the-spot decision making and problem solving. Emphasizing both the cognitive and the behavioral aspects of a task can lead to more comprehensive instructional goals and objectives and can also assist designers in explaining the reasoning behind learner performance (Smith & Ragan, 2005).

Social Learning Theory

Social learning theory expands notions of learning by focusing on the impact of the social environment. Here we will explore this theory through the work of J. B. Rotter and Albert Bandura.

The Foundations of Social Learning Theory

J. B. Rotter (1954) maintains that "the major or basic modes of behaving are learned in social situations . . ." (p. 84). His theory of social learning includes four main variables: (1) behavioral potential, (2) expectancy reinforcement, (3) reinforcement value, and (4) a psychological situation (Rotter, Chance, & Phares, 1972). Behavioral potential is the probability that a person will act in certain ways depending on the situation. This includes observable and nonobservable behavior. Expectancy reinforcement is the individual's belief that a specific behavior will likely lead to a particular reinforcement. Reinforcement value relates to how much a person values an outcome relative to other possible outcomes. The psychological situation includes the context of the behavior, focusing on how an individual views a particular situation; this in turn affects reinforcement value and expectancy (Pintrich & Schunk, 2002).

Social Cognitive Theory

Rotter's work was the forerunner of social cognitive theory, an expansion of social learning theory that focuses on observational learning (Bandura, 1997). Bandura and his colleagues discovered that a child will imitate the behavior performed by an adult if the adult was positively reinforced for that behavior. As stated by Burton, Moore, and Magliaro (2004), "virtually all learning phenomenon resulting from direct experience occur on a vicarious basis by observing other people's behavior and its consequences for them" (p. 12).

A basic assumption of social cognitive theory is that learners draw out information from observing the behaviors of others, and then make decisions about which of these behaviors to accept and perform. This observational and decision-making process is critical in acquiring and performing new behaviors. Bandura (1978) explains that learning possesses three factors: behavior, the environment, and the internal events that influence perceptions and actions. A three-way interlocking relationship exists among these three factors.

Social cognitive theorists maintain that learning and performance are two separate events in that individuals may acquire internal codes of behavior that they may or may not perform later. Learning is the acquisition of symbolic representations in the form of verbal or visual codes that serve as guidelines for future behavior. Visual codes are abstractions of the distinctive features of events such as activities, places, and objects, which could include a great deal of information (Bandura, 1986).

Social cognitive theory includes four components: (1) the behavior model, (2) the consequences of the modeled behavior, (3) the learner's internal processes, and (4) perceived self-efficacy. The function of the behavior model is to transmit information to the learner. This information can serve to strengthen or weaken the learner's existing tendencies to perform particular behaviors or to demonstrate new patterns of behavior (Bandura, 1973).

Similar to operant conditioning, the consequences of behavior are essential to learning in social cognitive theory. Consequences can be vicarious or self-imposed. When a learner observes a model being positively reinforced for a particular behavior, he or she may vicariously experience positive reactions. Self-reinforcement, however, is delivered by the learner as a result of his or her own behavior. Learners tend to establish their own performance standards; they respond to their own behavior in self-rewarding ways if they meet these standards or they can be critical if their performance fails to meet their standards. These self-imposed consequences operate in conjunction with external consequences (Gredler, 2001).

Cognitive processes play an important role in social cognitive theory. The learner's ability to code and store experiences in symbolic form and to represent future consequences in thought is essential to the acquisition and modification of human behavior. Cognitive processing of events and potential consequences guide the learner's behavior. There are four component processes responsible for learning and performance (Bandura, 1977a):

- Attention—noticing the critical factors of the modeled behavior;
- Retention—coding and transforming modeled information for storage and rehearsing and encoding it into memory;
- Production—translating visual and symbolic conceptions of modeled events into behavior; and
- Motivation—performing valued activities and those with expected positive consequences.

Perceived self-efficacy is the learner's belief in his or her capabilities to successfully manage situations that may include novel or unpredictable elements. Research indicates self-efficacy is a basic determinant of learner behavior; the greater people perceive their self-efficacy to be, the more active and longer they will persist in their effort to learn (Liaw, 2002). In other words, self-efficacy is the individual's confidence in her or his ability to perform a specific task.

Social cognitive theory states that the essential factor in achieving complex behavior is the individual's self-regulatory system (Bandura, 1986). This includes standards for one's behavior, self-observation, self-judgment, and self-reaction. It is important to have learners set goals and compare their performance with those goals. The development of a self-regulatory system also relies on learner behavior, the environment, and the internal events that influence perceptions and actions (Bandura, 1978).

Instructional Design Applications of Social Learning Theory

Principles of social learning theory have implications for designing instruction. These include using appropriate models and establishing value and self-efficacy.

Using Models

Teachers, peers, fellow workers, and others can serve as live models in learning and performance settings. A noteworthy application of social learning theory in ID is the use of symbolic modeling. Symbolic models such as pictures, cartoon images, and avatars are used frequently in electronic media. A symbolic model in an electronic source can be viewed multiple times depending on student needs.

Both live and symbolic models can teach abstract cognitive rules, problem-solving strategies, and sequences of integrated motor skills (Carroll & Bandura, 1982). In either case, it is critical that the model be credible, respected by the learner, and someone with whom learners can identify. Learners must also see the model's behavior as being either reinforced or punished (Martin & Briggs, 1986).

Establishing Value and Self-Efficacy

Instructional designers should attempt to establish learner expectancy for positive out-comes, thus increasing student attention to the learning task. If a student perceives that performing well in an instructional event will result in positive results, he or she may place greater value on the event (Bandura, 1977b). It is also important for designers to establish the value of learning something new (Keller, 1983).

Designers should also facilitate a learner's sense of personal efficacy. Self-efficacy can be increased by giving students the opportunity to observe the success of peers who possess similar abilities. This can be done by designing collaborative learning activities, such as peer tutoring or discussion groups, where learners work together.

The Philosophical Orientations of Learning Theory

The philosophical principles guiding most learning theory center primarily on empiricism, sometimes known as scientific empiricism. Empiricism, as previously discussed, views knowledge as being external to the learner and relies on observation and verification to determine reality. (See Chapter 3.) This directly aligns with all of the learning theories discussed in this chapter. Behaviorism, cognitivism, and social learning theory were all established via empirical research and the positivist tradition. Even though these theories project different explanations of the learning process, they all are rooted in the notion that there is an objective truth. Knowledge is factual in nature. Hence, there was often an attempt to establish laws, such as the Gestaltian Law of Good Fit or Thorndike's Law of Exercise. Such laws were verified by well-replicated research. Scientific attitudes tend to take precedence over logic and reasoning, although they did have a role in theorizing. The information processing model, for example, is fundamentally a product of logic and there is a wealth of research to support it.

Social learning theory, however, also reflects another philosophical orientation. It is concerned with the individual's internal conditions as they relate to self-efficacy, and as such it reflects the principles of humanism which emphasize human motivation and feelings. Humanists focus on the individual as the center of interest and one's ability to become a whole person through active engagement in the world (Lacey, 2005). The attempts to avoid feelings of failure (Atkinson, 1966), the wish for feelings of competence and achievement (Atkinson & Raynor, 1974), and the need for affiliation (Pintrich & Schunk, 2002) are examples of an individual's emotions and feelings that affect one's self-efficacy. Educators acknowledge that learners' feelings influence their ability to learn, and learner attitudes and values must be considered when designing instruction (Weinstein & Fantini, 1970).

TRENDS IN THE APPLICATIONS OF LEARNING THEORY TO INSTRUCTIONAL DESIGN

Learning theory remains a significant element in ID practice, especially as it guides designers in the selection of instructional solutions. Today, there is less focus on behavioral principles and a greater recognition of a broad range of factors involved in the learning process. Recent developments include the expansion of learner and environmental analysis in an effort to account for the impact of the learning and performance environments. We will briefly describe two trends in the applications of learning theory to ID: contextual analysis and the first principles of instruction.

Contextual Analysis

Context and environment issues are becoming increasingly important in ID, which is now moving beyond the traditional content emphasis (Richey, 1995). This coincides with learning theory and research recognizing the importance of learner attitudes, motivation, and behavioral modeling in cognitive processing. It also reflects society's need to demand transfer of training, especially in the workplace. Context "is a multilevel body of factors in learning and performance" (Tessmer & Richey, 1997, p. 87). Context influences learning and yet until recently, contextual analysis has been rare in ID. Contextual factors include the learner's work environment, work practices, technology, and individual attitude and background differences. Context is now seen as critical in ID and important to the achievement of performance-based learning (Tessmer & Richey, 1997). Tessmer and Richey (1997) propose a three-part view of context. It encompasses the orienting, instructional, and transfer contexts. (See Figure 4.2.)

There are three types of context addressed in this model. First is the orienting context, which occurs prior to the learning event and includes factors that influence the prospective student's motivation and preparation to learn. Second, the instructional context includes environmental factors that directly impact the delivery of instruction. Third, there is the transfer context which is the environment in which the learning is applied. In addition to the three different contexts, there are three contextual levels embedded within each: (1) the learner, including pertinent background characteristics; (2) the immediate environment, the physical place or event; and (3) the organizational environment, the broadest level.

Contextual analysis is considered to be a more holistic approach to analysis. This expands the needs assessment phase in the ID process to include gathering project-specific contextual data. Such data can isolate those factors that enhance and inhibit

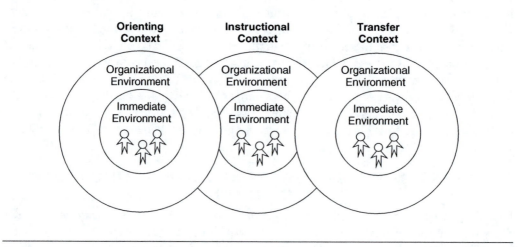

Figure 4.2 Contexts and Contextual Levels.

Note: From "The Role of Context in Learning and Instructional Design" by M. Tessmer and R. C. Richey, 1997, *Educational Technology Research and Development*, 45(2), p. 91. Copyright 1997 by the Association for Educational Communications and Technology. Used with permission.

learning and transfer, as well as identify important factors that are missing from the environment. These factors may be observable (e.g., intrinsic and extrinsic rewards) or they may be unobservable (e.g., organizational culture). Information from contextual analyses is used in the design of instruction to support effective transfer of learning to the environment, an ever-increasing goal of ID.

First Principles of Instruction

The First Principles of Instruction are research-oriented prescriptions for ID. Their focus is on the creation of effective learning environments and products, rather than simply describing how learners acquire knowledge and skill (Merrill, 2002). These principles encompass all of the major learning theories. As a whole, they suggest that learning occurs when it is structured around problem solving. There are five principles of instruction; the first relates to problem-centered instruction and the remaining four describe the four phases of effective instruction. Merrill's (2002, p. 44–45) principles state that:

1. Learning is promoted when earners are engaged in solving real-world problems.
2. Learning is promoted when existing knowledge is activated as a foundation for new knowledge.
3. Learning is promoted when new knowledge is demonstrated to the learner.
4. Learning is promoted when new knowledge is applied by the learner.
5. Learning is promoted when new knowledge is integrated into the learner's world.

The second principle prescribes the use of relevant previous experience in the facilitation of learning. The use of relevant prior experience requires the activation and modification of mental models enabling the learner's opportunity to incorporate new knowledge into existing knowledge (Merrill, 2002).

Social learning theory indicates the importance of the modeling of desired behavior in an effort to promote learner knowledge acquisition and the demonstration of new behavior. This is illustrated in the third principle which focuses on facilitating new knowledge through demonstration for the learner. The fourth principle stresses the importance of the learner applying what is learned. The final principle addresses the requirement of the learner to assimilate newly-learned knowledge with previous knowledge resulting in a new level of knowledge. Merrill (2002) maintains that "The real motivation for learners is learning. When learners are able to demonstrate improvement in skill, they are motivated to perform even better" (p. 50). Social cognitive theory is directly applied in this principle employing the tenets of self-efficacy. Merrill (2002) asserts that the First Principles are always true under appropriate conditions and that they can be implemented in a wide variety of programs and practices (Merrill, 2002).

RESEARCH, LEARNING THEORY, AND INSTRUCTIONAL DESIGN

Research supporting the applications of learning theory in ID is plentiful. Some of this research emerged from the field of psychology, but had implications for ID, while other studies have resulted from research in our field. Here we provide a brief overview of a few studies that inform ID practitioners of important and effective applications of learning theory, followed by recommendations for new avenues of research.

Empirical Support of Learning Theory Applications in Instructional Design

There is an abundance of research on the application of learning theory principles and its effects on human learning in instructional settings. We will explore only a representative set of topics here that pertain to applications of behavioral, cognitive, and social learning theory.

There are many conflicting results from the body of research on the use of behavioral objectives in instruction. For example, the early research on the effects of behavioral objectives on learning includes studies that found student awareness of objectives improves learning significantly (Doty, 1969; Olsen, 1972). However, other studies found student knowledge of objectives had no positive impact (Weinberg, 1971; Zimmerman, 1972). Similarly, Mager and McCann (1961) found that using objectives reduces student learning time, while Loh (1972) and Smith (1971) found no difference in efficiency with the use of objectives.

The effects of feedback have also been studied a great deal, and again without consistent results. Mory (1996) reviewed this research and found that in general the early studies viewing feedback as a type of reinforcement showed no systematic positive effects. The research after 1970, however, viewed feedback as information. Much of this research did find that feedback had positive effects on learning when it corrected inaccurate responses. Mory notes that this research tends to reflect an information processing point of view, and the learners are typically active participants in the process of correcting their errors. Feedback research continues. For example, Clariana, Wagner, and Murphy (2000) studied the effects of feedback timing—either delayed or immediate—on retention. They found that students had a greater memory of their initial lesson responses under delayed feedback conditions.

Research on cognitive theory applications includes studies on the use of advance organizers and mnemonics. Sui (1986) looked at the use of advance organizers with text to promote comprehension among Chinese seventh grade students. Results indicated that text with an advance organizer had a distracting effect for both good and poor readers. These results are supported by the various substantive reviews of the advance organizer research which do not show definitive support for this technique. However, West, Farmer, and Wolff (1991) also note that the studies had "no sensitivity to the fact that *the strength of the organizer is in long-term recall and transfer of general concepts*" (p. 120; emphasis in the original).

The most predominant area of mnemonic research relates to keyword mnemonics, and in general this literature shows that these mnemonics are effective (West et al., 1991). (The HOMES example previously discussed is a keyword mnemonic.) A more current example of such research is that of Kuo and Hooper (2004), who found that students who generated their own mnemonics demonstrated higher post-test scores and spent more time on the learning task.

Research based upon applications of social learning theory include studies of self-efficacy. For example, Ertmer, Evenbeck, Cennamo, and Lehman (1994) focus on the effects of student attitudes toward computers and judgments of self-efficacy for specific computer-based instructional tasks. They found no direct correspondence between computer time-on-task and student levels of confidence. This led them to conclude that the quality of the computer experience may be more critical to self-efficacy than the total amount of time that students spend engaged in computer-related activities. Extending this line of research, Joo, Bong, and Choi (2000) looked at the effects of students' self-efficacy for self-regulated learning in web-based instruction. They found that students' scores on tests of their ability to complete World Wide Web searches were significantly and positively predicted by student self-efficacy in using the Internet, but that Internet self-efficacy did not predict written test performance, which was predicted only by general academic self-efficacy. This demonstrates the complexity of self-efficacy as a motivational and achievement factor.

Recommendations for Continuing Research

Theories which help explain learning will continue to impact the field of ID. Therefore, continued research on the application of learning theory to ID is critical to advance the field. This is especially important as the use of emerging technology increases. For example, designers of technology-based instruction recognize the renewed possibilities of adopting behavioral learning principles when using multimedia that includes visuals and animations (Burton et al., 2004). Additionally, the use of computers as tutors presents opportunities to implement programmed instruction principles such as self-pacing, requisite mastery, and frequent student assessment (Bennett, 1999). As the use of technology-based instruction increases, further research on the application of these and other behavioral learning principles should be conducted.

Additional research on the application of cognitive learning theory to ID should also be undertaken. A particularly fruitful area is problem solving. (See Chapter 7.) For example, Merrill's (2002) first principle of instruction is that learning is promoted when students are engaged in solving real-world problems. While based on current cognitive learning theory, empirical evidence is required to determine the validity of this principle for different types of learners and contexts.

Finally, further research on social learning theory is important as the use of online, distance education grows. The perceived isolation felt by some learners in these settings suggests that studies on modeling and self-efficacy may increase our understanding of learning in online environments.

SUMMARY

Learning theory has had a profound effect on the ID knowledge base. This chapter began with an exploration of three major learning theories and provided examples of the application of behaviorism, cognitivism, and social learning theory in ID practice. Next, we described the philosophical orientation of learning theory as it relates to ID. Table 4.1 summarizes this material.

Learning theory is intricately tied to ID, as illustrated in Table 4.2. This table shows the ID elements that branch from learning theory and how they fit into the ID knowledge base.

Table 4.1 An Overview of Learning Theory and Instructional Design

---

1. **Key Principles:**
   - Learning occurs when an individual makes a connection between a stimulus and a reinforced response.
   - Memory traces include groups of items that are similar or that were presented in close proximity, are in a stable symmetrical shape, and are normalized into something familiar.
   - There are three types of memory: sensory, working, and long-term memory.
   - Schema is knowledge organized in the memory, and it aids in comprehension of new information and the storage and retrieval of previously learned information.
   - Learning occurs by observing other people's behavior in social situations and its consequences for them.
   - Self-efficacy is a basic determinant of learner behavior.

2. **Philosophical Emphases:** The following generalizations can be made:
   - Knowledge of the learning process can be described by general laws established and verified through scientific research.
   - Feelings and emotions impact learning in social settings.

3. **Basic Research Support:** Thorndike's research on connectionism; Pavlov's research on classical conditioning; Skinner's research on operant conditioning; Gestalt research and theory related to perception; Miller's research on memory capacity; Rotter's research on learning in social situations; and Bandura's research on observational learning.

4. **Early Contributors:** R.C. Atkinson, A. Bandura, K. Koffka, W. Kohler, K. Lewin, I. Pavlov, J. B. Rotter, R. M. Shiffrin, B.F. Skinner, E. L. Thorndike, and M. Wertheimer.

5. **ID Applications:**

• Advance Organizers	• Message Design
• Behavioral Objectives	• Mnemonics
• Behavioral Fluency	• Modeling
• Chunking	• Practice
• Cognitive Task Analysis	• Programmed Instruction
• Contextual Analysis	• Rehearsal
• Feedback	• Task Analysis

6. **Supporting ID Research:** Representative areas include the following:
   - Advance Organizers (e.g., Ausubel & colleagues, Sui, 1986)
   - Behavioral Objectives (e.g., Mager & McCann, 1961; Doty, 1968; Zimmerman, 1972)
   - Feedback (e.g., review by Mory, 1996; Clariana, Wagner & Murphy, 2000)
   - Mnemonics (e.g., review by West, Farmer & Wolff, 1991; Kuo & Hooper, 2004)
   - Self-Efficacy (e.g., Ertmer, Evenbeck, Cennamo, & Lehman, 1994)

7. **Related Concepts:**

• Instructional Context	• Performance Objectives
• Job Analysis	• Procedural Analysis
• Orienting Context	• Transfer Context

Table 4.2 Instructional Design Domains and Elements Related to Learning Theory

Learners and Learning Process
- Attention and Attention Mechanisms
- Cognitive Components (Memory Traces, Mental Schema)
- Factors Impacting Learning (Consequences, Context, Information Load, Readiness, Reinforcement, Rewards, Retrieval Cues)
- Laws of Effect, Readiness, and Exercise
- Laws of Similarity, Proximity, and Closure
- Learner Characteristics (Attitudes, Background Experiences, Information Processing Skills, Mental Models and Schema, Motivation, Perceptions)
- Learner Behavior Modeling (Attention, Retention, Reproduction, Reinforcement)
- Self-Efficacy
- Types of Learning (Behavior Modeling, Generalization, Response Strengthening with Reinforcement, Transfer)
- Types of Memory (Sensory, Short-Term, Working, Long-Term, Perceptual)

Learning and Performance Contexts
- Climate (External Influences and Constraints, Physical Resources, Organizational Culture)
- Instructional Environment (Interaction within Instructional Environment)
- Support Available (Practice, Reinforcement, Feedback)
- Types of Contexts (Orienting, Instructional, Transfer)

Instructional and Noninstructional Strategies
- Advance Organizers
- Behavior Modeling
- Content Chunking
- Feedback
- First Principles of Instruction
- Mnemonics
- Practice and Rehearsal
- Reinforcement
- Shaping

Designers and Design Processes
- Analysis Processes (Task, Job, Cognitive, Contextual)
- Content Identification (Behavioral/Performance Objectives)
- Criterion-Referenced Assessment
- Establishing Value for Learning and Self-Efficacy
- Message Design
- Sequencing (Part and Whole Task)

When you add these elements to those stemming from general systems theory (GST), and communication theory, you can see how the knowledge base is continuing to grow. The growth of the ID knowledge base continues in Chapter 5, which focuses on early instructional theory.

5

EARLY INSTRUCTIONAL THEORY

This chapter examines the contributions of early instructional theory to instructional design (ID). Many of the principles found in ID models today have their foundations in the early theories discussed in this chapter. Because ID and early instructional theory are closely aligned, some people confuse the two. We view this early theory as a precursor to the ID theories and models found in the current literature.

We have chosen to examine instructional theory developed before and during the 1970s because the application of ID models began to thrive during that decade and the term "instructional design" was used more widely in education than it had been in previous decades (Dick, 1987; Reiser, 2007a). While we discuss a range of early theoretical contributions to modern day ID, this chapter is not exhaustive. We will explore a few selected instructional theories that serve as a foundation to the ID field. The following will be discussed:

- Instructional theory that serves as forerunner to ID;
- Philosophical orientations of early instructional theory;
- Application of early theory to ID; and
- Research on early instructional theory.

INSTRUCTIONAL ANTECEDENTS OF INSTRUCTIONAL DESIGN THEORY

The instructional theories described below are forerunners to current ID theory and models. Some ID practices in use today have their roots in theories of curriculum development for schools. Other principles were developed during the Cold War when learning psychologists focused their research on issues of instruction to help close the missile gap between the United States and the Soviet Union (Bruner, 1960). In all cases, the theories we discuss provide important groundwork for ID. These include:

- Basic principles of curriculum and instruction;
- Theories of mastery learning and individualized instruction; and
- Early cognitive theory of instruction.

Basic Principles of Curriculum and Instruction

Ralph Tyler directed an evaluation of the progressive education movement in secondary education during the 1930s. The results of this eight-year study led him to conclude that curriculum and instruction should be based on evidence from empirical research. Tyler's intent was to provide a basis for studying the problems of curriculum and instruction, not to outline specific steps of curriculum construction (Tyler, 1949, 1980). However, his basic principles have been implemented by countless teachers and curriculum developers over the past 60 years. Furthermore, they include many of the elements found in the systems approach to ID.

Tyler's (1949) work provides an important foundation for our field because he indicated that curriculum and instruction includes four elements:

- Identifying the purposes of education;
- Selecting learning experiences that are useful for attaining objectives;
- Organizing these experiences; and
- Evaluating the effectiveness of these learning experiences.

Tyler (1949) proposes that goals and objectives are necessary to plan and make continuous improvement to an educational program. He indicates that three sources of information should be considered when objectives are formulated: (1) information about students, including their needs, interests, and level of development; (2) information about the problems of contemporary life so that meaningful outcomes are identified; and (3) information about the content and what subject matter experts consider important. He further suggests that information about learning psychology should be used to determine the appropriate sequence and relationship among objectives and the conditions under which students can attain these outcomes.

A learning experience "refers to the interaction between the learner and the external conditions in the environment to which he can react" (Tyler, 1949, p. 63). Tyler suggests the following general principles for learning experiences:

- Students must have the appropriate predispositions and prior knowledge to participate in a given learning experience.
- Students must gain satisfaction from participating in a learning experience and from attaining the desired behavior in an objective.
- Many learning experiences can be used to address a particular objective, and a wide range of experiences helps to maintain student and instructor interests.
- Students must have the opportunity to practice the behavior and deal with the content implied by the objective.
- Every learning experience is likely to have more than one outcome, and undesirable outcomes sometimes occur.

According to Tyler (1949) learning experiences should be organized to support each other and produce a cumulative, long-term impact on learning. He proposes three main criteria for organizing learning experiences: continuity, sequence, and integration. Continuity relates to the idea that instruction and practice should continually recur to help students learn important concepts and objectives. Sequence refers to having learning experiences build on each other to go deeper and more broadly into the content. Integration has to do with relating objectives and experiences in a particular subject matter to other content areas.

Finally, Tyler (1949) addresses the importance of evaluation in curriculum development and defines it as "a process for finding out how far the learning experiences as developed and organized are actually producing the desired results" (p. 105). He advocates that evaluation should include testing students before, during, and after they participate in an instructional program. He also suggests follow-up studies of graduates to determine if learning has become permanent.

Mastery Learning and Individualized Instruction

Proponents of mastery learning believe that most students can master new knowledge and skills if they are given enough time to achieve them, if there is specific criterion of what comprises mastery, if instruction is approached systematically, and if students who have difficulty learning are provided remediation (Bloom, 1971). Advocates of this approach suggest that traditional group instruction should be modified to give individual students the time they require to learn by working at their own pace (Joyce & Weil, 1986). Two theories of mastery learning that provide a foundation for ID are discussed below.

The Model of School Learning

John B. Carroll (1963) suggests that school learning can be described as a ratio between the amount of time required to learn something and the time a student actually spends on learning. His formula to represent learning is:

Degree of Learning = f(Time Actually Spent / Time Required to Learn).

The time actually spent is a function of two variables: perseverance and opportunity to learn. Perseverance is the amount of time a student is willing to spend on a learning activity; it is a time-on-task variable as opposed to lapsed time. Motivational factors such as interest and confidence are related to one's perseverance. Opportunity to learn is the amount of time given to students to master a new skill. Carroll (1963) notes that opportunity to learn is often less than the time a student requires to learn it.

Time required to learn is a function of three variables: aptitude, ability, and quality of instruction. Aptitude relates to the amount of time a student requires to learn a skill to an acceptable standard. A student who requires a small amount of time to learn a task is considered to have a high aptitude. Aptitude for any given task is dependent on the quality of instruction, which in turn affects a learner's ability to understand the instruction. Quality of instruction is based on how well content is organized and presented. Carroll (1963) indicates that quality of instruction is the most elusive of all the variables in his model. Ability to understand instruction relates to a learner's general intelligence, verbal ability, and learning strategies.

Therefore, of the five major variables in Carroll's model, three are student characteristics: perseverance, aptitude, and ability to understand instruction. The remaining two components are imposed on the learning process by the environment: opportunity to learn and quality of instruction. Typical environmental factors are instructional materials, media, and instructor performance.

Human Characteristics and School Learning

Benjamin Bloom notes that his thinking about mastery learning was influenced by Carroll's model. Bloom (1976) extends Carroll's theory by including three main variables that account for variations in learning: student characteristics, instruction, and learning outcomes. (See Figure 5.1.)

Bloom (1976) emphasizes the background of the learner in his theory by including the variable of student characteristics. These impact whether or not a student will master the objectives included in a learning task. One main characteristic that influences mastery is cognitive entry behaviors (i.e., prerequisite knowledge and skills). Bloom stresses the importance of this characteristic by stating, ". . . if all the students have the necessary prerequisites for a particular learning task, they would be able to learn it with less variation in level or rate of learning . . ." (p. 31). In addition to cognitive skills, Bloom highlights the significance of affective entry behaviors in his theory. These consist of students' general desire to learn, their interest in the content, and their confidence in their own ability. Affective entry behaviors also impact the mastery of a learning task.

Central to Bloom's (1976) instructional theory is a learning task. He indicates that a learning task is often referred to as a unit in a course or a topic in a curriculum. Learning tasks are made up of the ideas, procedures, and behaviors that students learn. They may include simple instructional objectives such as knowledge of facts and terms or they may contain complex objectives requiring skill application.

Bloom addresses the relationship among learning tasks by noting that complex cognitive tasks are often hierarchical in nature. Bloom (1976) states, "In such arrangements, each learning task becomes a prerequisite for the next task in the series and is, in turn, dependent on the achievement of certain prerequisites in the previous tasks" (p. 27).

Quality of instruction impacts whether students master a learning task. According to Bloom (1976), "The instructional variable of greatest importance is believed to be quality of instruction" (p. 11). He lists four essential components of instructional quality:

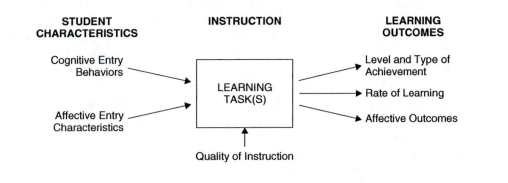

Figure 5.1 Major Variables in Bloom's Theory of School Learning.

Note: From *Human Characteristics and School Learning* by B. S. Bloom, 1976, p. 11. Copyright 1976 by McGraw-Hill. Used with permission.

- Cues and directions provided to students;
- Active participation of students;
- Feedback to help correct mistakes; and
- Reinforcement provided to students in relation to learning.

These components are found in many instructional theories based on psychological principles of learning. (See Chapter 4.)

Finally, Bloom (1976) includes learning outcomes as another main variable in his instructional theory. These consist of level and type of achievement, rate of learning, and affective outcomes. He suggests a causal relationship among these outcomes and the other variables in his theory. This implies that cognitive and affective student characteristics and quality of instruction impact student mastery of learning tasks, which in turn influences achievement, rate of learning, and affective outcomes.

Early Cognitive Theory of Instruction

Another early instructional theory that provides a foundation for ID was developed by Jerome Bruner. While his ideas include constructs found in behavioral learning theory, his thinking is greatly dependent on cognitive learning principles (Richey, 1986). Thus, Bruner is one of the key figures in the cognitive revolution in learning and instruction (Driscoll, 1994).

His theory includes four main concepts: predisposition, structure, sequence, and reinforcement. While recognizing the importance of culture, motivation, and personal characteristics that impact the desire to learn, Bruner (1966) indicates that learning and problem solving depends on a predisposition to explore alternatives. He suggests that instruction should facilitate the desire to explore alternatives through: (1) activation—providing an optimal level of uncertainty to peak learner curiosity; (2) maintenance—ensuring that the consequences of making mistakes are not severe; and (3) direction—making goals known to learners in some approximate manner.

Instruction must also address the optimal structure of a domain of knowledge or any problem in that domain, so it can be understood by learners. Bruner (1966) states:

> ... knowledge ... can be represented in three ways: by a set of actions appropriate for achieving a certain result (enactive representation); by a set of summary images or graphics that stand for the concept without defining it fully (iconic representation); and by a set of symbolic or logical propositions drawn from a symbolic system that is governed by rules (symbolic representation). (pp. 44–45)

These alternative forms of representing content—actions, pictures, and symbols—vary in difficulty and usefulness depending on age and learner background.

Instruction should also specify the most effective sequence of how to present material to learners. Bruner (1966) stated, "Instruction consists of leading a learner through a sequence of statements and restatements of a problem or body of knowledge that increase the learner's ability to grasp, transform, and transfer what he is learning" (p. 49).

Lastly, Bruner's (1966) theory of instruction addresses reinforcement by specifying the nature and pacing of feedback and rewards. He observed that effective instruction allows learners to determine whether they "got there" (p. 68) and suggested the use of intrinsic rewards and meaningful feedback.

Summary and Comparison of Early Instructional Theories

Table 5.1 shows the main elements in the early instructional theories discussed in this chapter. Information in the table provides a way to compare the theories and shows how they contribute to the foundation of ID.

All of the early instructional theories described above specifically address the importance of learner characteristics. These include factors such as ability, prior knowledge, interest, perseverance, and predispositions. All of the theories also include the concept of active learner participation. Most address sequencing particularly as it relates to complex skills and their hierarchical relationships. Two theories advocate providing meaningful feedback and reinforcement to learners, and two specifically include the use of instructional objectives. Two theories address the notion of aligning objectives, instructional activities, and assessment, while two others speak directly to time-on-task. Thus, most of the elements found in early instructional theory are also found in models of ID.

Table 5.1 A Comparison of Major Elements in Early Instructional Theories

Elements	Theories			
	Tyler's Principles of Curriculum & Instruction	Carroll's Model of School Learning	Bloom's Theory of Human Characteristics & School Learning	Bruner's Cognitive Theory of Instruction
Active Participation	X	X	X	X
Alignment of Objectives, Instruction & Assessment	X		X	
Alternative Forms to Represent Content				X
Feedback			X	X
Individualization		X	X	
Learner Characteristics	X	X	X	X
Objectives	X		X	
Reinforcement			X	X
Sequencing	X		X	X
Time-on-task		X	X	

The Philosophical Orientation of Early Instructional Theory

Early instructional theories adhere to tenants of logical positivism and objectivism. In this approach, knowledge exists outside the learner, conditions are arranged to promote the acquisition of predetermined goals, and learning is assessed by an external source such as a teacher (Hannafin & Hill, 2007).

Early instructional theories also represent an empirical, scientific orientation toward curriculum and instruction. N. L. Gage (1978) writes that "No one can ever prescribe all the twists and turns to be taken . . . to promote learning" (p. 15). Yet in promoting a scientific basis for the art of teaching, Gage supports the use of empiricism to discover the laws, generalizations, and trends that will improve teaching. This philosophical orienta-tion is shared by the early theorists discussed in this chapter. For example, Tyler's primary goal was to provide an empirical basis for studying the problems of instruction (see Tyler, 1980). Bruner's aim was observe how principles of learning work in effective day-to-day pedagogy (see Bruner, 1960). Thus, these early instructional theorists provide an empiri-cal foundation consisting of "knowledge of regular, nonchance relationships in the realm of events with which the practice [of teaching] is concerned" (Gage, 1978, p. 20).

EARLY INSTRUCTIONAL THEORY AND INSTRUCTIONAL DESIGN

The instructional theories discussed in this chapter provide a strong foundation for ID. This section focuses on how early instructional theory impacts the:

- Design and management of instruction;
- Identification of instructional objectives;
- Analysis of learner characteristics;
- Sequencing of objectives and activities; and
- Selection of instructional strategies.

The Design and Management of Instruction

According to Visscher-Voerman and Gustafson (2004), a majority of ID models in the literature follow an instrumental approach that starts with the development of goals and objectives. A basic principle of this approach is the alignment of objectives, instruc-tional activities, and assessment. Tyler (1949) was an early proponent of this system of planning curriculum and instruction. His ideas have been used to design curriculum and instruction for many children and adults in formal education settings (Cervero & Wilson, 1994; Kliebard, 1970). They are also implemented in the workplace through the use of learning management systems that link employee learning goals, attendance in training events, and assessment results (Merrill & Wilson, 2007).

Theories of mastery learning and individualized instruction proposed by Carroll (1963) and Bloom (1976) also impact the design and management of instruction. In the first edition of *The Systematic Design of Instruction*, Walter Dick and Lou Carey (1978) explain that their ID model has origins in individualized instructional theories. They note that "Systematically designed instruction . . . can be used to determine each student's instructional needs in order to tailor instruction to each student as much as possible" (Dick & Carey, 1978, p. 2).

Implementing individualized instruction has been difficult in traditional classrooms due to time limitations and other constraints faced by teachers. However, advances in interactive multimedia technology and web-based instruction serve as the basis for implementing theories of individualized instruction. For example, Reeves (1997) uses Carroll's model of school learning as a foundation for his own model of World Wide Web (WWW) Learning. Reeves expands on the concept of aptitude by noting the impor-tance of other individual differences that can be accommodated in WWW instruction, such as interests, attitudes, learning styles, anxiety, and tolerance for ambiguity. He also suggests that quality of instruction is influenced by task ownership, collaboration, meta-cognitive support, and opportunity to construct learning. These concepts are associated with constructivist philosophy. (See Chapter 8.)

Bruner's (1966) theory of instruction has also been applied to models of curriculum design and management. Proposing a new paradigm for instructional management, Heinich (1970) describes how Bruner's ideas pertain to ID. (See Figure 5.2.)

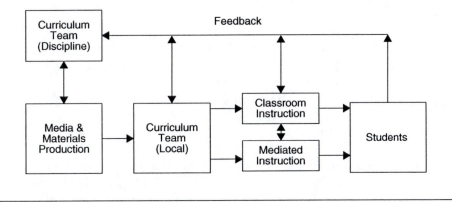

Figure 5.2 Bruner's Concept of Curriculum Construction.

Note: From *Technology and the Management of Instruction* by R. Heinich, 1970, p. 149. Copyright 1970 by the Association of Educational Communications and Technology. Used with permission.

In this approach, a team of teachers, subject-matter experts, and psychologists representing a discipline work together to identify content and prepare instructional activities, materials, and media. Local curriculum teams then examine these materials and decide whether to adopt them. If a positive decision is made, classroom and mediated instruction is implemented with students and feedback is obtained. This feedback is used to make the system adaptive and responsive. Heinich suggests that Bruner's theory is important to the management of instruction because teachers do not have the time to stay fully informed about their subject matter. He also indicates that Bruner's theory "is a systems approach made possible by well-developed technologies of instruction" (Heinich, 1970, p. 148).

Instructional Objectives

The identification of objectives is a major phase of systematic ID models (Dick, Carey, & Carey, 2009; Gustafson & Branch, 2002; Morrison, Ross, & Kemp, 2006; Seels & Glasgow, 1998). This element was influenced greatly by the principles of curriculum and instruction developed by Tyler. According to Reiser (2007a), "Ralph Tyler has often been considered the father of the behavioral objectives movement" (p. 25).

Tyler (1949) was an early advocate of writing objectives in terms of student behavior, even before behavioral learning theory exerted heavy influence on teaching. Prior to the introduction of his ideas, most objectives were stated in terms of instructional activities implemented by teachers or as a list of content topics covered in a course; they were not focused on learner outcomes. Furthermore, Tyler suggested several sources for obtaining objectives, including the learners themselves, contemporary life, subject specialists, and the psychology of learning. Following Tyler's recommendations, designers today consult a variety of sources when identifying the objectives of instruction. For example a designer who is developing training for a new computer system in a bank would confer with content matter experts who have knowledge of banking practices, bank managers with knowledge of federal and state regulations, employees who use the current system, and the information technologist who designed the new system. The designer would also consult existing training materials and other documents specifically related to the objectives of instruction.

Analysis of Learner Characteristics

Most ID models also include an analysis of learner characteristics. The early instructional theorists discussed in this chapter all provide a base for this component of ID. Carroll (1963) stresses factors such as general ability, the time required to learn a skill, and the amount of time a student is willing to spend learning. Bloom (1976) emphasizes the importance of learner background, especially as they relate to cognitive and affective entry behaviors. Tyler (1949) proposes that information about students, including their needs, interests, and level of development, should be considered when objectives are formulated. Bruner (1966) highlights the significance of students' predisposition to explore alternatives especially when they are asked to solve problems.

Instructional designers following a systems approach collect and use information about the general ability, prior knowledge, predispositions, and learning preferences of their target audience (Dick et al., 2009; Morrison et al., 2006). Designers also consider the motivation of the audience by collecting information about their needs, interests, values, expectations, and confidence (Keller, 1986; Klein, 1990). Furthermore, designers analyze learner attitudes about their job and work setting to address issues related to transfer of skills (Garavaglia 1993; Rossett, 1997).

Sequencing

Sequencing continues to be a major concern for instructional designers; it is one of the six domains of the ID knowledge base. (See Chapter 1.) Early instructional theories have implications for the sequencing of learning objectives and activities. For example, Bloom (1976) points out the hierarchical relationship among complex cognitive tasks and discusses how some skills are prerequisite to others.[1] Designers implement this principle when identifying subordinate and entry skills during task analysis (Dick et al., 2009).

Tyler (1949) and Bruner (1966) suggest that instruction should be sequenced to support cumulative, long-term learning. Both theorists support the proposition that learning experiences build on each other and that a recurrence of instruction on a particular concept helps learners retain and transfer knowledge and skills. Bruner (1960) proposes the concept of a spiral curriculum suggesting that curricula should be developed to address and build on basic ideas repeatedly until students grasp them fully. He hypothesizes that spiral curriculum can be used to teach any subject matter to any child at any stage of development.

---

1 Bloom cites early research conducted by Robert Gagné to support his point about the hierarchical relationship among complex skills. See Chapter 7 for a more detailed explanation of Gagné's research on this topic.

Instructional Strategy Selection

The work of early instructional theorists also has an impact on instructional strategy selection. Models of mastery learning suggest that students be allowed to work through instruction at their own pace and that remedial instruction be provided to those who have difficulties learning (Carroll, 1963; Joyce & Weil, 1986). Early instructional theories propose that students should actively participate in learning experiences and should have the opportunity to practice the behavior identified in an objective (Bloom, 1976; Tyler, 1949).

Early cognitive instructional theory suggests that content should be represented in alternative formats including actions, pictures, and symbols (Bruner, 1960). Early theory espoused by Bruner also serves as a basis for discovery learning, problem solving, and scaffolding. For example, Driscoll (2005, p. 234) writes, "Bruner believed that the process of discovery contributes significantly to intellectual development . . . through the exercise of problem solving." Later, Wood, Bruner, and Ross (1976) indicate that problem solving involves the use of effective scaffolding defined as ". . . controlling those elements of the task that are initially beyond the learner's capability, thus permitting him to concentrate upon and complete only those elements that are within his range of competence" (p.89). Scaffolding has recently been used in the design of technology-enhanced, problem-based learning environments (Brush & Saye, 2000; Sharma & Hannafin, 2007; Simons & Klein, 2007). (See Chapter 8.)

Feedback

Feedback is one of the main elements of effective instruction. Early theorists suggest providing meaningful feedback to help learners correct their mistakes (Bloom, 1976; Bruner, 1966). Building on this concept, Kulhavy and Stock (1989) propose two types of feedback: verification and elaboration. Verification feedback provides confirmation to help learners develop knowledge of their performance. Elaboration strategies provide corrective, informative, or reflective feedback (Dempsey & Sales, 1993). Elaboration involves giving learners feedback on the task itself and giving feedback regarding the process used to learn the task. Reflective feedback requires learners to justify their responses. All of these feedback strategies have their foundation in early instructional theory.

RESEARCH ON EARLY INSTRUCTIONAL THEORY

The early instructional theories described in this chapter were developed based on research on teaching and learning. Furthermore, studies which provide empirical support for some of the principles found in these theories have been conducted. Below, we discuss this empirical support and provide some recommendations for continued research on early instructional theory.

Empirical Support of Early Instructional Theory

Over the years, scholars in the field of curriculum and instruction have addressed the usefulness of Tyler's (1949) model. While recognizing the impact of the approach, some authors have also criticized it. For example, Kliebard (1970) writes that Tyler's theory is "the most persistent theoretical formulation in the field of curriculum" (p. 259). However, Kliebard questions whether stating objectives as external goals to be achieved through participation in learning experiences is a good method of curriculum planning. Furthermore,

Zahorik (1976) thinks that the model can result in effective and efficient instruction but states, "The Tyler planning model simply does not suit . . . programs or practices that emphasizes student independence, self-direction and responsibility" (p. 488).

These criticisms may be due to a lack of direct empirical evidence for the curriculum principles espoused by Tyler. In an extensive review of curriculum research, McNeil (1969) indicates that there is little support for the idea that principles of curriculum and instruction have a significant impact on how curriculum is developed in schools. Specifically addressing Tyler's work, McNeil (1969) writes, "Tyler (1967) cautioned against attributing change to any specific influence unless the relationship can be clearly demonstrated. Few such relationships have been shown" (p. 299).

There is some empirical evidence for the Carroll (1963) model of school learning. In 1989, Carroll published a 25-year retrospective in which he reviewed research conducted on components of his model. Based on these studies he indicated that the following conclusions can be made:

- Academic learning time is one of the most important factors related to student achievement.
- Time spent learning is an important predictor of achievement.
- Reducing the opportunity to learn relative to the time required to learn has a negative effect on achievement.
- Perseverance accounts for differences in student achievement even when researchers control for aptitude (i.e., amount of time required to learn).

Carroll (1989) admits that since his "model of school learning does not deal extensively with elements involved in quality of instruction, it has not been particularly influential in these studies" (p. 29).

Research has also been conducted on the impact of learner characteristics on educational outcomes. Establishing an empirical basis for his theory, Bloom (1976) indicates that studies show "cognitive entry behaviors can account for about 50 percent in the variation in achievement while affective entry behaviors alone can account for about 25 percent" (p. 108). He cites several longitudinal (macro) studies as well as a number of microstudies to support his proposition that learner characteristics should be considered when instruction is designed to enable mastery.

Furthermore, reviews of research on mastery learning generally support the notion that it is an effective instructional method. For example, a review by Block and Burns (1976) indicates that mastery approaches: (1) produce consistently large effects on student learning, but not as large as those advocated by their proponents; (2) require more student study time than nonmastery approaches; (3) impact affective consequences positively, but these effects may be due to novelty; and (4) sometimes help minimize the impact of individual cognitive differences among students, but do not eliminate them. A meta-analysis of mastery learning studies by Kulik, Kulik, and Bangert-Drowns (1990) shows that this approach has a positive impact on test performance and attitudes of students in college, high school, and upper elementary school. Their review also found that self-paced mastery approaches tend to increase student time-on-task but they often result in lower course completion rates for college students. However, a synthesis of the research on group-based mastery learning by Slavin (1987) found moderate, short-lived effects for this method when experimenter-made measures were used, and no evidence to support its effectiveness when standardized achievement measures were used.

Finally, the main concepts found in Bruner's (1966) theory of instruction have empirical support. In 2006, Bruner published a collection of his essays, book chapters, and articles that appeared in the literature from 1957 through 1976. Based on these works, we draw the following conclusions:

- There is much empirical support for the idea that humans move through enactive, iconic, and symbolic stages of development.
- Age and learner background should be considered when using alternative formats to represent content.
- The underlying principles of a subject matter give curriculum its structure, and learners should be taught new knowledge and skills in the context of this structure.
- The usefulness of corrective feedback depends on the form in which it is received by the learner and the conditions placed on how it can be used.
- While there is much research on the use of extrinsic rewards, these types of rewards should be de-emphasized, and instead intrinsic rewards, student interest, and curiosity should be emphasized in the design of instruction.
- Learning and problem solving should be organized hierarchically.
- When learning to solve problems, students formulate and test their own ideas by comparing their solutions to a criterion.

To summarize, research evidence does exist for many of the principles found in the early instructional theories discussed in this chapter. However, Bruner's (1960) advice still holds true today:

What is abundantly clear is that much work remains to be done by way of examining currently effective practices, fashioning curricula that may be tried out on an experimental basis, and carrying out the kinds of research that can give support and guidance to the general effort at improving teaching. (p. 32)

Recommendations for Continuing Research

It is clear that early instructional theory is based on results from empirical research. Tyler's principles of curriculum and instruction were developed based on evidence collected from his evaluation of the progressive education movement (Tyler, 1980). Carroll's model of school learning is supported by his observations and study of foreign language learning (Carroll, 1989). Bloom's theory of learner characteristics and school learning comes from evidence he and other researchers collected (Bloom, 1976). Bruner's theory of instruction is based on research conduced by him, his colleagues, and other cognitive psychologists.

We believe that future studies should be conducted by ID researchers to validate these early theories and their related elements. These studies could be conducted using model validation and use research techniques. (See Richey & Klein, 2007.) For example, multimedia instruction and online education allow learners to work at their own pace. They are also used with learners who may have cognitive and affective entry characteristics that differ from learners in face-to-face settings. We think design and development research should be conducted to determine if the models proposed by Carroll and Bloom are applicable in these newer environments. Design and development research can also be used to investigate and identify the components of theories and models (Richey & Klein, 2007). For example, this type of research could examine the application of Bruner's recommendation for enactive, iconic, and symbolic knowledge representation when designers use wikis and blogs for the purpose of facilitating learning.

SUMMARY

This chapter has examined selected theories of instruction and described how they contribute to the ID knowledge base. We discussed basic principles of curriculum and instruction, mastery learning and individualized instruction, and an early cognitive instructional theory, as well as the philosophical orientations of these theories. This was followed by a description of how early instructional theory impacts ID, including the design and management of instruction, identification of instructional objectives, analysis of learner characteristics, sequencing, feedback, and the selection of instructional strategies. This chapter closes with a summary of research conducted to provide empirical evidence for the ideas advocated by early instructional theorists and some recommendation for future studies using design and development research.

Table 5.2 provides a summary of key principles, theoretical foundations, philosophical orientations, contributors, and applications of early instructional theory. Furthermore,

Table 5.2 An Overview of Early Instructional Theory and Instructional Design

1. **Key Principles:**
   • Cognitive and affective learner characteristics impact learning.
   • Curriculum and instruction include interrelated elements.
   • Instruction must address the optimal structure and sequence of a domain of knowledge or any problem in that domain.
   • Objectives are the basis for instruction; they should align with instructional activities, assessment, and evaluation.
   • Theories of instruction should be based on empirical evidence.
   • Traditional group instruction should be modified to give individual students the time they require to learn.

2. **Philosophical Emphasis:** The following generalizations can be made:
   • Knowledge exists outside the learner and instruction promotes the acquisition of predetermined goals (i.e., logical positivism and objectivism).
   • Laws, generalizations, and trends that will improve instructional practices can be established (i.e., empiricism).

3. **Basic Research Support:** Research on operant conditioning; research on memory capacity.

4. **Major Contributors:** Benjamin Bloom, Jerome Bruner, John B. Carroll, and Ralph Tyler.

5. **Applications to ID:**
   • Analysis of Learner Characteristics
   • Design and Management of Instruction
   • Identification of Instructional Objectives
   • Sequencing of Objectives and Activities
   • Selection of Instructional Strategies

6. **Research Support: Studies of:**
   - Academic Learning Time (e.g., Carroll and his colleagues)
   - Cognitive Learning (e.g., Bruner)
   - Learner Characteristics (e.g., Bloom)
   - Mastery Learning (e.g., Bloom and his colleagues)

7. **Related Concepts**
   - Curriculum Design
   - Discovery Learning
   - Individualized Instruction
   - Problem Solving

Table 5.3 offers a synopsis of how early instructional theory relates to the six domains of the ID knowledge base.

Table 5.3 Instructional Design Domains and Elements Related to Early Instructional Theory

Learners and Learning Processes
- Learner characteristics (ability, aptitude, attitudes, background, beliefs and values, expectancies, and motivational factors such as predisposition, perseverance and desire to learn, prerequisite knowledge and experience).
- Learning is impacted by the amount of time required to learn and the amount of time a student is willing to spend.

Learning and Performance Contexts
- Classroom environments

Content Structure and Sequence
- Content classified as cognitive, affective, or psychomotor.
- Instruction consists of a sequence of statements and restatements of a body of knowledge or problem.
- Many learning outcomes are hierarchical, moving from simple to complex.
- Sequence instruction to support cumulative, long-term learning.

Instructional and Noninstructional Strategies
- Allow learners to have control over pace.
- Give meaningful feedback.
- Provide opportunities for active participation and practice.
- Provide reinforcement.
- Provide remedial instruction and scaffolding to learners having difficulties.
- Represent content using actions, pictures, and symbols.
- Use discovery and problem-based learning.

Media and Delivery Systems
- Individualized instruction in classrooms and technology-based environments

Designers and Design Processes
- Identification of goals and objectives
- Learner analyses
- Task analyses

Chapter 6 focuses on media theory which is a cluster of theories developed primarily by those within the IDT field. It provides the foundations for mediated instruction and the use of technology.

6

MEDIA THEORY

In the instructional design (ID) field, media is defined as "the physical means via which instruction is presented to learners" (Reiser, 2007a, p. 18). In past years, educators spoke of media as audio-visual aids; today they more commonly use the term "technology" when they talk about media. The term "media" implies devices which provide learning experiences, experiences which typically involve sound, visuals (either static or moving), concrete objects, or actual physical movement. The theoretical emphasis, however, is not on the machine, or even upon the software that contains the instruction, but rather on the learning that occurs as a result of interacting with the media. Consequently, media theory addresses those aspects of mediated instruction that facilitate learning, and in doing so attempts to explain how the learning process occurs when media is involved. This complex procedure is the focus of this chapter.

Over the years various technological innovations have fascinated the public and captured the imaginations of pioneering educators. At one time, the camera, motion pictures, television, computers, and the web were thought to provide answers to many of education and training's most vexing problems. Even though mediated instruction has never fully delivered on its promises, it has brought much progress and innovation to the field. Media theory seeks to explain how and why this has happened.

Unlike the other theory bases that we have discussed thus far, media theory is to a great extent a direct product of the scholarly efforts of those in the ID field. Even so, it does rely on the research and theory of other disciplines, especially communications and psychology. It also utilizes the work of scholars who are outside of the field, but who are nonetheless interested in the use of media in teaching and learning. Here we will examine media theory by describing:

- The various interpretations of the manner in which media impacts learning;
- The manifestations of media theory in ID over the years; and
- The research that supports both the theory and the various ID applications.

MEDIA AND LEARNING

Media theory has not been defined as succinctly as has learning theory, for example. (See Chapter 4.) Nevertheless, media has been a focal point of ID research and theoretical principles relating to media have evolved. Here we will examine the key principles of media use in instruction that have shaped ID thinking. We are using the media theorist Joshua Meyrowitz's (1993) three views of media as a way to organize these principles. These three metaphors present media as conduits of content, as languages, and as environments.

Media as Conduits of Content: Representations of Reality

Instruction in general has been characterized as a process of providing specific experiences that enable one to form generalized concepts (Dale, 1946). These concepts can relate to abstract knowledge (i.e., verbal information), they can relate to motor and intellectual skills (including cognitive strategies), or they can become the foundation of attitudes (Gagné, 1985). Media play a role in this concept formation process, and reflect designers' concerns with Meyrowitz's (1993) emphasis on "getting our message across". When the emphasis is on accurately conveying the instructional content, it is at times difficult to totally separate content from the general character of the media, especially the extent to which the content represents reality.

Elements of Realism

One of the basic media characteristics is how closely the media facilitates presentation of content that corresponds to reality. In 1937 Hoban, Hoban, and Zisman asserted that "the value of visual aids is a function of their degree of reality" (p. 22). To a great extent the goal of mediated instruction through the years has been an effort to create realistic learning experiences. Such experiences may be rooted in everyday problems, involve concrete representations calling upon all of our senses (sight, sound, perhaps even smell), and reproduce real-life activity and events. These are elements of fidelity and accuracy.

Another aspect of realism is the notion of "being there". Seels, Fullerton, Berry, and Horn (2004) characterize this as the sense of immediacy that learners feel. It is as if they were experiencing "the representation of the thing or event as [being] almost simultaneous with its occurrence" (p. 252). This can be the case with television, film, video clips, and the web.

Representations of reality have increased greatly in terms of both fidelity and in the sense of "being there" as technologies have become more sophisticated. For example, virtual reality tools allow learners to not only see and hear, but also to touch in the learning environment. The instruction can be truly experiential, and it has been especially useful in medical education and in surgical simulators (McLellan, 2004). These tools bring new meaning to Hoban et al.'s principle of aids functioning to their degree of reality.

The Cone of Experience

One of the earliest attempts to describe the role of media in instruction was Edgar Dale's (1946) Cone of Experience. Dale's Cone (as it has long been known) visualizes the role of media as links between doing (i.e., actual involvement in experiences) and symbolizing (i.e., reading words or visuals such as charts or diagrams). It classifies the audio-visual aids of that time in terms of their concreteness or abstractness with direct, purposeful experience being the most concrete and verbal symbols being the most abstract. Between the two extremes lie contrived experience, dramatized experience, field trips, demonstrations, exhibits, television, motion pictures, recordings or radio or still pictures, and visual symbols. One could easily update the Cone by substituting modern technology.

One implication of Dale's Cone is that abstract concepts are easier to grasp if presented first in terms of concrete examples and experiences. A close analysis of the Cone shows that these various activities and aids involve multiple senses, and the more concrete experiences typically involve audio and visual perception occurring at the same time. These activities tend to be closer to direct experience.

Dale was quick to support the importance of each of the Cone's parts, be they activities that involve doing, observing, or symbolizing. This same position was taken by Hoban et al. (1937) when they said "Mere concrete experience, in itself, is no guarantee of generalization; it merely supplies the situation by which this generalization becomes possible and meaningful" (p. 24). Dale's work was the beginning of what many call realism theory in media.

Media as Language: Elements of Structure

Meyrowitz's (1993) media-as-language metaphor focuses upon the way in which the various media are structured and emphasizes "the plasticity of the medium in altering the presentation and meaning of the content elements" (p. 59). Here we will discuss basic structural elements of instructional media: visuals, and the combination of various elements, most typically audio and visual.

The Role of Visuals

To a great extent the language of media is the language of visuals, and as early as 1922, it was suggested that research showed that 40 percent of conceptual learning could be attributed to visual experiences (Weber, 1922). In the past, visuals typically included photographs, drawings, diagrams, maps, and film. Today, they also include video, computer-generated animations, and icons.

Instructional visuals can be described in terms of what they look like or of their function. The latter approach speaks more to the role visuals play in learning with media. Knowlton (1966) suggested that pictures were either realistic or analogical or logical. Realistic pictures make reference to the real world. Analogical pictures visually portray comparisons. Knowlton saw maps and circuit schematics as examples of logical pictures. Duchastel (1980) provides another organizing scheme for instructional visuals. He sees them "as having attentional, explicative, and/or retentional roles" (p. 286). These two interpretations imply that illustrations add to the learning process by motivating (i.e., gaining attention, being realistic), facilitating understanding of the content (i.e., analogical, logical, explicative), or aiding in recall of the content.

While a large body of research supports the power of visuals as an instructional tool, Baker and Dwyer's (2000) series of studies provide a somewhat more tempered conclusion. Even though visuals do have a largely positive influence on learning, they found that not all visuals are equally important in terms of their given instructional function. Color did arouse interest and relate to achievement, but the realistic details at times seemed to distract students from the primary task.

Cue Summation and Dual Coding Theory

An important element of media structure relates to the number of cues or stimuli that are included in a mediated presentation. The guiding principle has been that "learning is increased as the number of available cues or stimuli is increased" (Severin, 1967, p. 237). Cues are details in a presentation (e.g., color, sound, and text). These are the factors that tend to make a presentation more realistic. This principle is consistent with realism theory, and it is also reminiscent of the assumed superiority of multiple-channel communication. (See Chapter 3). One implication of cue summation theory is that it is better to use multimedia with sound rather than use instructional materials that emphasize only text or static images.

The superiority of visual instructional presentations over solely verbal presentations also has been explained through the work of Paivio (1991, 2007). Paivio's dual coding theory suggests that there are two separate, but interconnected, memory systems: one for verbal information and another for visual information. Since visual information tends to include some text, both memory systems are used. Consequently, visual information is more likely to be retained than purely verbal.

Paivio's theory has been generally supported empirically. This has provided a rationale for not only using visuals, but for using more complex multimedia presentations in teaching-learning situations. However, there are conflicting research results in this regard. Mayer and Anderson (1992) found that instruction with animation and narration positively impacted problem solving, even though it did not show any advantages over traditional instruction in simple recall. However, other researchers have not found that animated instruction surpasses instruction using only static visuals (Lin & Chen, 2007). It may be that such visuals are important only when animation is specifically demanded by the content. This conclusion reinforces the long-standing design assumption that content, goals, and technique should mesh.

Media as a Learning Environment: Interacting with Technology

There is now a new approach to viewing media known as media ecology. This orientation is:

> ... based upon the assumption that media are not mere tools that humans use, but rather constitute environments within which they move and shape the structure of their perceptions, their forms of discourse, and their social behavior patterns. (Heise, 2002, p. 151)

This is reminiscent of general systems theory (GST) (see Chapter 2) since "when a new factor is added to an old environment, we do not get the old environment plus the new factor, we get a new environment" (Meyrowitz as cited by Heise, 2002, p. 157). Hence from this point of view, in teaching and learning environments it may be more appropriate to examine interactions with media, especially interactions shared among groups of learners and interactions between the learner and the tool itself. This reflects the current distinctions made between learning *from* technology and learning *with* technology (Kozma, 1991; Jonassen, Peck, & Wilson, 1999), but this is not a new idea.

Media-Learner Interaction Effects

In the late 1960s and 1970s it became popular for educational scholars to study aptitude-treatment interaction (ATI) effects. This research grew out of Cronbach's proposal that the best way to deal with individual learner differences was to adjust the instructional methods to fit the aptitude patterns of the learners (Parkhurst, 1975). Such thinking reflected a rejection of research that resulted in recommendations only for the average student, and a corresponding belief in the efficacy of individualized instruction. It also reflected a shift from the dominance of behavioral learning theory to that of cognitive learning theory. This orientation was also applied to instructional media research and practice.

Some of the initial efforts relating to ATI and media were simple. They thought of learner aptitude primarily in terms of mental ability, and media in terms of either verbal versus pictorial presentations or multi-channel and motion presentations. Typically, the latter research pertained to television or motion pictures (see Allen, 1975). Snow and Salomon (1968), however, reflected a more modern interpretation of learner characteristics when they suggested that "the term 'aptitude' refers to any individual difference variable which . . . appears to facilitate learning in some students and some instructional treatments while limiting or interfering with learning in other students and other instructional treatments" (pp. 347–348). Thus, learner characteristics also included other demographic variables, background, attitudes, and personality traits.

The practical implications of this line of thinking were that alternative media could be selected for small groups of students (Snow & Salomon, 1968) or that mediated presentations could be designed so that they would augment the mental operations of students performing a certain task (Salomon, 1974).

The interest in ATI effects of mediated instruction led fairly naturally to positions such as Salomon's (1994) media attributes theory. In summary, his theory builds upon the view that one of the inherent characteristics of a medium is its symbol system[1] (i.e., a way of structuring and presenting information). The human mind also uses symbols to control information, and some of these symbol systems are acquired from media. When there is a match between the media symbol systems, the content, and the way learners represent information in their minds, instruction is easier to understand (Clark & Salomon, 1986). Moreover, "symbolic features of media *can be made* to cultivate cognitive effects, not that those effects necessarily occur naturally as a result of uninvolved exposure to a medium" (Clark & Salomon, 1986, p. 469). Consequently, using certain media (and taking advantage of the media's important attributes) can actually lead to new cognitive skills among learners. This is a manifestation of complex interactions between treatments (i.e., the media) and learners—the ATI effect.

The Role of Media in Distributed Cognition

The previous discussion of learner interactions with media was rooted in the assumption that cognition is something that occurs "in the head". However, today cognition is "widely seen as being more typically 'distributed' than individual" (Cobb, 1997, p. 30) or as a "joint cognitive system in a cultural context, not the individual mind" (Angeli, 2008, p. 272). Pea (1993) views this as distributed intelligence and characterizes such distribution as when "recourses that shape and enable activity are distributed in configuration

---

1 Olson (1974) suggests that it is impossible to understand media effects without first understanding their underlying symbol systems. Moreover, these symbol systems (along with the medium) should be considered tools which can amplify a person's abilities, as well as the medium's instructional potential.

across people, environments, and situation. In other words, intelligence is accomplished rather than possessed" (p. 50).

The major interest here concerns interaction specifically between humans and media when the immediate physical learning resources are seen "not just as a source of input and a receiver of output, but as a vehicle of thought" (Perkins, 1993, p. 90). Learning is not only a shared activity, it is an activity that could not be accomplished without either the human or the tool that operates much as an instructional system.

What is the function of media when distributed cognition takes place? There have been two major points of view. First, media (and increasingly media is thought of in this context as computers or computer networks) can be seen as a vehicle for handling difficult tasks, tools that augment human capabilities. We can complete statistical computations at ease, or search through vast quantities of information for answers to our questions. On the other hand, media and technology can enhance cognition or become "reorganizers of mental functioning" (Pea, 1993, p. 57). Instead of simply making work less arduous, computer visualization and simulations, for example, can actually lead to different abstract concepts (Angeli, 2008). Intelligence can no longer be viewed exclusively as an individual characteristic; it is a joint product of a complex environment. Cognitive processes are actually shaped by the environment even though some efforts are "off-loaded" to this environment when possible (Hollan, Hutchins, & Kirsh, 2000). Mediated teaching and learning environments can assume these same characteristics.

The Philosophical Orientations of Media Theory

Over the years the ID field has been criticized as being mechanistic and inhumane. This was due in part to the role of media and technology in the teaching-learning process. There were fears that technology use in teaching leads to uniformity and less contact with inspiring teachers (Oettinger, 1969). There were concerns that while technology use in education and training projected the aura of progress, it also reduced the amount of human choice inherent in the process. At the same time the rush toward technology often captures a growing portion of the precious resources devoted to education (Taylor & Johnsen, 1986). Nonetheless, media and technology have continued to proliferate as instructional tools, not just because they are a sign of the times, but because of a number of ingrained beliefs and values.

Support for Realism and Object Manipulation

As we have seen, the value of media is closely related to how realistic it is. This faith in realism stems from an underlying belief that those objects directly presented to our senses represent the objects that actually exist in nature (Bittle, 1936). In other words, the object is independent of the mind. From a philosophical point of view, realism is an observable matter with physical attributes. It can be opposed to idealism which suggests that "what is real is in some way confined to or at least related to the contents of our own minds" (Hamlyn, 2005, p. 414). Realism serves as a philosophical foundation for Dale's Cone of Experience and for using visual aids and technology to tie abstract ideas to concrete objects and experiences. It rejects idealism as a philosophy, not as a standard of what is good or something to be sought.

Mediated learning typically involves experiencing concrete learning objects. Seeing, touching, and hearing all become ways of learning rather than simply exploring one's own reasoning. The various interpretations and renditions of phenomenology explore such a position. This thinking was based on Edmond Husserl's explorations into how people experience actual objects (Tomasulo, 1990). It is "dependent on the explicitly visual experiences of time, space, perception, signification, and human subjectivity" (Tomasulo, 1990, p. 2), and because of the importance of visuals to media, this has been a particularly appealing orientation of much media theory. The emphasis on manipulating concrete objects is consistent with the tenets of active learning as opposed to learning that relies on pure reflection. Phenomenology also leads to an examination of individual visual representations, and in turn the role of individual notions of reality.

Support for Individual Technology Interactions

Mediated instruction promoted various forms of individualized instruction. An individualistic philosophy places primary value on the individual, a very humanistic orientation. Much of the very early media use tended to perpetuate traditional lecture-demonstration techniques. However, there were early calls to use the capabilities of the new technologies to promote individual discovery learning and at the same time accommodate a wide variety of individual differences (see Kilbourne, 1961).

Those espousing anti-individualism philosophies tend to emphasize the role of the physical and social environment in determining individual behavior (Burge, 1979). This somewhat reflects constructivist principles, although constructivists believe that ultimately knowledge is internal to the individual. Distributed cognition is seen as a bridge between individual and social cognition since distributed learning occurs "between individuals in the context of the socio-cultural milieu, rather than in the head" (Schwartz, 2008, p. 395). Moreover, these social determinants are viewed by many as part of a cognitive system. This is not simply a middle-ground viewpoint, but is instead a "sensible and reconciled position" (Schwartz, 2008, p. 396).

MEDIA THEORY AND INSTRUCTIONAL DESIGN

Media is an integral part of much instruction, and as such it is also a critical part of the ID process. We will discuss two major ways in which media is integrated into the ID process. The first, media selection, is a standard part of most ID models. It is a critical part of the design of instructional strategies. The second, media use, is not typically highlighted in the ID models. It is, however, incorporated into the delivery strategies, and often becomes the dominant element of these strategies. Media use has aroused the passions of both media advocates and antagonists. While the media and technology options have changed drastically over the years, it continues to reflect fundamental principles of media and learning.

Media Selection

There are a wide variety of media selection models. The early models tended to deal with traditional instruction, whether it be self-instructional or in groups. These models could be as simple as Gropper's (1976) process, which he summarized in only four steps, or they could be as complicated as Romiszowski's (1981) two-level process with various subprocesses constructed at each level.

More recent models focus on e-learning situations, corporate communication, and the use of advanced technologies. There is, nonetheless, considerable overlap between the old and the new, and ultimately they all pertain to media's role in facilitating learning. Each model is built upon principles which address topics such as visual or verbal instruction effectiveness, the requisites for using realism, or interaction.

Major Elements of Media Selection Models

Most media selection models address five general factors:

- Content;
- Learner characteristics;
- Instructional strategies;
- Environment; and
- Management.

In these models, media selection is basically a process of matching media and their attributes to the needs of the situation at hand. We will explore how these factors are embedded into media selection models.

Instructional content is typically specified in behavioral objective format, and in many models the objectives are also classified as to the type of learning task they represent. Typically, Gagné's (1985) conception of the types of human capabilities is used to classify the learning tasks and these learning outcomes then serve as the basis for identifying the required instructional conditions. (See Chapter 7 for a full explanation of these conditions-based theories.) For example, the Department of the Air Force (1979) provides a guide that relates learning objectives, learning strategies, and media. (See Table 6.1.)

This basic approach is still recommended by Gagné, Wager, Golas, and Keller (2005). However, their matrix encompasses learned capabilities (i.e., types of learning tasks), events of instruction, instruction delivery methods and strategies, and effective media.

Media were not considered appropriate without considering the nature of the learners. The Reiser and Gagné model (1983), for example, identifies media that are suitable for both readers and nonreaders. Gagné (1985) cites the importance of learner age in the media selection decision. Romiszowski (1981) considers the impact of learning styles, attention span, and motivation. Huddlestone and Pike (2008) speak of the importance of considering student confidence to use technologies. Media selection cannot be successful without accounting for who will be using the media.

In the early years, instructional designers often saw the ideal instructional strategy as being individualized. Many media selection models reflected this orientation. The Reiser and Gagné (1983) model has two separate media decision paths: one for individualized instruction and another for grouped instruction. This was often the first macro-level strategy decision. Another general strategy decision was related to the function of the learning task. In the Air Force example (see Table 6.1) instructional strategies are viewed in terms of their function: presentation, practice, or feedback. Function has also been interpreted in terms of the medium's capability (e.g., to show motion or provide sound) (see Kemp, 1985). Another standard way of interpreting instructional strategy in the media selection process is by viewing the strategy as one of Gagné's Events of Instruction. This tactic was employed by Briggs, Gagné, and May in 1967, but it was also a part of Huddlestone and Pike's (2008) model. However, the newer models often make their strategy-related media decision in terms of the interaction required. Caladine (2008), for example, speaks to the need for interaction with materials, interaction between learners, and interaction with the facilitator.

Table 6.1 An Excerpt from the Department of the Air Force Identification of Suitable Media Given the Learning Objective and Learning Strategy

Learning Objectives and Elements of Learning Strategy	Verbal Chains			Classifying, Rule Using, and Problem Solving			Attitudes, Opinions, and Motivation		
	Presentation	Practice	Feedback	Presentation	Practice	Feedback	Presentation	Practice	Feedback
Rep. Instructional Media									
Classroom Instructor									
• Lecturer	YES	NO	NO	YES	P	P	YES	P	P
• Demonstrator	YES	NO	NO	YES	P	P	YES	P	P
• Tutor/Coach	YES	YES	YES	YES	YES	YES	YES	YES	YES
Instructional Aids									
• Overhead Projector	YES	P	P	YES	P	P	YES	P	P
• 35 mm Slides	YES	P	P	YES	P	P	YES	P	P
• Chalkboard	YES	NO	NO	YES	NO	NO	YES	NO	NO
Multimodal Media									
• Prenarrated Filmstrip	YES	YES	YES	YES	YES	YES	YES	YES	P
• Movies (sound)	YES	P	P	YES	P	P	YES	P	P
• TV	YES	P	P	YES	P	P	YES	P	P

Code: Yes—is effective   P—under certain circumstances, effective use is possible; or there are inherent limitations in the effective use
No—is not effective

Note: Adapted from *Instructional System Development AF Manual 50-2* by the Department of the Air Force, 1979, pp. 5–14. Public Domain.

The nature of the instructional environment also directs many designers to using one medium over another. Leshin, Pollack, and Reigeluth (1992), for example, emphasize the learning context, which they define in terms of factors such as group size. Romiszowski (1981) speaks to the availability of resources, whether the environment is well adapted to the use of a given medium, and whether the conditions in the instructional area permit acceptable operation of the medium. Both Gagné (1985) and Department of the Air Force (1979) explore how the instructional setting can limit media choice. They are especially concerned with whether the instructional setting bears a close resemblance to the transfer setting. Then, being concerned with online learning, Huddleston and Pike (2008) assess the type of connectivity available in the learning environments.

Finally, media selection typically involves considering the implications of management issues for ease of media use. Often these factors are considered in conjunction with a contextual analysis (Tessmer & Richey, 1997), and many models simply refer to all of these factors as issues of practicality. Most notable of the management issues is the medium's cost effectiveness. Cost issues are recognized by scholars such as Reiser and Gagné (1983), Dick, Carey, and Carey (2009), and Huddlestone and Pike (2008). However, there are many other management factors that impact media use. Gagné, Briggs, and Wager (1992) identify a large number of these practical factors, including storage facilities, technical support, teacher training requirements, and general disruption that may be caused by use of the medium. Huddlestone and Pike (2008) address a wide variety of other instructional management concerns, such as the effects of limited bandwidth and pressures to use existing classroom facilities.

In spite of the broad range of factors that impinge on educational media decisions, the overwhelming emphasis has been on matching the media function to the learning task at hand. Nonetheless, there are alternative ways of characterizing media. One approach is described in Daft, Lengel, and Trevino's (1987) media richness theory. Media are considered rich if they are capable of providing instant feedback, and if they have multiple communications cues, a variety of languages types, and a personal focus. For example, face-to-face communication would have the highest degree of media richness since immediate feedback can be provided; there are multiple cues (e.g., body language and tone of voice), natural language is used, and it can be very personal (Sun & Cheng, 2007). Another similar approach to media selection is presented by social presence theory. Here the social presence factor is seen as the extent to which other people are felt to be physically present during an interaction (Carlson & Davis, 1998). Both of these theories— media richness and social presence—lead us to the examination of two more recent media selection theories that were developed specifically for e-learning environments.

Trends in Media Selection

Many of the newer media selection models focus on e-learning environments, whether they involve web-based instruction or any other type of computer-based instruction that facilitates any time, any place learning. These are highly mediated learning environments which typically employ realistic static and animated visuals. Color, sound, and text all play critical roles in much of this instruction. Learning occurs via interaction with the technology itself, but the technology can also facilitate learning by providing for additional interaction between learners and between learners and instructors. Moreover, in these environments media can be employed with very small units of instruction since it can be embedded fairly easily in instruction on an objective by objective basis.

The new media selection models also provide ways of dealing with some long-standing issues in the field. For example, Gropper (1976) argued that media should be oriented towards student responses rather than being seen only as a way of delivering stimulus material. While this behavioral perspective is no longer generally accepted, media still are typically seen primarily as vehicles for information presentation. However, the new models which emphasize interaction address Gropper's concerns in many respects since they tend to put more emphasis on learner activity and engagement. We will explore these trends by examining two new media selection models: Huddlestone and Pike (2008) and Caladine (2008).

In many respects Huddlestone and Pike present an updated model that continues to recognize the traditional elements of media selection. Even though this model could be viewed as generic, it has been constructed to accommodate current trends in e-learning.

Not unlike the early media selection models, Huddleston and Pike see the learning task as the factor that primarily shapes the process. E-learning instruction can involve groups of varying sizes or it can be individualized. The grouping strategies, however, are dependent upon the media attributes which can support either interactions or the transmission of information. Instructional interactions depend to a great extent upon whether the learning experience is synchronous or asynchronous and on whether the players are co-located at any time (Huddlestone & Pike, 2008).

In this model, the learning context is not simply the delivery context, but it also encompasses factors such as support and maintenance, as well as design and development. Instructional management is similarly expanded to include not only scheduling and allocation of resources, but it also includes the use of a learning management system to handle student enrollment, tracking and recording results of the instruction. Cost effectiveness includes calculating the return on investment. All of these decision factors are interrelated and each factor impacts the operation of the others (Huddlestone & Pike, 2008).

The second current model we will review is Caladine's (2008) technology selection method. The Caladine model is directed toward what has been called flexible learning (i.e., learning that is flexible in terms of time or place). Here the instructor's voice is no longer the prime means of delivering information, and media systems are required to manage interactions. This model is presented in Figure 6.1.

While Caladine (2008) also incorporates many traditional components of media selection, his emphasis is on a combination of learning activities and learning technologies. Technologies are viewed as being either representational (requiring one-way interaction) or collaborative (requiring two-way interaction). Representational technologies (e.g., printed materials or a film) are used with learning activities that involve simply the provision of instructional materials or interaction with such materials. On the other hand, collaborative technologies (e.g., e-mail or video conferencing) are used with learning activities that involve interaction between learners, interaction with the facilitator, or intra-action. This latter activity involves interaction *within* the learner, such as reflection or critical thinking. Technology selection is also influenced by the capabilities required of the media (i.e., the mechanics of the subject), the learner, the facilitator, and the related costs. The technology is ultimately selected for a given situation by analyzing and matching these various factors.

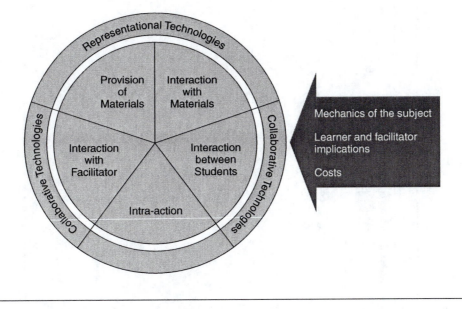

Figure 6.1 The Caladine Technology Selection Method.

Note: From *Enhancing E-Learning with Media-Rich Content and Interactions* by R. Caladine, 2008, p. 138. Copyright 2008 by Information Science Publishing. Used with permission.

The Caladine model is made possible because of the new technologies, especially the web, which makes such interaction and flexibility possible. However, the web also supports the use of a wide variety of other media, including those used in traditional face-to-face instruction. It also makes the use of materials from many disciplines and many sources far more feasible than was previously possible. Such instruction is typically structured around a learning management system.

These newer media selection models are put into the context of past models in Table 6.2. Here we compare seven models that represent the development of media selection processes over the years.[2]

Media Use

Media use parallels the development and availability of technologies at any given point of time, but media functions have been more constant. Here we will describe media use in terms of two major functions that media have served: being a vehicle of instructional automation and being a means of bringing realism and interactivity into the learning environment.

Automating Instruction

Since Sidney Pressey's introduction of the "Automatic Teacher" in the 1920s, there have been a variety of efforts to use technology to individualize instruction and to relieve teachers of the manual, routine aspects of instruction. Pressey's device provided a way

---

2 This table is similar to Reiser and Gagné's (1983) comparison of then-prominent media selection models on their page 15.

Table 6.2 A Matrix of Representative Media Selection Models and Their Components

COMPONENTS	MODELS						
	Briggs, Gagné, & May (1967)	Gropper (1976)	Dept. of the Air Force (1979)	Romiszowski (1981)	Reiser & Gagné (1983)	Caladine (2008)	Huddlestone & Pike (2008)
Content							
• Behavioral Objectives	X	X	X	X	X	X (pre-task)	X
• Type of Learning Task and Required Conditions	X	X	X		X		X
Learner Characteristics							
• Previous Experience		X	X	X	X	X	X
• Learning Rates and Abilities		X	X	X	X	X	X
• Motivation and Attitudes			X	X			X
Instructional Strategy							
• Individualized/Grouping	X		X	X	X		X
• Instructional Function	X	X	X	X	X	X	
• Media Capabilities Required	X	X	X		X	X	X
• Events of Instruction	X				X		X
• Interaction Requirements						X	X
Environment							
• Resources and Facilities			X	X	X	X	X
• Instructional Setting Characteristics			X	X			X
• Co-location of Students and Instructor					X	X	X
• Instructor Skills and Support			X	X		X	
Management							
• Cost Effectiveness			X	X		X	X
• Maintenance and Technology Support			X	X		X	X

for students to drill and test themselves, two processes that he saw as being intricately connected. The machine (initially made of old typewriter parts) "regulated the rate of instruction, allowed for self diagnosis, and liberated the teacher from time-consuming routine" (Petrina, 2004, p. 314). Students took multiple-choice tests and received feedback on their performance. This was a forerunner of Skinner's teaching machine.

Moving beyond Pressey's testing device, Skinner's machine employed programmed instruction based upon his behavioral theories. Here, learned behavior was developed by having students pass through very small sequences of steps (or frames) that led them slowly to the final desired behavior. Each correct performance was systematically reinforced (Skinner, 1958). Learning occurred through self-instruction and self-pacing. Ultimately, programmed instruction incorporated audio and video stimuli in addition to the textual presentation of information. Teaching machines and programmed instruction were one attempt to adapt instruction to the wide range of individual differences and eliminate failure from education and training.

Pressey and Skinner looked to single "machines" to automate the teaching and learning process. Others sought to combine the available technologies and processes to automate the entire classroom. For example, Finn (1957a, 1957b, 1960) made a coordinated proposal for full classroom automation. He saw automation as a way to increase educational efficiency and to deal with existing teacher shortages even as it raised the quality of teaching. Automated classrooms were intimately connected with the new instructional technologies of the time, especially television. Finn's view of classroom automation was also tied to systems theory (see Chapter 2) since he saw automation as involving the coordination of instructional management processes, personnel, and machinery. It was also dependent upon analysis and long-range planning.

These attempts to automate instruction reflect the view of media as a learning environment and they also emphasize learners interacting individually with the technology. Ultimately the efforts to automate classrooms were largely aborted, not because of technology failure, but because of apprehensions concerning mechanization and dehumanization. To many, automation conjured up images of mass production in the classroom. Nonetheless, there are elements of these innovations still alive today.

Creating Realistic, Interactive Learning Environments

As computer technologies advanced and became more accessible, computer-based media assumed a dominant role in instruction. Such technology soon integrated video, still and animated graphics, and the ability to establish links between all aspects of instruction and supporting information. Much of the early computer-based instruction often reflected elements of the Skinnerian teaching machine. For example, learners still controlled pacing and sequencing, and feedback was immediate.

With the advent of the World Wide Web, new instructional strategies emerged. Instruction no longer needed to be bound by time or space, and communication among learners and between learners and instructors could occur at any time. The web also provided access to sources of information that had previously not even been considered a remote possibility.

Advances in computer-based media were influenced by more than technology innovations. They were also influenced by new thinking related to pedagogy and the psychological aspects of learning (Hannafin, Hannafin, Hooper, Rieber, & Kini, 1996). For example, advocates of constructivism, anchored instruction, and situated cognition readily looked to the computer and the web as a way of providing instructional activities rooted in true-to-life contexts. (See Chapter 8.)

At first, making contextual descriptions realistic was approached simply from a technological point of view. For example, Strang, Badt, Kauffman, and Maggio (1988) described their use of simple microcomputer-based simulations to help preservice teachers to learn feedback and classroom management skills. The computer provided verbal exchanges between classroom teachers and their students. These exercises and subsequent debriefings with the instructor provided learning activities in addition to traditional lectures and field experiences.

Then the materials became more complex. Interactive video clips and large data sets were embedded in problem-solving instruction to provide the relevant contextual information, and some programs allowed students to model and practice problem solving. Other instruction established context through the use of high-fidelity images that captured the essence of real-life activities (Hannafin et al., 1996).

The possibilities for interaction during the teaching-learning process also grew dramatically with the introduction of the Internet, web-based instruction, and online learning. For example, Harris (as cited in Hill, Wiley, Nelson, & Han, 2004) identified six types of interpersonal exchanges taking place on the Internet. These included activities such as global classrooms (i.e., classrooms studying common topics together), electronic appearances (i.e., student correspondence with guests on electronic bulletin boards), and electronic mentoring (i.e., expert guidance of novice students). Creative instructors and designers will continue to expand interactions among students and subject matter experts. They will provide even more collaborative learning and an increased social presence.

Trends in Media Use

Today, technology permeates instruction at all levels. The more complex technology-based designs, however, relate to learning environments, not classrooms, since the new technologies have in effect removed traditional walls from instructional settings. These new settings have been called technology-enhanced learning environments (TELE). "TELEs are technology-based learning and instructional systems through which students acquire skills or knowledge, usually with the help of teachers or facilitators, learning support tools, and technological resources" (Wang & Hannafin, 2005, p. 5).

TELEs tend to be learner-centered with a high degree of learner control. They are likely to employ strategies that reflect experiential or situated learning principles, and they use primarily individualized methods. The technology resources help students access data often on a global basis and they establish social communities revolving around the learning tasks. They also provide for ongoing assessment and feedback, and help students develop a deep understanding of the content (Chen, Calinger, Howard, & Oskorus, 2008).

A recent TELE example is provided by Kim and Hannafin (2008). They describe a technology-enhanced, case-based learning activity in which students use a web-based library consisting of cases of expert teachers developing technology-enhanced lesson plans. These multimedia cases include interviews with the experts, authentic context data, work samples, and archival data. The tools provide for instruction that is self-regulated and situated in real life contexts. These tools facilitate learning by engaging students in experiences that demand task-related action, reflection, and problem solving.

TELEs also frequently make use of other technologies that replicate real-world experiences such as simulations, games, virtual reality, online worlds, and other immersive technologies. While some designers use the terms "simulation" and "game" interchangeably, Johnson (2008) views simulations as being driven by one person interacting with characters in different scenarios. Gredler (2004) sees a simulation as a case study of "a particular social or physical reality" (p. 573). On the other hand, games are competitive activities, even though they too may incorporate simulations. "An online world is typically a 3D representation of the real world and a place to host events or learning experiences" (Johnson, 2008, p. 30). Second Life is one of the most popular examples of an online world. Virtual reality is also related to these technologies. It "can be defined as the use of computers and related technology to produce an artificial environment that simulates a target one" (Connolly, 2005, p. 13). Learners are able to move about and manipulate these various worlds, often through very life-like avatars.

Collectively, these tools are known as immersive technologies. However, they are modern applications of the fundamental principles of media and learning. They are expressions of a belief in the value of hands-on learning couched in life-like materials that facilitate high degrees of interaction. They are expressions of a belief in the value of learning experiences which impact all of the senses, and of instruction which adapts to the needs of individual students. Today's technologies facilitate a far more complete application of these long-held principles than do the media of the past.

RESEARCH, MEDIA THEORY, AND INSTRUCTIONAL DESIGN

There is a huge body of media research. Allen (1959) estimated that in the 40 years between 1919 and 1959 there had been between 2500 and 3000 separate educational media studies. We would not attempt to update this figure, but it surely has more than doubled. In general, all of this research has sought to:

- Substantiate media effectiveness and superiority over traditional teaching methods;
- Explain how media attributes and techniques of classroom use facilitate learning;
- Explain the impact of media on learners; and
- Document processes of media design and development.

Periodic reviews of media research as a whole have attempted to determine the extent to which these goals were achieved. For example, see Allen (1956, 1959, 1971), Lumsdaine (1963), Campeau (1967), Torkelson (1977), Wilkinson, (1980), and Clark and Salomon (1986). In addition, there were the reviews that served as the basis of the now famous Clark-Kozma debate in the literature (See Clark, 1983; Kozma, 1991). Our task here is to briefly summarize what have we learned about media in general from this mammoth body of work.

Empirical Support of Media Theory Applications in Instructional Design

In an effort to tie media to learning, there have been many studies that compare one media to another. As Clark and Salomon said in 1986, these studies attempt to answer the question Who is the fairest of them all? Typically the comparison is between the newest medium which has captured disciplinary attention and nonmediated traditional classroom instruction delivered in a face-to-face setting. These studies have usually resulted in no significant differences, and there have been loud cries in the literature that they be discontinued (Allen, 1959; Lumsdaine, 1963; Campeau, 1967; Torkelson, 1977; Clark & Salomon, 1986). As a result of these findings of no differences, some researchers (notably Clark, 1983 and Winn, 1984) have concluded that there are "no learning benefits to be gained from employing any specific medium to deliver instruction" (Clark, 1983, p. 445).

However, Kozma (1991) argued that the capabilities of a given medium interact with the teaching methods and the two in combination can influence the manner in which learners process information. Therefore, media can make a difference. Others in their reviews of media research have pointed out the value of studies of the unique *attributes* of particular media (Allen, 1971, Levie & Dickie, 1973, Clark & Salomon, 1986). Wilkinson (1980) concluded that the research does suggest that when both media attributes and learner characteristics are considered that data show that media do impact student achievement. By and large Kozma (1991) agrees.

These views of media research fundamentally speak to the question of whether media are interchangeable in a given instructional situation with their selection being primarily a matter of cost, availability, or motivational qualities. Still, many wonder if the newer technologies have attributes and capabilities that are so unique that indeed they can not be viewed as interchangeable objects. Clark and Salomon saw this as a possibility in 1986 since the new technological materials tended (even at that time) to be better prepared and could provide an impetus for curriculum reform.

Current research on learning with multimedia seems to show that retention, problem solving, and transfer of training are positively impacted due to multiple and richer representations of content, multiple ways of retrieving information, and the possibilities of more cognitive flexibility (Graesser, Chipman, & King, 2008). The conclusions with respect to Internet-based instruction, simulations, and games are mixed (Hill et al., 2004; Graesser et al., 2008).

There is also a body of research directed toward the design and development of media. Some of this research confirms the effectiveness of certain design techniques (e.g., animation, learning objects, placement of words and pictures on a screen, whether to use narration or text). Other research examines the entire process of designing and developing specific products or tools (Richey & Klein, 2007). This research has been far less controversial and has provided direction for the design of the new and emerging technologies.

Recommendations for Continuing Research

With each review of media research there have been recommendations for it to continue, but with a new focus. In addition, individual researchers often offer more specific suggestions for new research agendas. Recent recommendations have included:

- Research on learning via the Internet in formal and informal contexts, including an exploration of best practices and ethical considerations (Hill et al., 2004);
- Studies of virtual environments, serious games, and learning (Graesser et al., 2008);
- Demonstration projects that analyze the role of immersion in learning (Summers, Reiff, & Weber, 2008);
- Practice-based studies of mobile technology and learning (Romiszowski & Mason, 2004);

- Research and development projects that view the computer as a cognitive tool (Kim & Reeves, 2007); and
- Meta-analyses of existing research on selected media, such as the effects of interactive simulations (Graesser et al., 2008).

This list could be much longer, but some commonalities are already apparent in these representative projects. Each addresses cutting-edge technology topics, and there are no suggestions to repeat the media comparison approaches of the past. We also expect media attribute and media use research to flourish, and there should be a substantial amount of research on the design and development of the emerging technologies.

SUMMARY

Today, technology dominates ID practice. This chapter has described the underlying media principles that provide direction for the selection and use of this technology in education and training. Specifically we addressed media in terms of its position in the teaching and learning process, including the importance of realism, visuals, stimuli in a mediated presentation, interaction, and media's role in distributed cognition. As with other chapters in this book, the logic behind these various viewpoints was explained from a philosophic perspective.

Media theory has, by and large, been a product of ID scholars. As such there is a close relationship between its principles and ID practice. Media selection was explained in terms of the various models that have been presented over the years, including forward-thinking models pertaining to e-learning. Media use was explained first in terms of how instruction was automated and then in terms of creating even more realistic and interactive instruction. This latter effort has been expanded through the use of TELEs and immersive technologies. Table 6.3 summarizes these points.

Table 6.3 An Overview of Media Theory and Instructional Design

1. **Key Principles:**
   - The value of media in the learning process is a function of their fidelity and the extent to which the experiences seem to be occurring simultaneously with real-life events.
   - Concrete experiences facilitate the acquisition of abstract generalizations.
   - Learning is increased as the number of audio and visual stimuli increase.
   - Visual information is retained more than verbal information since it is processed in both the visual and the verbal working memories.
   - Media selection and design should adapt to the characteristics of the learners, the content, and the learning environment.
   - Media can influence the development of student cognitive skills and the internal representation of information.
2. **Philosophical Emphases:** The following generalizations can be made:
   - Objects directly presented to our senses represent the objects that actually exist in nature.
   - Reality can be based upon directly experiencing and manipulating concrete objects.
3. **Basic Research Support:** Skinner's research on contingencies of reinforcement, Paivo's research on dual coding.
4. **Early Contributors:** William Allen, Edgar Dale, Charles Hoban, Jr., and Arthur Lumsdaine

Table 6.3 *Continued*

5. **ID Applications:**
   • Automating Instruction
   • Media Selection (Face-to-Face and Online Settings)
   • Multimedia Computer-Based Instruction
   • Online Worlds
   • Simulations and Games

6. **Supporting ID Research:**
   • Media and Learning Research
   • Media Attributes Research
   • Media Comparison Research
   • Media Design and Development Research
   • Media Use Research

7. **Related Concepts:**
   • Aptitude-Treatment Interactions
   • Cone of Experience
   • Flexible Learning
   • Immersive Technologies
   • Teaching Machines and Individualized Instruction
   • Technology-Enhanced Learning Environment (TELE)

Media theory has a special place in the ID knowledge base. While it does influence many of the domains, it primarily shapes the domains of media and delivery systems and instructional and noninstructional strategies as shown in Table 6.4.

Table 6.4 Instructional Design Domains and Elements Related to Media Theory

Learners and Learning Processes
   • Learner Characteristics (aptitude, demographics, background)
   • Distributed Learning Process

Learning and Performance Contexts
   • Instructional Environment (e.g., location of instructor and students, group size, delivery conditions, connectivity, storage and facilities)
   • Instructional Resources Available
   • Similarity Between Learning and Performance Contexts
   • Support Available (technical and maintenance)

Content Structure and Sequence
   • Visualization of Content

Instructional and Noninstructional Strategies
   • Facilitating Activity and Engagement
   • Facilitating Communication Online
   • Facilitating Interaction (between learners, between learners and instructors)
   • Individualizing Instruction
   • Providing Concrete Experiences
   • Reproducing Real-Life Activities and Events

Media and Delivery Systems
   • Media Capabilities and Attributes (e.g., richness, social presence)
   • Media Costs

- Media Functions (e.g., presentation, feedback, practice, manager of interactions)
- Media Selection (cues, interaction, symbol system, relating to content, learner characteristics, instructional strategy, environment, management)
- Role in Learning Process (e.g., part of stimulus, part of response)
- Type of Delivery (e.g., synchronous or asynchronous)

Designers and Design Processes
- Design of Online Learning
- Multimedia Design (e.g., increasing cues, sound over visuals)
- Product Development

The second major theory base that stems from ID research and practice is that of conditions-based theory, which is discussed in Chapter 7. To many scholars in the field, this is the heart of ID.

7

CONDITIONS-BASED THEORY

To many in the field, the core principles of instructional design (ID) are rooted in what is known as conditions-based theory. Conditions-based theory is basically a cognitive orientation that is especially pertinent to the selection and design of instructional strategies. It is closely related to the work of Robert M. Gagné, a pioneer of ID theory and research. While Gagné saw his key principles as elements of instructional theory, his work has been applied directly to the development of the conditions-based genre of ID theory and practice. Today, there are a number of conditions-based ID theories and models which are consistent with most (if not all) of Gagné's original principles. Recent thinking expands his original premises and often emphasizes new aspects of the learning and performance improvement processes.

Conditions-based theory evolved originally from instructional psychology research, highlighting the direct lineage between this branch of psychology and the field of ID that emerged in the late 1960s and 1970s. At one point during this period, the term "psychoeducational design" was used to emphasize the relationship between psychological principles and improved practice (Snellbecker, 1974). Today, conditions-based theories continue to be rooted in psychological research to some extent, but also rely on the findings of ID research as well.

In this chapter, we will describe:

- The foundations of conditions-based theory by identifying and exploring illustrations of its key elements;
- The expansion of conditions-based approaches to ID; and
- The research supporting conditions-based approaches to ID.

THE FOUNDATIONS OF CONDITIONS-BASED THEORY

Conditions-based theory has been called "commonplace, if not universal, in current instructional psychology and instructional design thinking" (Ragan, Smith, & Curda, 2008, p. 384). Nonetheless, many scholars struggle to specifically decide what constitutes such a theory, or what practice truly reflects the principles of conditions-based theory. Here we describe conditions-based theory in terms of three key premises. These principles are rooted in Gagné's work, but generalized to accommodate new interpretations of the theory. These premises are:

- There are different types of learning outcomes, and each type of learning calls for different types of instruction.
- Instructional sequencing relies upon relationships among the various learning outcomes.
- Instructional strategies should facilitate the internal processes of learning.

Others have described these principles somewhat differently, although we believe their essence is fundamentally consistent with our interpretation (Wilson & Cole, 1991; Ragan et al., 2008). Essentially, conditions-based theory encompasses the belief that all learning is not the same. Good instructors recognize this and modify their teaching to accommodate the unique nature of the content, being especially mindful of the relationships and complexities of various aspects of the subject matter. These variations in teaching, in effect, create a match between the internal conditions of learning (i.e., what is going on inside the learner's mind) and the external conditions of learning (i.e., the manner in which instruction is delivered). Thus, learning is enhanced and made more efficient. We will explore each of these ideas by describing the contributions of the foundational theorists.

Types of Learning Outcomes

The notion that there are different types of learning is not new. However, scholars originally categorized these differences in terms of how learning occurs. Thus, the literature included topics such as stimulus-response learning, incidental learning, or rote learning. On the other hand, when researchers directed their attention to topics such as verbal learning, concept learning, or learning perceptual-motor skills, they were venturing into thinking of variations in learning from a content perspective. This is the orientation of the various learning types in conditions-based ID theory. Here we will discuss the initial ways in which learning tasks were categorized by Benjamin Bloom, Robert Gagné, and David Merrill.

The Classification of Educational Goals

From 1949 to 1953, experts in psychology, education, and psychometrics worked to identify taxonomies of educational goals in the cognitive, affective, and psychomotor domains. The result of this work is now commonly called Bloom's taxonomies. These taxonomies are hierarchical, with outcomes moving from simple to complex. Objectives in each category build upon those in previous categories. According to Krathwohl, Bloom, and Masia (1964), the largest proportion of educational objectives are in the cognitive domain. These range from recalling simple facts to synthesizing new ideas when solving problems. The framework includes six main categories of cognitive objectives: knowledge, comprehension, application, analysis, synthesis, and evaluation (Bloom, 1956). Each of these groupings also include subcategories of outcomes. For example comprehension is supported by the subcategories translation, interpretation, and extrapolation.

Objectives in the affective domain represent interest, attitude, values, emotion, and bias. This framework includes five main categories of affective objectives: receiving, responding, valuing, organization, and characterization (Krathwohl et al., 1964). Psychomotor objectives focus on motor skills and the manipulation of tools and objects for a particular job. Bloom and his associates did not identify categories in the psychomotor domain since there were few examples of these objectives in the literature when the classification systems were introduced.

The taxonomies developed by Bloom and his colleagues have noteworthy implications for the systematic design of instruction. As van Merriënboer (2007) points out, the cognitive, psychomotor, and affective domains identified by Bloom generally correspond to the knowledge, skill, and attitude (KS&A) outcomes at the center of most traditional ID models. They are general behavioral descriptors of content addressed in education and training programs. In addition, since the content classifications are arranged from simple to complex, they also highlight the relationships between content areas. Bloom (1956) and his colleagues viewed their taxonomy as also serving as a vehicle for test development and curriculum construction. (See Chapter 5 for a discussion of Bloom's approach to curriculum.)

The Domains of Learning

Robert M. Gagné explicitly recognized the pioneering work of Bloom and his colleagues when he reasoned that different categories of learning domains are required for measuring outcomes regardless of the subject matter being taught (see Gagné, 1972/2000). Gagné's (1964, 1965) early identification of the various learning types strongly reflected the then dominant influence of behavioral psychology. However, over the years, he modified his views. Table 7.1 shows Gagné's various attempts to distinguish among the types of learning tasks and the relationships among these classification systems.

Initially, Gagné (1964) identified six categories of learning: response learning, chaining, verbal learning, concept learning, principle learning, and problem solving. With the publication in 1965 of the first edition of his landmark book, *The Conditions of Learning*, these categories were somewhat expanded. Response learning was divided into signal learning and stimulus-response learning. Verbal learning was then seen as verbal associations, and the notion of multiple discriminations was included as a precursor to concept learning.

Gagné's initial approach to categorizing learning tasks blends learning process concerns with learning content concerns. He provides examples across subject areas of content in each category. Teaching soldiers to be alert when hearing the command "Attention" is signal learning. Teaching a child the meaning of the word "middle" is an example of concept learning (Gagné, 1965). However, Gagné has two rationales for determining the various types of learning: (1) to show the simple to complex relationships among the categories (not unlike Bloom) and (2) to demonstrate common circumstances (i.e., external conditions) that facilitate each type of learning. He is concerned with both how learning occurs and the nature of the learning content.

This dual concern was also evident when Gagné made the transition from "types of learning" to "domains of learning". His initial presentation of domains was motor skills, verbal information, intellectual skills, cognitive strategies, and attitudes (Gagné, 1972/2000). On the surface this category system seems more content-oriented, and

Table 7.1 A Summary of Gagné's Interpretations of the Types of Learning from Least to Most Complex

Gagné (1964) Type of Learning	Gagné (1965) Type of Learning	Gagné (1972/2000) Domains of Learning	Gagné, Briggs, & Wager (1992) Intellectual Skills Commonly in Education and Training
	Signal Learning		
Response Learning	Stimulus-Response Learning		
Chaining	Chaining		
Verbal Learning	Verbal Associations	Verbal Information (or Declarative Knowledge, see Gagné, 1984)	
	Multiple Discrimination	Intellectual Skills (or Procedural Knowledge, see Gagné, 1984)	Discrimination
			Concrete Concept
Concept Learning	Concept Learning		Rules and Defined Concepts
Principle Learning	Principle Learning		Higher-Order Rules
Problem Solving	Problem Solving		Problem Solving
		Cognitive Strategies Motor Skills* Attitudes*	

* Domain outside of the complexity hierarchy

indeed he does consider them to be "classes of instructional objectives" (Gagné, 1972/2000, p. 103). They are similar in some ways to Bloom's taxonomy. However, he is still profoundly concerned with how learning occurs and sees these classes of objectives as each having a "different set of critical conditions to insure efficient learning" (Gagné, 1972/2000, p. 103). Thus, each category would be taught in a similar manner regardless of whether one was teaching physics or poetry. In addition, each domain tends to require different ways of assessing the learning outcomes, again similar to Bloom.

Gagné went on to expand the intellectual skill domain. Ultimately, he saw the intellectual skills (also arranged in a simple to complex fashion) as being discriminations, concrete concepts, rules and defined concepts, higher-order rules, and problem solving (Gagné, Briggs, & Wager, 1992). This classification system drew from his early identification of types of learning.

Gagné's thinking about the types of learning has greatly influenced ID practice. Classifying the learning task is one of the first steps designers typically take. This decision then provides direction for many subsequent design steps, especially strategy selection. Gagné's position on types of learning also establishes his conviction that there are general types of learning that cut across all disciplines; there are not types of science learning or mathematics learning, for example (Gagné, 1984). This assumption suggests that ID itself is a generic process that can be applied to all disciplines.

The Performance-Content Matrix

Merrill and Boutwell (1973) and Merrill (1983) proposed another configuration for classifying learning tasks. This was known as the Performance-Content Matrix. It shows the learning task as a combination of two independent phenomena: the content categories and the behaviors students demonstrate when they have met the instructional objective. This scheme does not directly address how learning occurs. The matrix is presented in Figure 7.1.

The types of content (fact, concept, procedure, principle) build upon Gagné's categories, a variation of the domains of verbal information, intellectual skill, and cognitive strategies (Gagné & Merrill, 1990). The alternative types of student behaviors are remember, find, and use. Merrill and Boutwell (1973) saw this system of classifying learning outcomes as being a more complete taxonomy than those previously suggested. It reflects the basic underlying assumption "that there is more than one kind of learning and perhaps more than one kind of memory structure" (Merrill, 1983, p. 300). Thus, Merrill is subscribing not only to multiple types of learning, but also to the notion of internal conditions of learning.

In 1992, Merrill, Jones, and Li identified 13 classes of instructional transactions as a precursor to Merrill's continued development of his theoretical position. Merrill (1999) defines an instructional transaction as "all of the learning interactions necessary for a student to acquire a particular kind of knowledge or skill" (p. 402). These transaction classes are shown in Table 7.2.

In essence, Merrill has expanded the performance component of his matrix.

Integrative Goals

Gagné and Merrill (1990) also worked together to expand both of their classification systems. The addition dealt with instruction that addresses comprehensive activities

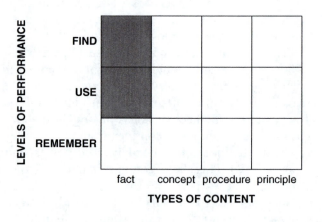

Figure 7.1 The Performance-Content Matrix.

Note: From "Component Display Theory" by M. D. Merrill, 1983. In C. M. Reigeluth (Ed.) *Instructional-Design Theories and Models: An Overview of Their Current Status*, p. 286. Copyright 1983 by Lawrence Erlbaum Associates, Publishers. Used with permission.

Table 7.2 Classes of Instructional Transactions

Component Transactions	
IDENTIFY:	Name and remember information about parts of an entity
EXECUTE:	Remember and do steps in an activity
INTERPRET:	Remember events and predict causes in a process
Abstraction Transactions	
JUDGE:	Order instances
CLASSIFY:	Sort instances
GENERALIZE:	Group instances
DECIDE:	Select among alternatives
TRANSFER:	Apply steps or events to a new situation
Association Transactions	
PROPOGATE:	Acquire one set of skills in the context of another set of skills
ANALOGIZE:	Acquire steps of an activity, or events of a process, by likening to a different activity or process
SUBSTITUTE:	Extend one activity to learn another activity
DESIGN:	Invent a new activity
DISCOVER:	Discover a new process

Note: From "Instructional Transaction Theory" by M. D. Merrill, 1999. In C. M. Reigeluth (Ed.) *Instructional-Design Theories and Models, Volume II: A New Paradigm of Instructional Theory*, p. 405. Copyright 1999 by Lawrence Erlbaum Associates, Publishers. Used with permission.

involving multiple types of learning tasks directed toward a common, integrative goal. Gagné and Merrill called this type of activity an enterprise. Moreover, they suggest that:

> . . . different *integrated goals* of various enterprises are represented in memory as different kinds of cognitive structures . . . a schema that reflects the purpose or goal of the enterprise category, the various knowledges and skills required to engage in the enterprise, and a scenario which indicates when and how each piece of knowledge or skill is required by the enterprise. (p. 25; emphasis in the original)

The integrative goals of an enterprise are critical to designers who are concerned particularly with transfer. The enterprise scenario relates the various knowledge and skill objectives to a final goal and often to a larger project that encompasses this goal. Instruction of this type incorporates a number of learning outcomes into a holistic and integrated teaching-learning activity and results in unique learning conditions and instructional strategies (Gagné & Merrill, 1990).

Sequencing Learning Outcomes

In a conditions-based orientation, decisions concerning instructional sequencing are dependent to a great extent upon the nature of the learning task and its connection to other related tasks. Each of the original systems of classifying learning tasks implied prerequisite relationships between the various learning outcomes. This dominant conditions-based position on sequencing was presented initially by Gagné, and then this thinking was extended by other theorists, such as Charles Reigeluth.

Learning Hierarchies and the Theory of Cumulative Learning

One of Gagné's fundamental beliefs was that "behavioral development results from the cumulative effects of learning" (Gagné, 1968/2000a, p. 40). He suggested that learning is an ordered process, involving new learning being built upon the foundations of past learning. This principle was empirically supported by Gagné's own research and that of many others (see Gagné, 1973). The components of this theory of cumulative learning are those hierarchical classes of human performance shown in Table 7.1, especially the various intellectual skills.

Cumulative learning theory has obvious implications for the sequencing of instruction, a task Gagné (1973) carefully distinguishes from the sequencing of learning. However, instructional sequencing is dependent upon first identifying and diagramming the knowledge and skills that are subordinate to the intended outcome of instruction. This diagram is known as a learning hierarchy. To Gagné (1973) learning hierarchies are "descriptions of successively achievable intellectual skills, each of which is stated as a performance class" (p. 21). Figure 7.2 shows a generalized example of such a hierarchy.

This example shows the relative level of complexity of all tasks, and identifies those which are essential prerequisites to the higher level tasks. It also shows the relationships of the tasks in the three major strands of skills (i.e., 3–4–7–10, 1–5–8–10, and 2–6–9–10).

One can use learning hierarchies to determine the most effective instructional sequence. However, Gagné (1968/2000b) clearly noted that the sequences suggested by these hierarchies were not the only path students could take to the final objective. While there seems to be evidence of increased efficiency when instruction requires systematic recall of prerequisites (Gagné, 1973), hierarchy-directed sequences may not necessarily be the most efficient route for a particular learner given the broad range of individual differences. What is likely, however, is that the learning hierarchy sequence has "the most probable expectation of greatest positive transfer for an entire sample of learners" (Gagné, 1968/2000b, p. 69).

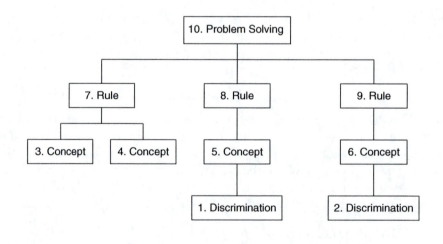

Figure 7.2 A Sample Learning Hierarchy.

Elaboration Theory

Reigeluth's Elaboration Theory provides direction for sequencing large units of instruction dealing with many ideas, often at the course level. At its inception, it extended Merrill's early ID theory which dealt primarily with the microdesign of individual lessons. In addition, Elaboration Theory originally pertained exclusively to Bloom's cognitive domain, covering "all of the levels of Bloom's taxonomy, plus an additional level which is often referred to as 'meta-cognition'" (Reigeluth & Darwazeh, 1982, p. 23). In later explanations of the theory, Reigeluth (1999) emphasized the holistic and learner-centered aspects of this approach to sequencing and its role in building firm cognitive foundations, and meaningful, motivated learning. This is possible because of the relationships (i.e., superordinate, coordinate, and subordinate) among the concepts to be sequenced. Such relationships must be first identified through a theoretical analysis resulting in a hierarchical structure of the concepts or principles to be taught (Reigeluth, 1999).

In essence, Elaboration Theory prescribes a general-to-detailed sequence that is another variation of the simple-to-complex approach. The initial generality presented is called an epitome, a special kind of content overview.

> Epitomizing always entails identifying either very *general* or very *simple* ideas, but *not abstract* ones. . . . [and presenting] a small number of the most fundamental, representative, general, and/or simple ideas . . . including whatever of the other types of content that are highly relevant (including learning prerequisites). (Reigeluth & Stein, 1983, p. 346; emphasis in the original)

For example, the various economic principles (such as the law of supply and demand) serve as the epitome for an introductory course in economics, and concepts such as price or quantities supplied are examples of supporting content (Reigeluth & Stein, 1983).

The epitome is followed by presenting various levels of content elaboration, each of which provides additional content detail or complexity (Reigeluth & Stein, 1983). These elaborations provide more comprehensive versions of the task at hand. These versions may be more complex and more realistic than the preceding example, or they may show less representative cases (Reigeluth, 1999). For example, in the economics course example, elaborations might include the effects of changes in supply schedules on price (Reigeluth & Stein, 1983). This elaboration process may be interrupted to return to the general epitome to reestablish the context and to review the instruction to date, but then further elaboration of the content would take place. Reigeluth and Stein (1983) call this the "zoom lens" approach.

The lessons end with the use of an internal summarizer and an internal synthesizer. The summarizers review the original generality, a specific example, and some self-test practice situations. The synthesizers show the relationships among the various ideas in the lesson (Reigeluth & Darwazeh, 1982).

Elaboration Theory itself has a multifaceted theoretical foundation. It is primarily a type of conditions-based theory, because it is based upon the assumption that there are different types of learning tasks and instruction varies in terms of each type. Moreover, Elaboration Theory integrates Gagné's hierarchical approach to sequencing into its structure by recognizing the place of teaching prerequisite skills. It expands Merrill's generality-instance-practice pattern. It also reflects Ausubel's notion of subsumptive sequencing (see Chapter 4), and Bruner's concept of a spiraling curriculum (see Chapter 5) (Reigeluth & Darwazeh, 1982; Reigeluth & Stein, 1983).

Facilitating Internal Learning Processes

The third major premise of conditions-based theory is that instructional strategies should facilitate the internal processes of learning. In many ways, this is the heart of conditions-based theory. The effective external conditions of instruction (i.e., the teaching strategies, the instructional materials, and the student activities) facilitate learning which is fundamentally an internal process. These external conditions, however, are dependent upon the type of learning task and the sequencing of the activities. Our discussion once again will begin with the groundbreaking work of Robert Gagné. It will then continue with David Merrill's theories that expanded Gagné's thinking to account for new cognitive interpretations of learning and new technologies.

The Events of Instruction

Gagné's views of learning primarily reflect the cognitive orientation, and more specifically that of information processing. Consequently, the learning process was seen as involving sensory perception, working memory, encoding and storage in long-term memory, and retrieving information from long-term memory. (See the more complete discussion of cognitive learning theory in Chapter 4.) Effective instruction consists of activities that facilitate these various aspects of the learning process. Gagné (1985) summarized these activities in his Events of Instruction. They begin with gaining students' attention, letting them know what the goals of the lesson are and how the goals relate to things they already know, presenting the content and helping students with its complex aspects, providing opportunities for practice and information on how well they are doing, testing, and helping students to remember and use what they have just learned. These events are the general steps teachers would follow in any lesson. They are the external conditions of learning. Table 7.3 identifies these nine events. In addition, it shows how each event relates to the learning process as seen from a cognitive point of view.

The order of these events is one that is typically followed, although Gagné never suggested that the order or even the use of each event was required in every lesson (Gagné et al., 1992). Instead, designers should ask themselves a simple question: "Do these learners need support at this stage for learning this task?" (Gagné et al., p. 190).

While the Events of Instruction provide a general design approach, the framework is modified to match the different instructional conditions associated with the different types of learning. These modifications are made typically in Event 3 (Stimulating recall of prior learning), Event 4 (Presenting the stimulus material), and Event 5 (Providing learning guidance). For example, intellectual skills demand the recall of prerequisite facts, rules, and concepts, while cognitive strategies depend upon the recall of their component tasks. Concept learning requires guidance in terms of many examples of the concept, but learning verbal information may utilize a memory aid such as mnemonics for guidance (Gagné et al., 1992).

The Events of Instruction provide a basic structure for designers to follow after they complete the analysis phase of ID and proceed into determining the strategies that will be employed to facilitate student learning. On the surface, the Events appear to be a simple, almost intuitive approach to instruction. However, a careful examination of the

Table 7.3 The Relationship Between Gagné's External Events of Instruction and the Internal Processes of Learning

Event of Instruction	Process of Learning
1. Gain attention	• Reception of stimuli in sensory memory
2. Inform learner of the objective	• Expectancies and cognitive strategies
3. Stimulate recall of prior learning	• Retrieval from long-term memory to working memory
4. Present the content	• Selective perception of distinctive features
5. Provide learning guidance	• Encoding for long-term storage
	• Cues for retrieval
6. Elicit performance	• Activates response organization
7. Provide feedback	• Establishes reinforcement
	• Correct errors
8. Assess performance	• Retrieval from long-term memory
	• Response organization
	• Reinforcement and feedback
9. Enhance retention, and transfer	• Cues for retrieval and retention
	• Generalization for transfer

events shows that they serve as a link between the tenets of cognitive learning theory and everyday ID practice.

Component Display Theory and Instructional Transaction Theory

Merrill provided a second approach to applying the conditions-based ideal of using external conditions to facilitate learning. He developed two major theories of ID: Component Display Theory (CDT) and Instructional Transaction Theory (ITT). In the process of evolving these theories, there were intervening descriptions of what he called ID$_2$. Each of these emerging points of view is fundamentally conditions-based with instructional strategies varying by the type of learning outcome. (Note the earlier discussion of Merrill's performance-content matrix.)

A central feature of Merrill's (1983) Component Display Theory (CDT) is that all instructional content can be presented using a series of what he called "primary presentation forms". These presentations forms are based upon the propositions that all types of learning can be represented in two dimensions:

- By presenting either a generality or a particular instance of the topic; and
- By using either expository (telling) or inquisitory (asking) techniques.

Table 7.4 shows how Merrill's (1983) combines these elements to form a type of taxonomy of general instructional strategies.

Each of these presentation forms can also be elaborated. Expository presentations, for example, can be expanded by providing prerequisite knowledge, additional context information, or mnemonic aids. Inquisitory presentations can be elaborated with feedback, or additional examples. These elaborations are called secondary presentation forms.

These presentation forms serve as the "displays" that combine the type of presentation with the targeted level of performance and the targeted content. In addition, Merrill (1983) recognizes that the various displays can themselves be related. Designers select

Table 7.4 The Primary Presentation Form Taxonomy

Type of Presentation	Type of Presentation Technique	
	Expository	**Inquisitory**
Generality	Instructor tells, shows, illustrates, or demonstrates a rule or generality.	Students practice and test their understanding of a generality by completing a general statement.
Instance	Instructor tells, shows, illustrates, or demonstrates an instance or a specific case.	Students practice and test their understanding of an instance by applying a given generality to a specific case.

Note: Adapted from "Component Display Theory" by M. D. Merrill, 1983. In C. M. Reigeluth (Ed.) *Instructional- Design Theories and Models: An Overview of Their Current Status*, p. 306. Copyright 1983 by Lawrence Erlbaum Associates, Publishers. Used with permission.

instructional strategies by determining the proper display for the content and then determining when each display should be presented in isolation or related to another display.

Merrill (1983) suggests that the CDT approach to structuring learning activities implies a sequence of presenting first a generality, then an example, followed by practice. For example, if one were teaching the concept of conifer, the first step would be to provide the general definition of the term. Next, specific examples of conifers would be given. Finally, students would practice picking out the conifers from large groups of trees. However, the empirical support for this approach to sequencing varies. Some of the most robust findings conclude that it is best to present generalities before instances, and it is best to include practice, but the order in which this occurs is not critical (Merrill, 1983).

Merrill subsequently expanded the notion of primary and secondary presentation forms into the concept of an instructional transaction. A transaction "is characterized as a mutual, dynamic, real-time give-and-take between the instructional system and the student in which there is an exchange of information" (Merrill, Li, & Jones, 1990, p. 9). It typically consists of multiple displays and multiple interactions with the learners. There are various types of transactions, but they employ many of the traditional aspects of an instructional strategy. They include the content (known as the knowledge structure), presentation techniques, practice opportunities, and learner guidance (Merrill, 1999).

There were two major reasons why Merrill and his colleagues turned to the transaction format. The first related to the "assumption that learning results when mental models are organized and elaborated in memory" (Merrill et al., 1990, p. 9). Consequently, instruction should encompass everything necessary to facilitate the acquisition of a particular mental model. Because these models are typically complex, there should be many integrated instructional interactions between learners and teachers or the instructional materials (Merrill et al., 1990). Hence, there is a need for a more complex transaction, as opposed to a simple display which usually demands only a single student response.

There was a second reason for using transactions, however. Transactions, by definition, emphasize interaction rather than simply delivering information to learners. One way of promoting complex types of student interactions during the teaching-learning process is through the use of computer-based instruction, a rapidly growing instructional tool. Merrill explored new ways of designing such instruction, and in doing so became involved in the development of a computer-based ID system called ID Expert. This system used transaction shells which were "pieces of computer code that, when delivered to a student via an appropriate delivery system, cause a transaction or set of transactions to occur" (Merrill, Li, & Jones, 1991, p. 8). ID Expert sought not only to automate the ID process, but also to create learning environments that are adaptive to students; instruction could be tailored on the spot to the needs and characteristics of individual students (Merrill, 1999). Instructional Transaction Theory was developed in conjunction with this computerized design and development system which produced instruction that not only facilitated the acquisition of many types of knowledge and skills, but also attempted to truly individualize instruction.

The Philosophical Orientations of Conditions-Based Theory

The various approaches to ID are influenced not only by the theories that we have been discussing, but also by the beliefs and values of the designers (Smith & Ragan, 2005). One could certainly say that those espousing conditions-based theory were scholars who only advocated a particular position if it had research support. They were empiricists at heart. This position is similar to that of the learning theorists, the early communications theorists, and others whose theories are primarily rooted in research, rather than pure reasoning. With respect to conditions-based theory specifically, this implies an empirically supported explanation of the learning process and of the instructional activities which facilitate knowledge acquisition and transfer of learning to new settings.

Strike (1972), however, points out one complexity of the empiricist point of view for those studying human behavior:

> When the social scientist claims to understand an action, he is grasping its meaning by seeing it as governed by a particular set of rules. But seeing an act as the following of a rule is very different from seeing it as an instance of some regularity or law. Rules can be broken, laws cannot. Rules give meaning to action, laws merely relate the condition under which they occur. Thus, to understand an action is not at all like giving a scientific *explanation* of it. (p. 41; emphasis in the original)

Perhaps this is why today we seldom see educational theories constructed in terms of laws. Perhaps this is why the ID "rules" of conditions-based theory are often stated with caveats, such as recognizing the effectiveness of instructional sequences that do not match those implied in a learning hierarchy.

As one examines the work of Gagné and Merrill especially, it is clear that their theories evolved over time. This is in keeping with Petrie's (1972) admonition for "empirical researchers constantly to be theorizing . . . and to be elaborating their theory with its presuppositions as they go" (p. 73). However, these presuppositions can provide interesting entanglements for an empiricist, because they may not be totally based upon evidence; instead they may well be influenced by personal (or perhaps disciplinary) values. Strike (1979) suggests that "facts and values come in integrated conceptual packages" (p. 14).

Conditions-based theorists do seem to share some common values. Smith and Ragan (2005) identify a number of these values or assumptions, including: (1) the notion that "learning goals should be the driving force behind decisions about activities and assessment" (p. 23), (2) the generic role of principles of instruction, and (3) the importance of instructional effectiveness and efficiency. These values do seem to imply an acceptance of generalizations and a predisposition towards objectivist viewpoints. It is not implausible that the views of conditions-based theorists reflect philosophical empiricism. Or perhaps as Smith and Ragan (2005) again suggest, there is more of a pragmatic flavor to the theory. In this light they see instructional designers as proposing "that knowledge is built up by testing [the] 'truth for now' hypothesis and revising or discarding this 'truth' as common experience and interpretation implies it should be modified" (p. 22).

THE REFINEMENT OF CONDITIONS-BASED INSTRUCTIONAL DESIGN THEORY

Theorists have expanded the notion of conditions-based ID in recent years to include principles found in the latest theories of learning, motivation, and instruction. These developments relate to advances in cognitive psychology, social learning theory (see Chapter 4), and constructivism (see Chapter 8). Below we discuss four such developments in conditions-based theory including:

- Supplantive and generative instruction;
- Complex learning;
- Problem solving; and
- Motivational design.

Each of these theoretical approaches includes elements of conditions-based ID theory. They recognize the relationships and complexities of various kinds of outcomes, address the internal processes of learning, and have implications for the external conditions of instruction.

Supplantive and Generative Strategies

A key development in conditions-based ID theory can be found in the work of Patricia Smith and Tillman Ragan, who sought to extend Gagné's theory by addressing strategies for providing learning guidance to students. Smith and Ragan (2005) address the question "Which should be the locus of control of information processing – the instruction or the learners?" (p. 141). They contend that the answer depends on the learning task, the amount of prior knowledge held by the learner, and the quantity and variety of learning strategies the learner possesses. They propose a continuum of supplantive-generative instructional strategies to deal with these issues.

Supplantive instructional strategies provide more support to learners than generative strategies. Smith and Ragan (2005) argue that supplantive strategies are appropriate for novices with low prior knowledge and few learning strategies because they limit responsibility for structuring their own learning. However, they also caution that learners may engage fewer internal processes of learning when supplantive strategies are used incorrectly. Examples of supplantive strategies are found in expository instructional methods.

Generative instructional strategies allow learners to construct their own meaning from instruction by "generating their own educational goals, organization, elaborations, sequencing and emphasis of content, monitoring of understanding, and transfer to other contexts" (Smith & Ragan, 2005, p.141). Smith and Ragan (2005) suggest that learners with extensive prior knowledge and well-developed learning strategies can be given control of their own learning. They propose the use of a generative environment where learners provide many events of instruction for themselves. Examples of generative strategies are found in learner-centered environments such as problem-based learning.

Based on research findings, Ragan et al. (2008) suggest that instruction should use as many generative strategies as possible. However, they caution that supplantive strategies that provide support to learners may be more appropriate when a limited amount of time is available for instruction or when generative strategies may lead to frustration, anxiety, or danger. They recommend that instructional designers use a problem-solving approach to determine "the amount of cognitive support required for the events of instruction based on careful consideration of context, learner, and learning task" (Ragan et al., 2008, p. 392).

Designing for Complex Learning

Another expansion of conditions-based ID theory can be found in the work of Jeroen van Merriënboer and his colleagues, who focus on how to design instruction to achieve complex learning. According to van Merriënboer and Kirschner (2007):

> Complex learning involves the integration of knowledge, skills and attitudes; the coordination of qualitatively different *constituent skills*, and often the transfer of what is learned in the school or training setting to daily life and work settings. (p. 4; emphasis in the original)

Complex learning centers on integrated learning goals and multiple performance objectives that comprise tasks found on the job or in life. These coordinated goals and objectives promote the application and transfer of skills that make up complex learning (van Merriënboer, Clark, & de Croock, 2002). They are similar to the integrated goals that Gagné and Merrill (1990) proposed to expand their classification systems.

Sequencing decisions are important when designing for complex learning. van Merriënboer et al. (2002) state "a sequence of learning tasks is the backbone of every training program aimed at complex learning" (p. 43). van Merriënboer et al. (2002) propose a hierarchy to account for two types of relationships between skills that must be taken into account when designing for complex learning. The first type of relationship in a hierarchy is a horizontal relationship between coordinated skills that can be sequential (e.g., first you do this; next you do that). The second type of relationship in a hierarchy is vertical, where skills at the lower part of the hierarchy enable (or are prerequisite to) skills at the higher levels of the hierarchy. van Merriënboer acknowledges that Gagné's work on learning hierarchies influenced his own thinking about sequencing for complex learning tasks.

Complex learning includes both recurrent and nonrecurrent skills. Designers identify different performance objectives for both types of skills (van Merriënboer et al., 2002). Recurrent (i.e., routine) skills are those that can be applied in similar complex situations. They consist of rules that generalize from one situation to another. Nonrecurrent (i.e., novel) skills vary from situation to situation.

According to van Merriënboer et al. (2002) "for the nonrecurrent aspect of a complex skill and the complex skill as a whole, the main learning processes that must be promoted are related to schema construction" (p. 42). Schemata facilitate the use of skills from one situation to another because they contain generalized and concrete knowledge. (See Chapter 4 for a discussion of schemata.) To help them construct and reconstruct schema, learners are provided with concrete experiences and encouraged to "abstract information away from the details" (van Merriënboer & Kirschner, 2007, p. 20).

Other internal processes of learning are addressed by van Merriënboer and his colleagues. They hypothesize that when a new schema is constructed, mental models facilitate reasoning because they reflect how content is organized. In addition, cognitive strategies also affect problem solving because they impact how a problem is approached. For example, the processes of discrimination and generalization impact the reconstruction of existing schema to align them with new experiences (van Merriënboer et al., 2002).

van Merriënboer and his colleagues developed the Four-Component Instructional Design (4C/ID) model that centers on the integration and coordination of skills that make up complex learning (van Merriënboer et al., 2002; van Merriënboer & Kirschner, 2007). The four-component model includes ten steps that designers follow to address complex learning. (See Table 7.5.)

Learning tasks for complex learning can be performed in either real or simulated environments; they provide learners with whole-task practice of all the constituent skills that make up a complex skill (van Merriënboer et al., 2002; van Merriënboer & Kirschner, 2007). These authentic whole-task experiences facilitate rule generalization for recurrent tasks and support schema construction for nonrecurrent tasks.

Supportive information "provides the bridge between learners' prior knowledge and the learning tasks" (van Merriënboer et al., 2002, p. 43). It is used to support the construction of schemata through the elaboration of relationships between new information and prior knowledge. Supportive information for each successive task is an elaboration of previous information that assists learners to do things that they could not previously do. Expository or inquiry strategies can be used for this type of information. These ideas extend Merrill's (1983) CDT discussed above. Supportive information also includes

Table 7.5 Components of the 4C/ID Model with Corresponding Steps

Components of 4C/ID	Ten Steps to Complex Learning
Learning Tasks	1. Design Learning Tasks 2. Sequence Task Classes 3. Set Performance Objectives
Supportive Information	4. Design Supportive Information 5. Analyze Cognitive Strategies 6. Analyze Mental Models
Procedural Information	7. Design Procedural Information 8. Analyze Cognitive Rules 9. Analyze Prerequisites Knowledge
Part-Task Practice	10. Design Part-Task Practice

Note: From *Ten Steps to Complex Learning: A Systematic Approach to Four-Component Instructional Design* by J. J. G. van Merriënboer & P. A. Kirschner, 2007, p. 10. Copyright 2007 by Lawrence Erlbaum Associates, Publishers. Used with permission.

cognitive feedback to encourage learners to reflect on the quality of their approach to problem solving and their solutions. It is also provided to enhance learners' cognitive learning strategies (van Merriënboer & Kirschner, 2007).

Procedural information provides learners with the steps they require to perform a recurring skill. Also referred to as "just-in-time information" (van Merriënboer et al., 2002), it is given when learners require it to work on recurring tasks. It includes demonstrations of how rules and procedures are applied, as well as corrective feedback on errors (van Merriënboer & Kirschner, 2007). Procedural information is organized in small units, called information displays. Based on Merrill's Component Display and Instructional Transaction Theories (1983, 1999), van Merriënboer et al. (2002) suggest that information displays should consist mostly of generalities and examples:

> For instance, rules are general in that they can be applied in a variety of situations, and prerequisite concepts are general in that they refer to a category of objects or events. It is often desirable to present examples that illustrate or exemplify those generalities. For rules, such examples are called demonstrations; for concepts, plans, and principles, they are called instances. (p. 52)

The final component in the 4C/ID model is part-task practice. Part-task practice supports the strengthening of rules and procedures which often require extensive amounts of practice (van Merriënboer et al., 2002). While a whole-task approach is used to facilitate schema construction, a part-task strategy breaks a complex task into component parts, each of which are taught separately. Then the various parts are combined into the whole task. van Merriënboer and Kirschner (2007) think this approach will facilitate rule learning more quickly.

A Design Theory for Problem Solving

A further refinement in conditions-based ID theory can be found in David Jonassen's work on problem solving. His contributions can be viewed as conditions-based theory because they speak to:

- A typology of problems with each category requiring different instructional support;
- Identification of the relationships among problem types in terms of their structure, complexity, and specificity; and
- Internal processes and individual differences that impact problem-solving learning.

Jonassen (1997) states that problems vary in terms of their structure, complexity, and abstractness. He also distinguishes between well-structured and ill-structured problems. Well-structured problems have known solutions that require the application of a fixed number of concepts, rules, and principles. Ill-structured problems have multiple solutions, unknown elements, and inconsistent relationships among concepts, rules, and principles. Types of well-structured problems include logic and story problems, while instances of ill-structured situations include design problems (e.g., constructing an expansion bridge) and dilemmas (e.g., how to withdraw from a country at the end of a war).

Problem types also differ in terms of their complexity, defined in terms of the number of variables or issues involved in solving the problem (Jonassen, 1997). Simple problems involve fewer cognitive operations than complex ones. Simple problems are also more static than complex ones. Jonassen (2000) states "the most complex problems are dynamic, that is, those in which the task environment and its factors change over time" (p. 68). He also thinks problems are domain specific, situated, and embedded in a specific context. Figure 7.3 shows a sample of types of problems and how they differ based on Jonassen's classification scheme.

In discussing structural relationships and problem solving, Jonassen (2000) distinguishes between his theory and other approaches to sequencing. He believes that the hierarchical structure of intellectual skills advocated by Gagné and Merrill does not adequately address the complex relationships found in problems solving. Jonassen (2000) writes:

> Problem solving, as an activity, is more complex than the sum of its component parts. Without question, problem solving necessarily engages a variety of cognitive components, such as propositional information, concepts, rules, and principles . . . However, it also involves structural knowledge . . . metacognitive skills. . . . motivation/attitudinal components . . . [and] knowledge about self. (p. 64)

Like other conditions-based theorists discussed in this chapter, Jonassen indicates that elements internal to the learner affect how to solve different kinds of problems. Jonassen (2000) hypothesizes that "problem solving skill is dependent on a schema for solving particular types of problems" (p. 65). He suggests that learners construct mental models consisting of structural, procedural, strategic, and reflective knowledge (Jonassen &

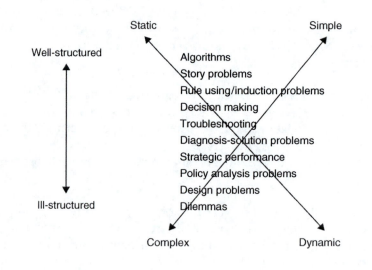

Figure 7.3 Typology of Problems.

Note: From *Learning to Solve Problems: A Handbook for Designing Problem-Solving Learning Environments*, by D. Jonassen, 2011, p. 12. Copyright 2011 Taylor & Francis. Used with permission.

Henning, 1999). Jonassen (2000) indicates that individual differences within learners mediate problem solving. These factors include:

- General problem-solving skill;
- Familiarity with the problem type;
- Domain knowledge;
- Structural knowledge (i.e., knowledge of how concepts in a domain are interrelated);
- Cognitive and meta-cognitive processes; and
- Affective, motivational, and volitional factors.

Based on his typology of problems, the internal conditions impacting problem solving, and knowledge of how humans solve problems, Jonassen (1997) proposes an ID model for well- and ill-structured problem solving. This model provides the steps and activities (i.e., external conditions) designers should follow when developing instruction for the two major kinds of problems: well-structured and ill-structured problems. (See Table 7.6.) He also suggests a number of instructional strategies to engage learners in problem solving, including authentic cases, simulations, modeling, coaching, and problem-based learning.

Jonassen (2010) thinks that it is not enough to merely teach learners about problem solving if they are expected to actually solve problems. If the outcome is for students to learn how to solve problems, Jonassen believes that learners must be engaged in problems centered on job tasks or other real-life activities.

Table 7.6 Jonassen's (1997) Model for Designing Problem-Solving Instruction

Well-Structured Problems	Ill-Structured Problems
1. Review prerequisite component concepts, rules, and principles.	1. Articulate the problem context.
2. Present conceptual or causal model of problem domain.	2. Introduce problem constraints.
3. Model problem solving performance using worked examples.	3. Locate, select, and develop cases for learners.
4. Present practice problems.	4. Support knowledge base construction.
5. Support the search for solutions.	5. Support argument construction.
6. Reflect on problem state and solution.	6. Assess problem solution.

Motivational Design of Instruction

Another development in conditions-based ID theory is found in the writing of John Keller on motivational design. As shown in Figure 7.4, his model of motivation, performance, and instructional influence (Keller, 1983) includes:

- Outcomes of instruction consisting of effort, performance, consequences, and satisfaction;
- Characteristics internal to learners such as expectancies, values, prerequisite knowledge, and skills; and
- Environmental inputs including motivational design, learning design, and contingency management.

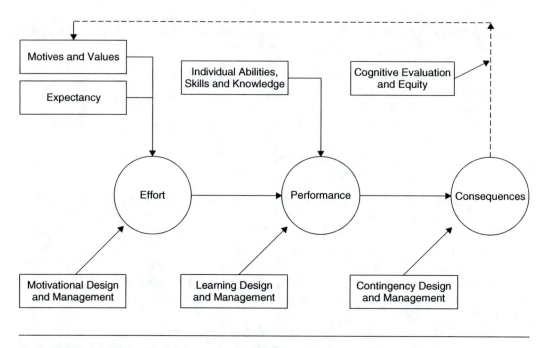

Figure 7.4 A Model of Motivation, Performance, and Instructional Influence.

Note: Adapted from "Motivational Design of Instruction" by John M. Keller, 1983. In C. M. Reigeluth (Ed.) *Instructional-Design Theories and Models: An Overview of Their Current Status*, p. 392. Copyright 1983 by Lawrence Erlbaum Associates, Publishers. Used with permission.

According to Keller (1983), "the primary concern with this theory . . . is to illustrate a systematic basis for a motivational-design model" (p. 384). Like other ID theorists, Keller (1979) explains how learning design, along with an individual's abilities, skills, and prior knowledge, impact learning and performance. Yet the bulk of his ideas center on designing instruction to address learner motivation. As defined by Keller (1983), motivation equals the choice a person makes to approach or avoid a task plus the effort applied to completing it. He theorizes that effort is influenced by a learner's curiosity, interest, motives, values, and expectations. Designers can impact effort by following principles of motivational design. Effort impacts performance, which in turn leads to positive or negative consequences. Consequences are evaluated by the learner, who may or may not feel satisfied by them (Keller, 2010).

The motivational design model (Keller, 1987a, 2010) includes the same components found in most general systems models of ID. (See Chapter 2.) It is an overlay model that can be used in conjunction with other ID models. The motivational design model includes the steps for designing instruction that have a positive impact on learner effort and satisfaction. Following this model, a designer analyzes learners and the instructional environment to identify any motivational problems that may exist. The process begins with obtaining information about the course, including its setting and delivery system. Learner analysis is completed to construct a motivational profile focusing on student attitudes, motives, and expectations. Current course materials are also analyzed, with special attention given to the strategies used to motivate learners. Next, motivational objectives, measures, and strategies are designed and implemented. These are integrated into instructional materials and are then evaluated, tested, and refined.

Motivational problems and strategies relate to the four main components in Keller's (1987b, 2010) attention, relevance, confidence, and satisfaction (ARCS) model of motivation:

- Attention—learner interest and curiosity must be aroused and maintained;
- Relevance—learners must perceive their personal needs are met in an instructional situation;
- Confidence—learners must have appropriate expectations about themselves, others, and the subject matter; and
- Satisfaction—learners must receive the appropriate intrinsic and extrinsic rewards from instruction.

According to Dick, Carey, and Carey (2009), Keller's work addresses the criticism that designers who follow the systems approach often produce instructional materials that lack appeal to learners. Therefore, we think Keller's ideas extend the notion of conditions-based ID and provide an important foundation to the field.

RESEARCH ON CONDITIONS-BASED INSTRUCTIONAL DESIGN THEORY

Many of the constructs embedded in the conditions-based ID theories discussed in this chapter have been empirically investigated. While a few studies have examined the total application of a particular theory to the design of instruction, most studies have been conducted to examine one or more components. Below we provide a summary of representative research that informs ID practitioners of the important findings related to conditions-based theory. Then we suggest new avenues of research that could provide further support for this type of ID theory.

Empirical Support of Conditions-Based Applications in Instructional Design

Most of the research on conditions-based ID theory has been conducted by providing learners with a small number of instructional events or components. Very few studies have been conducted where the effects of a combination of elements have been tested. Sasayama (1984) compared the effects of providing rules, examples, and practice on learning concepts, principles, and procedures based on Merrill's CDT. The lesson that included rules, examples, and practice was more effective than that which provided rules only, examples only, or rules and examples only. Coats (1985) tested the impact of providing all of Gagné's nine events to an experimental group and only some events to two different control groups. No significant differences were found among the three treatment groups on achievement. Martin, Klein, and Sullivan (2007) compared the effects of several of Gagné's events including objectives, practice, examples, and review in a computer-based lesson. They found that of the instructional elements tested in the study, practice had the most impact on both learner achievement and attitudes.

According to Martin and Klein (2008) "some of these events produce a much different effect when they are studied individually than when they are combined into a more complete set that incorporates most or all of the events" (p. 172). Research on computer-based instruction consistently shows that practice with feedback has the most impact on learning, especially when compared to providing objectives and review opportunities to learners (Hannafin, 1987; Hannafin, Phillips, Rieber, & Garhart, 1987; Martin & Klein, 2008; Martin et al., 2007; Phillips, Hannafin, & Tripp, 1988).

In addition to the studies cited above, Ragan and Smith (2004) reviewed and summarized a number of other empirical studies of conditions-based ID theory. Results of their comprehensive review indicate:

- Strong empirical support for the validity of learning hierarchies and the extent to which they accurately describe relationships among subskills and prerequisite skills;
- Strong support for the notion that different events of instruction lead to different kinds of learning, especially for declarative and procedural outcomes;
- Some support for the effectiveness of instruction designed following principles of Component Display Theory and Elaboration Theory; and
- Weak support for the hypothesized relationship between internal process of learning and the acquisition of different learning outcomes.

Turning to research on supplantive and generative learning, Grabowski (2004) wrote an extensive review of empirical studies that have been conducted on these strategies. Her findings show:

- Some studies indicate that learner-generated organizational schemes are more effective than instructor-provided strategies.
- Cognitive ability impacts the effectiveness of learner-generated organizational strategies.
- Student-generated examples and questions improve retention and transfer, but not always more than instructor-provided elaborations.
- The difficulty of a task must be considered when a combination of generative strategies is used.
- Learners may become frustrated if they are not developmentally ready for a generative activity.

Research has also been conducted to validate the 4C/ID model. van Merriënboer and Kester (2008) summarized the findings from studies conducted by van Merriënboer and colleagues. These studies suggest:

- Teachers trained to use the 4C/ID model developed qualitatively better designs (as measured by experts) than teachers not trained to use the model.
- Low achievers benefited more from competency-based instruction developed using the 4C/ID model when they worked in teams rather than alone.
- Whole-task practice is more effective than part-task practice for learning complex tasks.
- Novice and advanced learners achieved better whole-task performance and better transfer performance when they received whole-task training.

In proposing his design theory for problem solving, Jonassen (2000) stated:

> It is important to note that the typology presented in this paper is not promulgated as a definitive theory, but rather as a work in progress. Experimentation, assessment, and dialogue about these problem types and the forthcoming models are needed to validate anything approaching a definitive theory for problem solving instruction. (p. 82)

Since the publication of that seminal article, Jonassen and colleagues have conducted several empirical studies to validate some of the constructs in his theory. Much of this research was done in the context of science and engineering. Findings from these studies suggest that the component skills required for solving well-structured problems and ill-structured problems may differ:

- Domain knowledge and justification skills are related to solving both types of problems (Shin, Jonassen, & McGee, 2003).
- Self-regulation and attitudes toward science are related to solving ill-structured problems (Shin et al., 2003).
- Metacognition and argumentation are related to solving ill-structured problems in simulations (Hong, Jonassen, & McGee 2003).
- Communication patterns in teams differ when groups solve well-structured and ill-structured problems (Cho & Jonassen, 2002; Jonassen & Kwon, 2001).

Findings also indicate how experts approach problem solving, including:

- Expert problem solvers index their knowledge by using their past experiences (Hung & Jonassen, 2006).
- Experts use their domain knowledge to impose structure, filter alternatives, test hypothesis, identify constraints, and propose solutions when solving problems (Wijekumar & Jonassen, 2007).

Furthermore, after reviewing contemporary research on story problems in instruction, Jonassen (2003) reported that:

- Story problems vary in terms of their context, structural relationships, and processing operations.
- Story problems require learners to construct a conceptual model that includes structural relationships that define the class of problem, situational characteristics of the problem situation, and a reconciliation of the structural and situational characteristics required to solve the problem.

Keller's motivation model is based on his own extensive review of behavioral, cognitive, and motivational theory and research. These include studies of curiosity, needs, motives, values, expectancies, and rewards (see Keller, 1979, 1983, 2010). Furthermore, some research has been conducted to examine the use of his models. Our review of this work suggests:

- There is some empirical evidence for Keller's (1987a) claim that his model of motivational design can be used along with other ID models (Main, 1993; Okey & Santiago, 1991; Shellnut, Knowlton, & Savage, 1999).
- There is evidence of alternative ways to design effective motivational messages using ARCS principles (e.g., Oh's (2006) study of the design and use of reusable motivational objects and Tilaro and Rossett's (1993) examination of motivational job aids).
- There is support that application of the ARCS model can lead to increased student motivation (Visser & Keller, 1990; Means, Jonassen, & Dwyer, 1997; Song & Keller, 2001; Visser, Plomp, Amirault, & Kuiper, 2002; Kim & Keller, 2008).
- There is also a little evidence that students can be taught to utilize ARCS strategies to increase their own motivation (Klein & Freitag, 1992).

Recommendations for Continuing Research

As we have noted, most of the research on conditions-based ID is aimed at examining certain components of each theory rather than looking at the entire theory. This suggests that additional research should be conducted to validate these theories when practitioners apply them to ID projects. A particularly useful approach for these kinds of studies is design and development research (Richey & Klein, 2007). This type of research would allow us to answer questions about the benefits and constraints of using each conditions-based theory.

The findings cited above also suggest another fruitful area for additional research. A basic tenet of conditions-based theory is that internal process impacts learning outcomes. However, there is little empirical support for the hypothesized relationship between the attainment of learning outcomes described in conditions-based theory and various cognitive processes of learning (Ragan & Smith, 2004). Future studies on this issue should be conducted using qualitative research methods such as think-aloud protocols to examine how learners are processing information.

Finally, future research on conditions-based theory should center on the application of knowledge and transfer of skills. This suggestion is particularly pertinent for theories related to complex learning, problem solving, and motivational design. The increased focus of the ID field on performance improvement (see Chapter 9) requires us to examine the impact of these theories on individual, group, and organizational outcomes.

SUMMARY

This chapter has examined conditions-based theory and its contribution to the ID knowledge base. We began by discussing the foundations of conditions-based theory by identifying and exploring illustrations of its three key elements. Next, we examined developments in conditions-based approaches by discussing generative instructional strategies, complex learning, and problem solving. We also reviewed a range of empirical research conducted to support conditions-based approaches to ID and provide some recommendations for future study in this area.

Table 7.7 provides a summary of the key principles, theoretical foundations, philosophical orientations, early contributors, and applications of conditions-based ID theory. Furthermore, Table 7.8 offers a synopsis of how the elements of conditions-based theory relates to the domains of ID.

Table 7.7 An Overview of Conditions-Based Theory and Instructional Design

1. **Key Principles:**
   - There are different types of learning outcomes, and each type of learning calls for different types of instruction.
   - Instructional sequencing relies upon relationships among the various learning outcomes.
   - Instructional strategies should facilitate the internal processes of learning.

2. **Philosophical Emphases:** The following generalizations can be made:
   - Conditions-based theory is based upon an empiricist philosophy with many pragmatic applications.
   - There are common beliefs and values supporting the theory that may not be empirically derived.
   - There is an emphasis on goal-directed instruction, efficiency, effectiveness, and process generalization.

3. **Basic Research Support:** Gagné's research on cumulative learning; research on prerequisite content relationships

4. **Early Contributors:** Benjamin Bloom, Robert Gagné, and M. David Merrill

5. **ID Applications:**
   - Domains of Learning
   - Events of Instruction
   - Generative and Supplantive Strategies
   - Problem Solving
   - Learning Hierarchies
   - Performance-Content Matrix
   - Complex Learning
   - Motivational Design

6. **Supporting ID Research:** Studies of:
   - Learning hierarchies (Gagné and colleagues)
   - Instructional events (Hannafin and colleagues; Klein and colleagues)
   - Generative strategies (Wittrock)
   - Designing for complex learning (van Merriënboer and colleagues)
   - Expertise and problem solving in science and engineering; story problems (Jonassen and colleagues)
   - Motivational design (Keller and colleagues)

7. **Related Concepts:**
   - Cumulative Learning Theory
   - Instructional Transaction Theory
   - Enterprise Scenario
   - Problem-Based Learning
   - ARCS Motivation
   - Component Display Theory
   - Elaboration Theory
   - Generative Learning
   - 4C/ID

Table 7.8 Instructional Design Domains and Elements Related to Conditions-Based Theory

Learner and Learning Processes
- All learning is not the same
- Internal conditions of learning
- Learner Characteristics (affective characteristics such as motivation, background, learning strategies, mental models, prerequisite knowledge, schema)

Learning and Performance Contexts
- Authentic and simulated settings for complex learning and problem solving

Content Structure and Sequence
- Learning Task Classifications (e.g., cognitive/affective/psychomotor)
- Instructional Sequences (e.g., simple to complex)
- Vertical and horizontal relationships among recurring and non-recurring component skills for complex learning
- Problem solving includes structural knowledge, metacognitive skills, and motivation components

Table 7.8 *Continued*

Instructional and Noninstructional Strategies
- External instruction conditions should match the internal learning conditions
- Events of instruction (e.g., provide learning guidance)
- Adapt strategies to type of learning task
- Primary presentation forms (generality or instance and expository or inquisitory)
- Secondary presentation forms (e.g., mnemonic aids)
- Generative strategies allow learners to construct their own meaning
- Supplantive strategies provide direct instructional support
- Part- versus whole-task practice
- Strategies for motivation

Media and Delivery Systems
- Use computer-based instruction to facilitate complex interactions between the learner and the instruction
- Use simulations for problem-solving outcomes

Designers and Design Processes
- Analysis (theoretical analysis of concepts, determine prerequisite relationships)
- Design (events of instruction, primary and secondary presentation forms, supportive and procedural information, integrative goals, part- and whole-task sequencing, motivational design)
- Design Tools (learning hierarchies, ID Expert)

Chapter 8 examines constructivist design theory as a foundation to the ID knowledge base. Constructivism expands the scope of ID by suggesting new ways of knowledge development that in many ways fundamentally alters designers' interpretations of how to facilitate the learning process.

8

CONSTRUCTIVIST DESIGN THEORY

Many scholars and practitioners of instructional deign (ID) now view themselves as constructivists. Their work is influenced by this philosophical orientation which holds that knowledge is individually constructed and often unique to each person. Correspondingly, they believe that the most effective learning occurs when people actively derive meaning from their experiences and the context in which they take place. There are, however, many interpretations and forms of constructivism. Two of the most common are individual constructivism (also known as cognitive constructivism), which emphasizes individual meaning-making, and social constructivism, which highlights the role of social interactions in knowledge development. These two orientations of constructivism have had the most impact on ID.

Smith and Ragan (2005) identify the key assumptions that characterize both of these orientations. They suggest that individual constructivists believe:

- Knowledge is constructed from experience.
- Learning results from a personal interpretation of knowledge.
- Learning is an active process in which meaning is developed on the basis of experience. (p. 19)

This position emphasizes the psychological processes of an individual, and views learning as a matter of cognitive reorganization (Duffy & Cunningham, 1996). In this approach, knowledge can be unique to a given person.

Social constructivists, on the other hand, expand this notion of learning and meaning-making. They assume that "learning is collaborative with meaning negotiated from multiple perspectives" (Smith & Ragan, 2005, p. 20). This stance emphasizes the role of social and cultural processes; therefore, learning is often a matter of acculturation (Duffy & Cunningham, 1996). In this orientation, knowledge is shared by a community of learners. There are members of both the individual and the social viewpoints of constructivism that also emphasize the importance of incorporating real-life contexts into the environment.

In keeping with these constructivist ideas, new approaches to ID and pedagogy have evolved. These beliefs have impacted the ways designers complete their most fundamental tasks (e.g., analysis, strategy selection, and assessment), as well as how they solve teaching and learning problems in general. In this chapter we will explore:

- The principles of constructivist design;
- Related philosophical issues;
- How constructivism is manifested in ID practice;
- Trends in constructivist ID; and
- Representative research on constructivist design theory.

THE NATURE OF CONSTRUCTIVIST DESIGN THEORY

A new design theory has evolved as a result of the growing interest in constructivism and its view of the learning process. This theory is rooted in three basic principles:

- Learning results from a personal interpretation of experience.
- Learning is an active process occurring in realistic and relevant situations.
- Learning results from an exploration of multiple perspectives.

These principles build on those of Smith and Ragan (2005) and encompass both individual and social constructivist orientations. The blending of these two positions not only reflects common design practice, but is also supported theoretically by Cobb (1994) and Fox (2001). For example, Cobb argues that "it is inappropriate to single out qualitative differences in individual thinking apart from their socio-cultural situation because differences in students' interpretations of school tasks reflect qualitative differences in the communities in which they participate" (p. 15). Taking a somewhat different stance, Fox (2001) argues that individuals can have both personal learning and still "share in common knowledge" (p. 30). We believe that these positions hold true for most types of education and training, and propose a set of integrated principles. In this section we will examine each of these constructivist design principles.

Personal Interpretation of Experience

Many scholars look to Piaget as a foundation for constructivism. As late as 1980, Piaget stated:

> Fifty years of experience have taught us that knowledge does not result from a mere recording of observations without a structuring activity on the part of the subject. Nor do any a priori or innate cognitive structures exist in man; the functioning of intelligence alone is hereditary and creates structures only through an organization of successive actions performed on objects. (Piaget as cited in Phillips, 1995, p. 6)

von Glasersfeld extended Piaget's ideas when he posited that "what we call knowledge does not and cannot have the purpose of producing representations of an independent reality, but instead has an adaptive function" (von Glasersfeld as cited in Fox, 2001, p. 27).

These conclusions provide a basis for our first constructivist design principle:

Learning results from a personal interpretation of experience.

While many interpretations of constructivism exist, most scholars subscribe to the view that knowledge is constructed by individuals as they attempt to make sense of their own experiences (Driscoll, 2005). We will explore this principle in terms how learners develop self-knowledge and how instructors facilitate learning.

Developing Self-Knowledge

Duffy and Cunningham (1996) present the concept of a self-world, "the worlds that organisms individually and collectively create and that serve to mediate their experience in the world" (p. 178). In the blend of individual and social constructivism, these self-worlds combine one's personal history of learning, as well as common knowledge (Fox, 2001). This is the essence of self-knowledge. These internal representations and personal interpretations of knowledge are constantly open to change (Bednar, Cunningham, Duffy, & Perry, 1992). Thus, learning evolves.

The self-world serves as the prior knowledge used to construct new knowledge. Prior knowledge, however, is more than simple information; it includes values, experiences, and beliefs as well (Smith & Ragan, 2005). It also encompasses the learner's self-reflective skills, a particularly critical component since it is through reflection that one is best able to build new knowledge.

A person's self-knowledge also includes an awareness of how knowledge construction works. Duffy and Cunningham (1996) call this understanding "knowing how to know" (p. 181). This self-knowledge often needs to be encouraged and nurtured in the learning environment, and Driscoll (2005) calls this nurturing process one of the basic conditions of a constructivist learning environment. Understandings of one's own knowledge construction can lead to learners not only feeling a sense of knowledge ownership, but also have "control over and responsibility for their beliefs" (Duffy & Cunningham, 1996, p. 182). Constructivist design involves creating environments and activities that are controlled by learners, and controlling one's own knowledge and beliefs is the ultimate mission of a mature learner.

Facilitating Learning

Fundamentally, constructivist designers view instruction as "a process of supporting [knowledge] construction rather than communicating knowledge" (Duffy & Cunningham, 1996, p. 171). Thus, learners should not be passive and simply receive, memorize, and recall information; instead they should be active by thinking, analyzing, understanding, and applying information (Gordon, 2009).

Instructors and instructional designers use a variety of techniques, often implemented with technology, to build these active learning environments. Shirvani (2009) suggests creating an atmosphere that:

- Allows students to freely question and express their own opinions, create their own meaning, share control of the classroom, and develop positive attitudes toward learning;
- Includes instructors who maximize student interactions, guide students in connecting new and previous experiences, provide frequent assessment and feedback, respect learner ideas, and encourage student autonomy; and

- Involves activities that are relevant, challenging, focus on large concepts, and encourage high-level thinking.

Certainly, other approaches to the design of learning environments employ many of these same strategies, but the concentration of their use in a single learning environment is now commonly seen as constructivism.

Active, Realistic, and Relevant Learning

In the early part of the twentieth century, "John Dewey began arguing for the kind of change that would move schools away from authoritarian classrooms with abstract notions to environments in which learning is achieved through experimentation, practice and exposure to the real world" (Karagiorgi & Symeou, 2005, p. 24). Constructivism builds upon this thinking by the second principle which suggests that:

Learning is an active process occurring in realistic and relevant situations.

This statement reflects the emphasis constructivists place on creating active, authentic, and contextualized learning environments.

Active Learning

The classic constructivist learning environment eschews instructor-led delivery of information in favor of those environments in which learners actively participate in the task at hand. Many theories of learning and ID, however, advocate the notion of active learning. Behavioral psychologists demand overt performance throughout the learning process. Discovery learning was a prominent cognitive strategy emphasized especially in the 1960s and 1970s (Bruner, 1966). This approach can be seen as a learning-by-doing strategy. These strategies are promoted as a way to facilitate skill development and information acquisition in practical contexts (Schank, Berman, & Macpherson, 1999).

The constructivist perspective of active learning, however, differs from other positions primarily because they tend to involve instructor-determined content. As Duffy and Cunningham (1996) describe in relation to discovery learning, "the learner has to discover the answer that the teacher already knows" (p. 182). Active learning for the constructivist involves more than processing information provided by the materials or the instructor; it involves more than physically participating in predetermined learning activities.

Active learning from the constructivist point of view involves interacting with information at a high level, elaborating upon this information, and interpreting it in light of one's previous knowledge and experiences (Perkins, 1992). Wu and Tsai (2005) found that over time the use of multiple constructivist teaching strategies can facilitate not only knowledge acquisition, but these techniques lead to further development of learner cognitive structures and to the advanced use of higher order information processing strategies.

Authentic and Contextualized Learning Activities

Constructivists also subscribe to the practice of situating instruction in real-life contexts, arguing that this not only makes the instruction more interesting and motivating, but also more likely to be transferred or applied in other settings. This approach is also based upon the belief that "knowledge and the conditions of its use are inextricably linked" (Hannafin, Hannafin, Land, & Oliver, 1997, p. 109). Smith and Ragan (2005) note that this type of instruction is often called "anchored instruction", and the resulting learning is called "authentic or situated learning". To be considered authentic, according to Young (1993), a situation:

> . . . must at least have some of the important attributes of real-life problem solving, including ill-structured complex goals, an opportunity for the detection of relevant versus irrelevant information, active/generative engagement in finding and defining problems as well as in solving them, involvement in the student's beliefs and values, and an opportunity to engage in collaborative interpersonal activities. (p. 45)

Brown, Collins, and Duguid (1989) define authentic activities as those which are "coherent, meaningful, and purposeful . . . the ordinary practices of the culture" (p. 34). They go on to posit that these actions "embed learning in activity and make deliberate use of the social and physical context" (p. 34). The context of authentic activity is that of practitioners rather than the classroom or the training site. Authentic learning activities then are built using everyday language, everyday problems, and everyday situations. These authentic activities are often complex; they have not been simplified or targeted information has not been isolated as is common in traditional instruction. Even though authentic activities have real-world foundations, the activity may be simulated, and often they are computer-mediated.

Exploration of Multiple Perspectives

The third principle of constructivist design theory is:

Learning results from an exploration of multiple perspectives.

This reflects the social facet of constructivism which is firmly rooted in the thinking of Vygotsky. His position is presented in a commonly quoted statement: "every function in the child's cultural development appears twice: first, on the social level, and later on the individual level" (Vygotsky, 1978, p. 57). The emphasis on multiple perspectives encompasses two major elements of constructivist design: rich learning environments and collaborative learning environments. Both of these elements are intrinsically social in nature.

Rich Learning Environments

Karagiori and Symeou (2005) define a rich learning environment as one which "encourages multiple learning styles and multiple representations of knowledge from different conceptual and case perspectives" (p. 20). By definition, rich learning environments provide multiple perspectives and are information rich. However, many of these environments are also those in which "learners engage in domain-related practices to carry out socially negotiated tasks" (Hay & Barab, 2001, p. 282). These situations are likely to be project-dominated, contextualized, and authentic.

Not surprisingly, many of the rich learning environments are networked, allowing full access to what has been called "knowledge webs" (Albion & Maddux, 2007). Consequently, they are likely to have multiple interpretations of the instructional content, and multiple sources of input.

Collaborative Learning Environments

One of the hallmarks of constructivist learning environments is that they "allow learners to share and collaboratively reflect" (Hay & Barab, 2001, p. 283). Collaborative learning, however, is not simply "sharing a workload or coming to a consensus, but allows learners to develop, compare, and understand multiple perspectives on an issue" (Karagiori & Symeou, 2005, p. 21). Thus, collaboration involves sharing, discussion, perhaps argument, reflection, and often negotiation. These learning environments can involve large or small groups, or an organized community of practice.

Collaborative environments are often electronic environments utilizing a variety of collaborative learning tools (e.g., online discussion boards). While the use of such tools does not automatically designate a learning environment as constructivist, they can be used to achieve constructivist goals. This is increasingly the case with online learning. Learning in such environments can be an individual event, but in some situations (especially those which are project-oriented), learning is distributed across a group. No one person may acquire all of the important knowledge, but across the group enough has been learned to accomplish a particular task. In the framework of this distributed cognition, the notion of learning is expanded and "cognition is propagated from mind to mind, from mind to tool, and tool to mind [and] . . . is shared between the constituents of the group" (Schwartz, 2008, p. 390). This is a unique form of collaboration.

CONSTRUCTIVISM AND RELATED PHILOSOPHICAL ISSUES

We view constructivism fundamentally as a philosophy, a set of beliefs that leads to a particular view of learning and a corresponding approach to instructional design (ID). However, constructivist thinking is also related to other philosophical orientations and debates. We have previously discussed rationalism as a view of truth based upon deduction rather than observation. This is in keeping with the evolution of constructivist philosophy which has been developed to a great extent through reasoning. Smith and Ragan (2005) go so far as to suggest that constructivism is a subset of rationalism.

Constructivism also shares some humanistic orientations. While humanism is mainly concerned with the welfare of individuals, constructivism is concerned with individual knowledge. Thus, the humanist element in constructivist philosophy is in its implied subjectivity, and the notion that truth can vary from person to person, or from culture to culture. This element of subjectivity, however, brings forth charges in some quarters of "epistemological relativism, where there exists no absolute truth and any truth is as good as other" (Liu & Matthews, 2005, p. 388). In keeping with this viewpoint, Phillips (1995) suggests that some versions of constructivism view knowledge as being only a matter of "sociopolitical process or consensus" (p. 11). This interpretation is not consistent with the notions of testable realities or knowledge that is adaptable to its environment (Kevinen & Ristelä, 2003). Such arguments can pertain to either individual or social constructivism, but it is more likely that they would apply to the stance of radical constructivists who argue that "knowledge is not a self-sufficient entity" (Liu & Matthews, 2005, p. 387).

Finally, Phillips (1995) has charged constructivists with having a quasi-religious or ideological fervor, calling this an ugly face of the movement. He speaks of the various constructivist "sects" and the common "distrust of nonbelievers" (p. 5). This zeal may have subsided in recent years, but constructivism and constructivist design theory is clearly greatly influenced by personal values, and the examination of such theory is often a minefield of strong emotions.

APPLICATIONS OF CONSTRUCTIVIST DESIGN THEORY

The three basic principles of constructivist design theory (i.e. personal interpretation of experience, active, realistic, and relevant contexts, and exploration of multiple perspectives) have implications for practitioners of ID. Below we discuss how the application of constructivism impacts analysis, instructional strategy selection, and assessment.

Analysis

Several scholars describe how constructivists conduct analysis (Bednar et al., 1992; Hannafin & Hill, 2007; Karagiorgi & Symeou, 2005; Perkins, 1992). These authors often compare instructional systems design (ISD) methods of analysis to constructivist approaches. For example, designers who follow the systems approach analyze instructional goals to identify prerequisite skills, knowledge, and attitudes or to determine the sequence of operations required to achieve a goal. Tasks are also broken down into their component parts when ISD analysis procedures are followed. Furthermore, the subordinate facts, concepts, rules, and procedures required to achieve a goal are identified during analysis.

While practitioners who subscribe to constructivist design theory also carry out analysis, they focus on ". . . tasks that display understandings, not just knowledge and smooth operations" (Perkins, 1992, p. 52). Constructivist designers typically do not prespecify content because they adhere to the principle that individuals must construct their own personal interpretation of knowledge. "Instead of dividing up the knowledge domains based on a logical analysis of dependencies, the constructivist view turns toward a consideration of what real people do in a particular knowledge domain" (Bednar et al., 1992, p. 23).

Thus context, not content, is the focus of analysis from a constructivist point of view. Constructivist designers analyze "the environments in which the knowledge, skills, and complexities naturally exist" (Karagiorgi & Symeou, 2005, p. 19). This reflects the constructivist principle that learning occurs in realistic and relevant situations. Analysis provides information that is used to identify the dimensions of a rich learning environment. "To guide the creation of context, the designer may focus on the description of a problem . . . and/or identification of key concepts related to the problem" (Hannafin & Hill, 2007, p. 58).

For constructivist designers, analysis leads to the identification of general learning goals that are related to authentic tasks rather than the specification of instructional objectives. As Bednar et al. (1992) state:

> Constructivists do not have learning and performance objectives that are internal to the content domain (e.g., apply the principle), but rather we search for authentic tasks and let the more specific objectives emerge and be realized as they are appropriate to the individual learner in solving the real-world task. (p. 25)

Systematic and constructivist approaches to ID both include an analysis of learners. A vital task for designers following an ISD approach is to identify the attributes most critical to the attainment of specific learning objectives (Morrison, Ross, & Kemp, 2007). These factors include general profile characteristics (e.g., age, gender, work experience, and ethnicity), learning styles, and prerequisite skills and knowledge. Constructivist designers also identify learner prerequisites. However, they focus on the unique perspectives of each individual as they enter a learning environment rather than on group characteristics (Bednar et al., 1992). For constructivists, a critical prerequisite is self-knowledge, the ability of students to be aware of their own role in the knowledge construction process (Duffy & Cunningham, 1996).

Instructional Strategies

While systematic and constructivist approaches to ID have contrasting views of analysis, designers with both points of view understand the importance of selecting instructional strategies based on how people learn. Below, we discuss a few strategies that are commonly associated with constructivist principles.

Cognitive Apprenticeships

The constructivist notion that learning is an active process occurring in realistic and relevant situations implies an abandonment of the "acontextual, one-size-fits-all perspective" (Cobb, 1994, p. 19). One prominent tactic to contextualize instruction has been through the use of cognitive apprenticeships. These are learning environments that provide students with the opportunity to participate in an expert's world rather than simply learning expert processes and acquiring expert knowledge in an abstract fashion. Learners are immersed in the expert's culture and are able to develop skills while being involved in authentic work. While teachers may serve in the expert role, they are more likely to serve as coaches than as dispensers of information. Duffy and Cunningham (1996) do not see the master-apprentice relationship as the critical part of a cognitive apprenticeship. Instead, they suggest that the important aspect of the approach is for the learner to operate as a "member of a larger community of practice who, through legitimate peripheral participation and the affordances of the environment, begins to assume greater responsibility in that community" (p. 184).

Problem-Based Learning

Problem-based learning (PBL) is an instructional strategy used to prepare students to be better problem solvers.[1] According to Hoffman and Ritchie (1997), PBL is "a student-centered pedagogical strategy that poses significant contextualized, real-world, ill-structured situations while providing resources, guidance, instruction and opportunities for reflection to learners as they develop content knowledge and problem-solving skills" (p. 97). The essential characteristic of PBL is the use of a problem to situate learning rather than exposing students to disciplinary knowledge before they solve problems (Albanese & Mitchell, 1993; Hmelo & Evensen, 2000). However, it is not the purpose of PBL to have students reach a perfect solution; rather, PBL emphasizes having students understand the causes of the problem and actively build knowledge that transfers to other problem situations (Hmelo & Evensen, 2000).

Scaffolding

The concept of scaffolding is grounded in the theories of Vygotsky (1978), who proposed that there is a cognitive distance between what learners know and can do independently,

---

1 We view problem solving as a learning outcome that can be approached from several different points of view and problem-based learning as an instructional strategy that mainly adheres to constructivist design principles.

and what learners can potentially achieve with the assistance of a more capable person. This is called the zone of proximal development (ZPD). Scaffolding is used to help learners cross the ZPD to extend their capabilities into a new domain with just enough support (Arts, Gijselaers, & Segers, 2002). Just enough support means that scaffolding should support learning while still making it challenging and allowing for independent thinking (Rommetveit, 1974).

Scaffolding can take a variety of forms such as encouraging, explaining, modeling, or questioning (Hogan & Pressley, 1997). Content scaffolds can be used to support students' understanding of the subject matter (Reid, Zhang, & Chen, 2003; Pedaste & Sarapuu, 2006). For example, a content scaffold could direct students' attention to key terms and principles as they gather specific information they require to approach a problem (Su, 2007). Metacognitive scaffolds are designed to facilitate learners as they plan and monitor learning activities or evaluate and reflect on their own learning (Reid et al., 2003; Pedaste & Sarapuu, 2006). For example, a metacognitive scaffold might encourage students to summarize, reflect on, and debrief information they learned after finishing a project (Su, 2007).

Saye and Brush (2002) proposed a taxonomy of scaffolds, grouping them into two types based on their flexibility. Soft scaffolds refer to dynamic and situational supports that require teachers to continuously diagnose learners' instructional situations and provide them with just enough support in a timely manner. Hard scaffolds are static supports that can be predicted and planned in advance based on anticipated typical difficulties students may have during learning (Saye & Brush, 2002).

Collaboration

Adherence to the constructivist principle that learning results from an exploration of multiple perspectives frequently leads to the use of collaboration. Collaboration refers to a variety of instructional strategies that encourage students to work together, including peer teaching, discussion groups, and learning communities (Goodsell, Maher, Tino, Smith, & McGregor, 1992). The terms collaborative learning and cooperative learning are often used interchangeably. However, collaborative learning is less structured than cooperative learning; it relates to ill-structured tasks for open and flexible solutions and to the acquisition of an ill-defined domain of knowledge and skills (Eastmond, 1995; Webb & Palincsar, 1996).

Some constructivists suggest that learning is more effective when students collaborate to discuss with their peers (Jonassen & Kwon, 2001; Kanuka & Anderson, 1998). This belief has led to a shift from individual knowledge construction to knowledge-building communities of learners (Chou, 2001; Ravits, 1997). A collaborative strategy often used by constructivist designers is computer-mediated collaboration (CMC). CMC can provide enhanced opportunities for dialogue, debate, and the potential for a sense of community (Naidu, 1997; Oliver & Omari, 2001). Theorists think CMC may have a greater impact on problem-solving and higher-order skills than other modes of interaction (Adelskold, Alklett, Axelsson, & Blomgren, 1999; Jonassen, Prevish, Christy, & Stavulaki, 1999). However, empirical evidence for the use of CMC to enhance problem solving is meager at best (Murphy & Collins, 1997; Uribe, Klein, & Sullivan, 2003).

Assessment

Constructivism also has implications for assessing student learning. According to Jonassen (1992), "An obvious implication of constructivism for evaluation of learning is that evaluation should be goal-free" (p. 139). Based on Scriven's (1991) principles of goal-free program evaluation, Jonassen believes that the learning process, and the assessment of it, will be biased if learning goals are known in advance. Constructivists often suggest assessing learners' thinking processes by asking them to solve problems in a domain and explain and defend their decisions (Bednar et al., 1992). In addition, constructivist designers use open-ended assessments to determine if learners understand and can the use knowledge they have constructed for themselves (Perkins, 1992). Because constructivists believe that learning results from an exploration of multiple perspectives, evaluation processes should allow for different perspectives rather than one right solution (Jonassen, 1992). Thus, constructivist designers would require learners to present alternative solutions to a problem and make arguments that support their position. These beliefs suggest that criterion-referenced assessments used by designers who follow the systems approach are not appropriate for assessing constructivist learning.

Summary

Many of the individual elements of constructivist design theory are often used in other approaches to instruction. However, the applications of the core principles together lead to the design of unique learning environments. The differences between constructivist design and instructional systems design are compared in Table 8.1.

Table 8.1 A Comparison of Instructional Systems Design and Constructivist Instructional Design

Task	Instructional Systems Design	Constructivist Instructional Design
Analysis	• Content (Tasks, Procedures) • Problem and Organization • Learner (Prerequisites, Profiles, Learning Style) • Context (Orienting, Instructional, Transfer)	• Context (Authentic Settings) • Problem • Individual Learners (Self-Knowledge, Perspectives)
Design	• Behavioral Objectives • Sequencing (Hierarchical, Simple to Complex) • Media Selection • Implementation Plans	• General Goals Related to Authentic Tasks • Learner-Controlled Sequencing • Rich Learning Environments
Development	• Instructional Activities • Instructional Materials	• Networked Environment • Electronic Collaborative Tools • Social Networking Tools
Implementation	• Variety of Strategies (e.g., Collaborative, Computer-Based, Large Group Direct Instruction, Individualized) • Instructor Roles (Delivery, Facilitation and Guidance, Evaluator)	• Active and Authentic Learning Strategies (e.g., Problem-Based Learning, Cognitive Apprenticeships, Computer-Mediated Collaboration, Learning Communities) • Scaffolding • Instructor Roles (Coach, Facilitator, Guide, Support)
Evaluation	• Criterion-Referenced Assessment of Learners • Formative, Summative, and Confirmative Evaluation (Program, Materials)	• Continuous Diagnosis • Goal-Free Assessment • Open-Ended Assessment • Multiple Perspectives

TRENDS IN CONSTRUCTIVIST INSTRUCTIONAL DESIGN

Constructivist design theory continues to expand how we approach ID. Starting originally as a general philosophical position, it was adapted to new ways of teaching and then to the design and development of instruction. Now constructivist design theory serves as the impetus for a re-examination of the design process itself and for the role of technology in furthering constructivist goals. We will address these two developments in this section.

Emergence of Constructivist Instructional Design Models

There is a call in some quarters for the adoption of "new theoretical stances and models, representing different views on learning and instruction" (Larson & Lockee, 2004, p. 32). This includes the move to a nonlinear, cyclical, and iterative design process using authentic problem-solving techniques (Willis, 2009a; Hakkinen, 2002). Constructivist-ID models (C-ID) may be one answer to this call.

Proponents of C-ID models recommend that designers focus on the local context of the design project and emphasize collaborative development procedures. They also suggest an iterative design process. Although many designers implementing ISD procedures also operate in an iterative manner, there is a fundamental difference between C-ID models and ISD models (Willis, 2009a). Most designers using ISD models tend to be objectivists who adhere to general explanations of the learning process which have been supported by empirical research. C-ID models, however, are based on the assumption that there are "no absolute laws of human behavior and learning that can be confidently generalized from one situation to another" (Willis, 2009a, p. 24). The contextual idiosyncrasies of each design project guide the decision-making process and determine what works and what may not work. Instruction designed using C-ID models is implemented with the assumption that there will be multiple perspectives during instruction and designers best serve learners when they help them confront as many of these perspectives as possible (Willis, 2009a). This reflects the view that learning results from an exploration of multiple perspectives; this was discussed earlier. The use of C-ID models results in instruction that promotes learning from a personal interpretation of experience, often through activities such as problem-solving and cognitive apprenticeships. Here we explore two examples of C-ID models: the Layers of Negotiation Model and the Recursive, Reflective Instructional Design (R2D2) Model.

Layers of Negotiation Model

The Layers of Negotiation ID Model was constructed during the design and development of a series of case-based interactive videodiscs for use in constructivist teacher education programs (Cennamo, Abell, & Chung, 1996). The model focuses on the process of knowledge construction which involves reflection, the examination of information multiple times for multiple purposes, and the social negotiation of shared meanings (Cennamo, 2003). The model uses a recursive process that spirals through the analysis, design, development, and evaluation phases of ID. Cennamo (2003) attempted to apply the same elements of a constructivist learning environment to the design of instruction:

1. Embrace the complexity of the design process.
2. Provide for social negotiations as an integral part of designing the materials.
3. Examine information relevant to the design of the instruction at multiple times from multiple perspectives.

4. Nurture reflexivity in the design process.
5. Emphasize participatory design. (p. 15)

Social negotiations become an integral part of the ID process by involving all participants throughout the project. Participants in the design process develop a set of shared
beliefs that are incorporated in the design and development of the instructional materials (Cennamo, 2003). Cennamo implemented and revised the model in a second project pertaining to elementary teacher professional development. Cennamo (2003) states
"throughout the design process, decisions were made based on the data that were available and relevant. As additional data became apparent or relevant; we spiraled back and
revisited prior decisions" (p. 16). The Layers of Negotiation Model was subsequently
refined in the Cennamo and Kalk (2005) rapid prototyping model previously described
in Chapter 2.

Recursive, Reflective Instructional Design Model

The R2D2 Model is another example of constructivist ID. This model was initially created
during ID projects conducted at the NASA Johnson Space Center (Willis, 2009b). R2D2
provides design guidelines rather than a set of required steps. The three general principles
or flexible guidelines in the Willis R2D2 Model relate to recursive, reflective, and participatory design.

The first guideline is design is recursive or iterative in nature. In this approach, design
is essentially nonlinear. The procedures are completed in the order that makes sense
for the design project. Designers have the opportunity to revisit issues again and again
throughout the process. Unlike a more sequential ISD approach, objectives, content, and
teaching-learning activities gradually emerge rather than being specified early in the
process (Willis, 2009b).

The second guideline is each effort to solve a design problem is seen as an opportunity
to reflect. In constructivist design, "the real world is constructed by the practitioner, who
then makes professional practice decisions from within that constructed reality" (Willis,
2009b, p. 302). Willis (2009b) describes this as both "artistic and reflective" (p. 302).

Finally, the third guideline is design is participatory in nature. As such the design project includes "the users as participants, not as observers" (Willis, 2009b, p. 303). All participants (including end-users and stakeholders) in a design project of this type are considered
experts in what they do. The designer is not viewed as the expert. Consequently, designers
must collaborate with participants while making design decisions (Willis, 2009b).

Willis (2009b) states the use of these general principles have been widely adopted in
other design fields and that a paradigm shift appears to be occurring in ID resulting in the
general acceptance and use of these principles. The R2D2 Model itself is portrayed as a triangle with three focal points: define, design and development, and dissemination (Willis,
2009c). Unlike many other ID models, the triangle does not imply a particular point of
entry or the need to follow a sequential order: "The model is based on the assumption
that designers will work on all three focal points of the process in an intermittent and
recursive pattern that is neither completely predictable nor prescribable" (Willis, 2009c,
p. 315). For example, in ISD writing objectives and test items is typically performed at
the beginning of the project by the instructional designer. Willis (2009c) maintains that
this is not the most effective type of design. Rather, he suggests that the designer should
be a facilitator of the design process, and that it should be undertaken by the entire design

team including end-users, subject-matter experts, and stakeholders. Once the design team determines the general approach to the new instruction, they move forward in a participatory manner knowing that this approach may be modified as the project moves into product development.

The Cennamo and Willis models both approach design as a recursive, reflective process. They both emphasize participation of all involved (including end-users) in all phases of the project. The difference between the two models, however, is in the role of the instructional designer. Cennamo (2003), who reflects a practitioner perspective, believes in the importance of a general ID expert; Willis (2009c), on the other hand, maintains that design is context-specific to the point that the designer serves more as a facilitator of the people and the process.

Applications of Constructivist Instructional Design to Online Learning

There is a growing need to address complex topics in education and training and to integrate learning and work in business settings. At the same time, there is often a need for education and training to be more flexible in terms of time and place in order to meet individual needs. We have discussed constructivist design strategies, including cognitive apprenticeships, problem-based learning, scaffolding, and collaboration. Online learning can provide one environment for these and other constructivist strategies. Here, we discuss two approaches to online learning: computer-supported collaborative learning environments (CSCL) and the use of social networking learning communities.

Computer-Supported Collaborative Learning Environments

CSCL presents a collaborative learning environment in which "the educational context is collaborative, the social context is the group, and the technological context is a computer-mediated setting" (Kirschner, Strijbos, Krejins, & Beers, 2004, p. 50). CSCL involves "designing, developing, and describing technologies to support collaboration in learning environments" (Satwicz & Stevens, 2008, p. 166). Technology is the environmental mediator between the social and educational contexts. The ability of the learner to successfully interact with others in this environment is essential (Kirschner et al., 2004). Interaction in a CSCL environment can provide learners with an opportunity for active learning in a realistic and relevant situation, a basic principle of constructivist design theory.

CSCL environments support those teaching and learning activities that rely heavily on social interaction among group members. These collaborative environments facilitate the emergence of a social space, and a human network of social relationships among group members (Kirschner, 2004). This social interaction among group members can foster an exploration of multiple perspectives of the instructional content and collaboration, also goals of constructivist design. In a review of the use of technology for collaborative learning in higher education, Resta and Laferriere (2007) conclude that:

> . . . the last 20 years have been highly productive for CSCL. The advances of the learning sciences, combined with the needs of the knowledge society, have heightened the requirements for flexible (time and space) and challenging (problem-solving and knowledge building) learning environments. (p. 77)

As technology continues to evolve, so too will these types of learning environments.

Social Network Learning Communities

Social networking learning environments are a result of the continuing evolution of technology and its use in promoting learner interaction and collaboration. Gunawardena et al. (2009) define social networking technology as "tools that facilitate collective intelligence through social negotiation when participants are engaged in a common goal or a shared practice" (p. 6). Social networking technologies include media such as weblogs, podcasting, audio blogs, and wikis. These tools support a constructivist approach to learning by providing an online community where learners can collaborate and interact with others as well as with the instructional content via the Internet. Social networking communities can provide a place where individuals form groups interested in learning and sharing knowledge (Snyder, 2009). Learners are actively seeking others, and in doing so are gaining the multiple perspectives of an identified area of interest.

Utilizing technologies to provide for online student interaction opportunities is not new to ID. Beldarrain (2006) describes how first-generation web tools (e.g., email, chat rooms, and discussion boards) have been used for over a decade. Second-generation web tools may make interactivity more feasible. For example, social networking tools can be used in conjunction with other applications to create engaging learning communities.

RESEARCH ON CONSTRUCTIVIST INSTRUCTIONAL DESIGN

Much like conditions-based ID (see Chapter 7), there is little research examining the comprehensive application of constructivist ID models. Yet, studies have been conducted to investigate instructional strategies commonly associated with constructivism. Below we discuss some representative research on cognitive apprenticeships, PBL, scaffolding, and CMC.

Empirical Support for Constructivist Strategies

A review of the literature on cognitive apprenticeships (Dennen, 2004) suggests that two research methods have been conducted on this strategy: in situ (i.e., qualitative) research and experimental research on designed interventions. In situ studies document cognitive apprenticeships in a specific context. Results of the in situ studies reviewed by Dennen (2004) indicate that in-depth examinations of an expert's actions and understandings in a specific context can lead to models that teachers can use to support their students. Furthermore, modeling and reflection can help students make sense of and internalize what they are learning. However, Dennen (2004) writes:

> The various theories of how cognitive apprenticeship works and the results from *in situ* research both need to be studied with rigor in the interest of attaining generalizability. Small pockets of experimental studies have been conducted to date, but many of these studies occur in isolation rather than in a related series. (p. 821)

A considerable amount of research has been conducted to evaluate the impact of PBL in the classroom or to compare it with conventional approaches to instruction. Many of these studies have been included in reviews of the PBL literature or in meta-analyses of research findings (Albanese & Mitchell, 1993; Gijbels, Dochy, Van den Bossche, & Segers, 2005; Norman & Schmidt, 1992; Vernon & Blake, 1993). This research indicates that PBL:

- Enhances student interest, attitudes, and motivation for learning;
- Decreases immediate acquisition of declarative knowledge outcomes; and
- Promotes long-term retention of information, application of skills, and self-directed learning.

Others report some difficulty associated with PBL, especially when it is implemented in technology-rich settings that allow students the freedom to explore multiple resources. For example, learners can become disorientated or lost during PBL; this often leads to feelings of frustration and lack of support (Edelson, Gordin, & Pea, 1999).

To address these issues, scaffolds are frequently used to support learners when PBL is used with complex multimedia. These hard scaffolds are static supports, are planned in advance, and are based on anticipated student difficulties (Saye & Brush, 2002). Research findings suggest that these types of scaffolds have a positive impact on information seeking, knowledge acquisition, concept integration, ill-structured problem-solving, and reflection (Cho & Jonassen, 2002; Davis & Linn, 2000; Roehler & Cantlon, 1997; Saye & Brush, 2002; Simons & Klein, 2007). However, other researchers report that many students lack the metacognitive skills required to use scaffolds in open-ended learning environments (Land & Hannafin, 1997; Oliver & Hannafin, 2000).

In addition to studies on PBL and scaffolds, there is extensive research on the use of collaborative strategies. Generally, findings show that collaboration has a positive impact on learning and motivation in classrooms and when students use technology (Johnson & Johnson, 2004; Sussman, 1998). However, most of these studies do not attempt to link collaboration with any of the constructivist design principles discussed in this chapter.

CMC is frequently hailed by constructivist designers as a way to increase problem-solving ability. Yet empirical evidence for the use of CMC to enhance problem solving is meager at best. According to Uribe et al. (2003), research on CMC has been limited to preference surveys or evaluative case studies. For example, a case study conducted by Gilbert and Driscoll (2002) indicated that students in a graduate course on instructional theory benefited from building and sharing information by means of CMC. Another case study by Scardamalia and Bereiter (1996) suggested that elementary school students using CMC displayed a higher level of knowledge construction when compared to those who did not collaborate. Furthermore, Uribe et al. (2003) note that many studies on CMC focus on affective outcomes, while ignoring learning and performance.

Recommendations for Continuing Research

Growing interest in the application of constructivism to ID requires that scholars conduct rigorous research on the principles of constructivist design theory. As we have pointed out, isolated studies have been conducted on some of the strategies that adhere to constructivist philosophy. We think that research on cognitive apprenticeships, PBL, scaffolding, and CMC should continue, but that findings should tie more directly to the basic tenets of constructivist ID discussed in this chapter.

Most strategy research compares constructivist to nonconstructivist approaches in an apparent effort to prove the effectiveness of these techniques and the wisdom of the philosophy. However researchers, such as Hay and Barab (2001), have begun to study the relative effects of various approaches to constructivist design by examining the impact of alternative learning environments. This seems to be a fruitful tactic, one that holds promise of providing a more solid foundation for constructivist design. In addition, such research can clarify the nature of constructivism itself by distinguishing the alternative "theories that are frequently grouped under the umbrella term of constructivism" (Hay & Barab, 2001, p. 318).

Finally, we think that more research should be done to validate constructivist ID procedures and models. Constructivist approaches to analysis, assessment, and evaluation, as well as the application of models such as the R2D2 Model (Willis, 2009b) require empirical validation. A fruitful method for these studies would be design and development research or design-based research.

SUMMARY

This chapter has explored the basic principles of constructivist design theory: personal interpretation of experience, active, realistic, and relevant contexts, and exploration of multiple perspectives. We examined how constructivism is applied in ID practice during analysis, strategy selection and design, and assessment. We also discussed some trends in constructivist ID and representative research studies conducted to investigate instructional strategies commonly associated with constructivism. Tables 8.2 and 8.3 provide a summary of the major themes covered in this chapter.

Table 8.2 An Overview of Constructivist Design Theory and Instructional Design

1. **Key Principles:**
   - Learning results from a personal interpretation of experience.
   - Learning is an active process occurring in realistic and relevant situations.
   - Learning results from an exploration of multiple perspectives.

2. **Philosophical Orientation:**
   - Constructivism is a philosophy itself.
   - Constructivism also reflects principles of rationalism.
   - Constructivism's implied subjectivity reflects some elements of humanism.

3. **Theoretical Foundations:** John Dewey, Jean Piaget, Ernst von Glasersfeld, and Lev Vygotsky

4. **ID Applications:**
   - Analysis of the Environment, Problems, and Individual Learners
   - Goal-Free and Open-Ended Assessment
   - Instructional Strategies (Cognitive Apprenticeship, Problem-Based Learning, Scaffolding, Collaboration)
   - Learning Environments (Computer-Supported Collaborative Learning, Social Networking Learning Communities)

5. **Supporting ID Research:** Representative areas include the following:
   - Cognitive Apprenticeships (e.g., Dennen, 2004)
   - Problem-Based Learning (e.g., Albanese & Mitchell, 1993; Gijbels et al., 2005)
   - Scaffolding (e.g., Cho & Jonassen, 2002; Davis & Linn, 2000; Land & Hannafin, 1997; Saye & Brush, 2002; Simons & Klein, 2007)
   - Computer-Mediated Collaboration (e.g., Johnson & Johnson, 2004; Scardamalia & Bereiter, 1996; Uribe et al., 2003)

6. **Related Concepts:**
   - Anchored Instruction
   - Individual Constructivism
   - Knowledge Construction
   - Learning Community
   - Situated Cognition
   - Social Constructivism

Table 8.3 Instructional Design Domains and Elements Related to Constructivist Design Theory

Learners and Learning Processes
- Distributed Cognition
- Knowledge Construction
- Learner Characteristics (beliefs and attitudes, self-knowledge, self-reflective skills)

Learning and Performance Contexts
- Computer-Supported Collaborative Learning Environments
- Learning Environments (rich, authentic)
- Social Networking Learning Communities

Content Structure and Sequence
- Learner-Controlled Instructional Sequences

Instructional and Noninstructional Strategies
- Active Learning
- Authentic Learning Activities
- Cognitive Apprenticeships
- Facilitation of Learning and Individual Knowledge Construction
- Interactive and Collaborative Learning
- Learner Control
- Problem-Based Learning
- Scaffolding

Media and Delivery Systems
- Computer Supported Collaborative Learning
- Electronic Collaborative Tools
- Social Networking Tools

Designers and Design Processes
- Analysis (context, individual learners, problems)
- Design and Development (general goal related to authentic tasks, participatory, recursive, reflective, strategy and media selection)
- Assessment and Evaluation (accept multiple perspectives, goal-free assessment, open-ended assessments)

Next, we turn to performance improvement (PI) theory and explain how this area of scholarship and practice provides a foundation to the ID knowledge base. We examine some models of PI and look at some of the trends and research findings in this field.

9

PERFORMANCE IMPROVEMENT THEORY

Theories and models of performance improvement (PI)[1] expand the scope of instructional design (ID) by employing the systems approach to address performance opportunities and problems. PI can be applied to improve the performance of organizations, processes, and individuals (Rummler & Brache, 1995). It is concerned with measurable performance and how to structure elements within a results-oriented system (Stolovitch & Keeps, 1999).

Practitioners of PI and ID follow a systems approach to analyze, design, develop, implement, and evaluate products and programs. Like ID, the origin of modern day PI can be traced back to World War II when the Training Within Industry project went beyond training individual workers to focus on organizational performance and used innovative tools such as job instructions, job methods, and job relations (see Swanson, 1999). Furthermore, PI and ID share many of the same theoretical underpinnings.

While PI and ID share many of the same roots, PI models and theories have impacted ID in recent years. The purpose of this chapter is to examine the contributions of PI to ID. The following will be discussed:

- The theoretical foundations of PI;
- Models of performance improvement;
- Evaluation and PI;
- The philosophical orientations to performance improvement;
- Trends in the application of performance improvement to ID; and
- An examination of PI research literature and suggestions for future studies.

---

1 We use the term performance improvement (PI) in this chapter rather than performance technology (PT), human performance improvement (HPI), or human performance technology (HPT). While many view the terms to be synonymous, we prefer PI because it is focused on outcomes rather than tools, and it is broader in scope. At times, however, we use the terms HPI or HPT when quoting from the literature. (See Stolovitch, 2007 for a further discussion of these terms.)

THEORETICAL FOUNDATIONS OF PERFORMANCE IMPROVEMENT

Various authors have identified the theories that form the basis of PI (Foshay & Moller, 1992; Rosenberg, Coscarelli, & Hutchison, 1999; Stolovitch, 2007; Sugrue & Stolovitch, 2000). According to a review of the literature by Huglin (2009), the most frequently cited cognate fields considered as foundational to PI are psychology, systems theory, organizational development, instructional systems design, and communications theory.

Some of the theoretical foundations of PI parallel those of ID. For example, general systems theory (GST) (see Chapter 2), communications theory (see Chapter 3), and learning theory (see Chapter 4) contribute to ID and PI alike. Stolovitch (2007) discusses the impact of behavioral learning theory on PI by stating:

> Thomas F. Gilbert is generally considered to be the father of HPT. As a graduate student of B. F. Skinner, Gilbert was steeped in the principles and practices of behaviorism . . . taking Skinner's principles and venturing into the workplace arena. (p. 139)

Organizational development (OD) theory also influences PI. Like PI, OD centers on results by emphasizing an organization's mission and objectives (Stolovitch, 2000). Nevertheless, OD practitioners "focus on humanistic rather than behavioristic strategies" (Rosenberg et al., 1999, p. 32). These strategies relate to culture, diversity, ethics, leadership, and team building (Dean, 1999; Van Tiem, Moseley, & Dessinger, 2004).

After conducting an extensive review of the organizational change and development literature, Beer and Walton (cited in Rosenberg et al., 1999) propose four views of the field: OD as general management, OD as creation of adaptive strategies, OD as human resource management, and OD as implementation of change. Each point of view impacts PI by providing a wide assortment of interventions that focus on the well-being of individuals within an organization (Beer & Walton, 1987).

Another way of describing the theoretical foundations of PI is to examine the lens it uses to view performance (Swanson, 1999). According to Rosenberg et al. (1999), "There appears to be general agreement that HPT ultimately stems from the work of a number of behavioral psychologists" (p. 26). As a result, early approaches to performance improvement focused mainly on individuals and the processes they used to accomplish a task or job. Someone viewing PI through this lens is focused on subsystem performance (Swanson, 1999). While still concerned with individual accomplishment, PI today is also focused on system-wide improvement—organizational performance is at the highest position of the lens (Rummler & Brache, 1995; Swanson, 1999). Furthermore, newer frameworks that center on the socio-cultural aspects of performance improvement to include complex group and organizational structures have recently been introduced into the PI literature (Schwen, Kalman, & Evans, 2006).

MODELS OF PERFORMANCE IMPROVEMENT

A number of models have been developed to address how to improve the performance of organizations, processes, and individuals. Below we discuss several of these models including:

- A model advocated by the International Society of Performance Improvement;
- Gilbert's Behavior Engineering Model;

- Harless's Performance Improvement Process Model;
- Rummler and Brache's Framework for Improving Performance; and
- Kaufman's Organizational Elements Model.

A Comprehensive Performance Improvement Model

A comprehensive model of performance improvement is shown in Figure 9.1. The model was originally generated by Deterline and Rosenburg (1992) and has been adopted by the International Society for Performance Improvement (ISPI). According to Stolovitch (2007, p. 142) it "has probably had the most global exposure" of any performance improvement model. It includes five interrelated components—performance analysis, cause analysis, intervention selection, design and development, implementation and change management, and evaluation (Van Tiem et al., 2004). Below we discuss each of these components.

Performance Analysis

Performance analysis is the first component in the comprehensive model of PI. According to Rossett (1999), performance analysis centers on the directions an organization wishes to go (i.e., desired performance) and the drivers that encourage or impede performance (i.e., current performance). During this phase, organizational analysis is conducted to identify the vision, mission, values, goals, and strategies of the organization where a performance issue is occurring (Van Tiem et al., 2004). Environmental analysis is also conducted to uncover factors related to the performance issue (Gilbert, 1996; Mager & Pipe, 1997). These factors may include the:

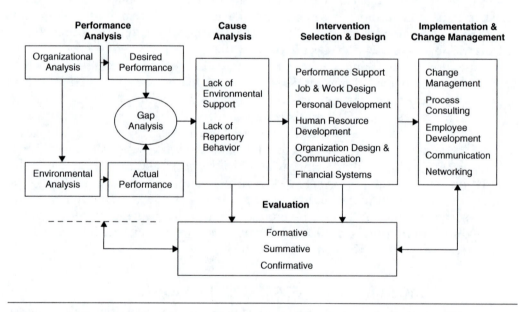

Figure 9.1 A Comprehensive Model of Performance Improvement.

Note: From *Fundamentals of Performance Technology: A Guide to Improving People, Process, and Performance* (2nd Edition) by D. M. Van Tiem, J. L. Moseley, & J. C. Dessinger, 2004, p. 7. Copyright 2004 by The International Society for Performance Improvement (http://www.ispi.org). Used with permission.

- Knowledge, skills, motivation, expectations, capacity, and ability of the workforce;
- Resources, tools, information, and feedback provided by the organization as well as the consequences, rewards, and incentives of performance or nonperformance; and
- Job tasks, processes, policies, procedures, and employee responsibilities.

A gap analysis is also conducted during this phase to identify optimal and actual performance, the gaps between these two conditions, and the organization's priorities for addressing these gaps (Kaufman, Rojas, & Mayer, 1993).

Cause Analysis

The second component in the comprehensive PI model is cause analysis, the critical link between identified performance gaps and their appropriate interventions. Cause analysis is based on Gilbert's Behavior Engineering Model; it is conducted to determine the root causes of a performance problem and why it exists (Gilbert, 1996). It also helps to identify potential barriers to a performance opportunity (Rossett, 1999). A range of possible causes or barriers are identified during this phase of a performance improvement project (Klein, 2010).

Intervention Selection, Design, and Development

Interventions are the strategies used to improve human performance. They are planned solutions to address gaps in results and facilitate change in behavior. They are implemented to influence individual and organizational performance.

Table 9.1 provides a list of 28 interventions that can be used to impact performance. The list, while not exhaustive, has been created using several sources, including Langdon, Whiteside, and McKenna (1999), Sanders and Thiagarajan (2001), Vadivelu and Klein (2008) and Van Tiem, Moseley, and Dessinger (2001).

Interventions can be classified in several different ways (Hutchison & Stein, 1998; Sanders & Thiagarajan, 2001). They are either instructional (e.g., classroom training, e-learning, and job aids) or noninstructional (e.g., coaching/mentoring, electronic

Table 9.1 Instructional and Noninstructional Performance Interventions

Intervention	Description
360-Degree Feedback	Employee development feedback obtained from subordinates, peers, and managers in the organization's hierarchy
Accelerated Learning	Programs to enable faster retention of specific issues using multiple mediums of learning such as projects, classroom teaching, e-learning, and team-building activities
Action Learning	Process for group-based problem solving
Classroom Training	Formal instructor-led programs delivered to develop specific employee skills
Coaching/Mentoring	Assigning coaches/mentors to employees for developing their skills
Compensation Systems	Providing bonuses, stocks, salary increases, and other rewards to motivate employees
Competency Assessment	Competencies evaluated through various assessments for employee selection, certification, and advancement
Conflict Management	System for handling of conflicts constructively

Table 9.1 *Continued*

Cultural Change Management	Process for altering the way people think, behave, interact, and perform within an organization
Diversity Programs	Initiatives designed to foster creativity by leveraging the cultural differences among employees
E-learning/Web-Based Learning	Programs enabling learning on the web (videos, recorded classes, and virtual resources)
Electronic Performance Support Systems	Digital programs that provide just-in-time, on-demand information necessary for accomplishing tasks
Employee Assistance	Programs designed to address work-life balance, professional development, and other personal issues
Employee Orientation	Introducing and welcoming new employees to the organization and helping them become productive quickly
Ergonomics	Modifying the physical workplace to enable increased productivity
Information Systems	Storing and retrieving employee information such as rate of pay, attended classes, vacation hours, etc.
Job Aids	Method for providing essential information when performer is carrying out the task that reduces amount of recall and minimizes error
Job Rotation	Changing workflow in order to ensure employees are provided opportunities to develop new skills
Leadership Development	Programs and initiatives that enable development of leaders focusing on the interpersonal linkages between individuals in a team
Management Development	Programs that enable development of managers within organizations
Meetings/Dialogue	Process for bringing people together to collectively share information, plan, make decisions and solve problems
Motivation Systems	Process for increasing employee performance by providing external rewards and feedback or by addressing intrinsic rewards by aligning projects with employee interests
Organizational Communication	Using the company intranet and other corporate communication tools to facilitate organizational change, receive feedback, etc.
Physical Resource Management	Providing physical resources and facilities that encourage employee performance
Performance Appraisal	Process for identifying, evaluating, and developing performance of employees
Succession Planning	Process designed to ensure the continued effective performance of an organization by making provision for the development and replacement of key people over time
Teambuilding	Creating a small group of people with complementary skills who are committed to a common goal, and hold themselves mutually accountable
Virtual Communication	Tools and processes that enable remote collaboration of employees in different parts of the globe

performance support systems, ergonomics, incentives, and compensation). Interventions can also be classified by the root causes of a performance problem in terms of whether they improve knowledge and skill, motives, information and feedback, physical resources, structure and process, or health.

The principles of systematic design are followed when performance interventions are planned and implemented. Additional factors that contribute to the success of an intervention are cost, sustainability, and accountability (Sanders & Thiagarajan, 2001; Spitzer, 1999). Designers should consider how much time and money a client is willing to spend on the intervention in relation to the cost of the problem. Interventions should be cost effective, comprehensive, and systemic. Time and money should be budgeted for intervention design and implementation; interventions should save more than they cost. They should address the entire problem or opportunity and be integrated into the organization. Furthermore, successful interventions are easily maintained. They also require a sponsor who will be accountable for them and who will guarantee their maintenance (Spitzer, 1999).

Spitzer (1999) provides the following suggestions for designing successful performance interventions:

- Identify the objectives of the intervention. Objectives should be aligned with the performance opportunity or the problem and its causes.
- Determine and prioritize requirements by distinguishing between mandatory and desirable results.
- Consider multiple interventions and build the most cost effective solution that meets the organization's requirements. Two categories of requirements for interventions are technical and human.
- Prepare a high-level intervention design. Use visual or verbal descriptions to outline the proposed intervention and all its elements to the client.
- Develop several alternative designs then select the best one to use.
- Complete a detailed intervention plan by identifying specific events, activities, tasks, schedules, and resources.

Intervention, Implementation, and Change Management

Once an intervention is selected and designed, it is implemented and change must be managed. According to Van Tiem et al. (2004) the four methods for executing this component of the PI model are:

- Communication, networking, and alliance building;
- Employee development activities;
- Change management; and
- Process consulting.

Effective communication, networking, and alliance building are the quickest techniques to obtain support for a new intervention. Employee development includes strategies such as training, job aids, and mentoring. Change management and process consulting are rooted in organizational development theory and are time consuming and difficult to implement. Change management relates to an organization's culture and structure, is concerned with ownership and empowerment, and includes various key stakeholder groups (Van Tiem et al., 2004). Tactics for managing change consist of leadership development, problem solving, and project management. Process consulting is a centralized approach that "involves major redesign of processes and jobs leading to significant organizational reengineering" (Van Tiem et al., 2004, p. 133). It is typically completed when large performance issues at the organizational level are being addressed.

Evaluation and Measurement

Evaluation and measurement occurs throughout the life of a performance improvement project (Shrock & Geis, 1999). The general model of PI includes three types of evaluation: formative, summative, and confirmative (Dessinger & Moseley, 2004). Formative evaluation is an ongoing process that begins during performance analysis, continues through cause analysis, and is completed during intervention design and implementation (Geis & Smith, 1992). Summative evaluation is conducted after an intervention is implemented to determine its effectiveness (Dessinger & Moseley, 2004). Confirmative evaluation "places a value on knowledge or skill transfer to the job, organizational impact, and return on investment" (Van Tiem et al., 2004, p. 158). The concept of confirmative evaluation was first introduced by Misanchuk (1978) to expand the formative-summative dichotomy and to suggest how instructional designers can determine the impact of a product after it has been implemented and used for a period of time.

The Behavior Engineering Model

As we previously discussed, Thomas F. Gilbert's ideas have a profound impact on PI practice. In fact, the cause analysis phase of the general PI model is based on his Behavior Engineering Model. Gilbert (1996) adheres to principles of behavioral learning theory (see Chapter 4) by writing "all behavior can be described in terms of stimuli (S) and responses (R) . . . For behavior to be maintained it must be reinforced" (p. 82). He extends these principles to workplace settings by including two components in his Behavior Engineering Model: an individual's repertory of behavior and the environment that provides performance support. The three main individual aspects that influence performance are knowledge, capacity, and motives. The three factors in the environment that impact performance are information, resources, and incentives.

Causes of performance problems are rooted either in the environment or in individual performers. According to Dean and Ripley (1997):

> Gilbert claimed that the absence of performance support factors in the work environment is the single greatest block to exemplary performance . . . Gilbert believed that performance improvement usually could be achieved by addressing environmental support factors alone, yet traditional managers and human resource specialists assume that the individual, not the environment, needs "fixing." This leads to training as the performance intervention of choice. (p. 48)

The Performance Improvement Process Model

The performance improvement process (PIP) model developed by Joe Harless (1970) introduced the term "front-end analysis" to the field (Dean & Ripley, 1997). According to Stolovitch (2007), Harless "had a marked influence on practitioners of training, especially instructional designers . . . [he] laid the foundation for numerous performance improvement models that were to follow" (p. 140) Harless's goal was to increase the quality of human performance in organizations by the use of interventions generated from thorough analysis, design, and testing (Harless, 1994).

The PIP model (see Figure 9.2) includes the following components:

- Organization alignment—This initial step requires a review of organizational goals and actual conditions to identify performance gaps and determine which to address.

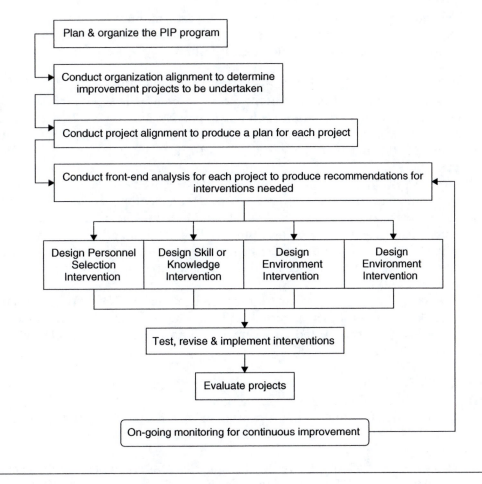

Figure 9.2 The Performance Improvement Process Model.

Note: From *Performance Quality Improvement System* by J. H. Harless, 1994. Copyright 1994 by J. H. Harless. Used with permission.

- Project alignment—This stage of the model produces a project plan to determine who will be involved and the strategies that will be used.
- Front-end analysis—During this phase of PIP, either diagnostic front-end analysis or new performance analysis is conducted depending on whether a client is experiencing a shortfall in reaching a current goal or if he or she wants to support new performance.
- Intervention design—Once front-end analysis is conducted, interventions are selected, designed, and developed. This may include strategies for personnel selection, skills and knowledge, environment, or motivation/incentives.
- Intervention testing, revision, and implementation—This phase of PIP is similar to formative evaluation and includes designing performance measures, conducting validation tests, and pilot-testing of interventions.
- Project evaluation—This involves examining the performance improvement process to determine if it worked and how to modify it.
- Monitoring for continuous improvement—The last stage of PIP includes ongoing

investigation after solutions are implemented to monitor performance and to determine if changes in the workforce or new problems arise. When this occurs, additional front-end analysis and a new PIP study may be required.

Managing the White Space in Organizations—The Rummler and Brache Model

According to Stolovitch (2007), "one of the most important milestones in the evolution of HPI was the appearance of another volume, *Improving Performance: How to Manage the White Space on the Organization Chart*" (p. 141). Written by Geary Rummler and Alan Brache (1995), this book proposes a framework that centers on organizational performance.

The framework "is based on the premise that organizations behave as adaptive systems" (Rummler & Brache, 1995, p. 9). As such, each component in the organization (e.g., people, tools, processes, etc.) is interconnected to the other components in the system. (See Chapter 2 for a discussion of GST.) Rummler and Brache (1995) think that PI practitioners must understand these connections in order to improve performance and they specify the interdependent variables of performance in their model.

The model applies a systems view to three levels of performance: the organization level, the process level, and the job/performer level. The model also includes three performance needs: goals, design, and management. Rummler and Brache (1995) describe these factors as follows:

- Goals—The organization, process, and job/performer levels must have specific standards that reflect customer expectations.
- Design—The structure of the organization, process, and job/performer levels should include the necessary components, configured to enable the goals to be met efficiently.
- Management—Each of the three levels requires management practices that ensure that goals are current and are being achieved. (p. 19)

The framework combines the three levels of performance with the three performance needs to produce nine variables of performance. Rummler and Brache (1995) suggest that managers can use their model to improve the performance of organizations, processes, and individuals.

The Organizational Elements Model and Megaplanning

According to Kaufman, Thiagarajan, and MacGillis (1997) many approaches to performance improvement are reactive because they respond to an existing problem. These authors advocate for a proactive approach to PI that is designed to avoid performance problems and assist organizations make positive contributions to society.

The Organizational Elements Model (see Table 9.2) is used to identify and align results and their consequences (Kaufman, 2006, 2009). This model includes three levels of organizational needs (i.e., results in performance): mega, macro, and micro. It also includes two levels of quasi-needs: processes and inputs. There is an associated planning level for each organizational element. Strategic, mega-level planning examines the entire organization in a societal context. The focus of megaplanning is organizational results and their consequences for external clients and society. Organizations may decide instead

Table 9.2 The Organizational Elements Model

Name of the Organizational Element	Brief Description and Level of Focus	Type of Planning
Mega	The results and their consequences for external clients and society (shared vision)	Strategic
Macro	The results and their consequences for what an organization can or does deliver outside of itself	Tactical
Micro	The results and their consequences for individuals and small groups within the organization	Operational
Process	Means, programs, projects, activities, methods, techniques	
Input	Human, capital, and physical resources; existing rules, regulations, policies, laws	

Note: From *Changes, Choices, and Consequences: A Guide to Mega Thinking and Planning* by R. Kaufman, 2006, p. 38. Copyright 2006 by Roger Kaufman. Used with permission.

to center on other levels of results. Tactical macro-level planning examines results and their consequences for what the organization delivers. Operational micro-level planning focuses on results and their consequences for individuals and small groups within the organization. Gaps in processes and inputs (i.e., resources) are examined to the extent they relate to results.[2]

Evaluation Models for Performance Improvement

Several models have been proposed to evaluate the impact of a performance improvement effort. Three such models that provide a foundation to both ID and PI are examined below. These include:

- The Four-Level Model of Evaluation;
- An Integrated Model of Evaluation; and
- A System for Assessing the Results of Performance Improvement.

The Four-Level Model of Evaluation

Donald Kirkpatrick originally developed his evaluation model in 1959 to assist managers determine the impact of training programs (see Kirkpatrick, 1996). In addition to determining the results of training for five decades, the model has been adopted by PI practitioners to evaluate different types of instructional and noninstructional performance interventions (Klein, 2002).

Kirkpatrick's model includes four levels of evaluation: reaction, learning, behavior, and results. (See Table 9.3.) Reaction is related to attitudes and perceptions toward an intervention. It is typically measured using surveys and questionnaires. Learning is connected to the acquisition of skills and knowledge; that is, does an intervention such as a job aid or electronic performance support system assist workers gain new skills or knowledge? Learning can be measured by performance assessments or written

---

2 Refer to Kaufman (2006, 2009) for a detailed discussion of the Organizational Elements Model and levels of planning.

Table 9.3 Kirkpatrick's Four-Level Model of Evaluation

Level	Factors Measured	Data Collection Techniques
Reaction	Attitudes and Perception	Surveys and Interviews
Learning	Skills and Knowledge	Performance and Achievement Tests
Behavior	Transfer, Job Performance, and Application	Observations, Surveys, and Interviews
Results	Organizational Impact	Return on Investment and Cost-Benefit Analysis

achievement tests. Behavior is synonymous with on-the-job application. Observations and interviews are used to determine if an intervention works in a job setting. Finally, results are measured to determine if an intervention provides a positive return on investment. This includes financial and other outcomes that impact organizational success such as quality, safety, and worker satisfaction.

Kaufman, Keller, and Watkins (1995) propose that societal benefits be added to Kirkpatrick's model to evaluate the consequences of an intervention on society and the people in it. Factors such as self-sufficiency and work-life balance are indicators of the effect of an intervention on the community.

Kirkpatrick's four-level model of evaluation continues to have a profound impact on ID and PI. According to Dick and Johnson (2007),

> Kirkpatrick's model can be used as part of both instructional design and human performance technology . . . It is often applied after training is completed to measure reaction, learning, and subsequent behavior and results . . . Kirkpatrick's model is consistent with the performance technology approach . . . The long-term solution should solve the underlying problem that led to the development of the solution. Thus there is a direct fit with the four levels of Kirkpatrick's model and the evaluation of the solution to an organization's performance problem. (pp. 101–102)

While Kirkpatrick's evaluation model has been used extensively over the past five decades, it is not without its critics. Some of those who find fault with the four-level model have developed their own approaches to evaluate the impact of a performance improvement effort. Two of these models are presented below.

An Integrated Model of Evaluation

Brinkerhoff (1988) suggests that Kirkpatrick's model narrowly focuses on training discrete skills that readily transfer to the work environment. He indicates that some programs may not produce immediate results and laments that the impact of these efforts would not be detected using the four-level evaluation model. Brinkerhoff further proposes that the Kirkpatrick model is biased toward bottom-line outcomes and does not account for evaluation of programs as they occur. In response to this criticism, Brinkerhoff offers a six-stage, integrative model of evaluation.

Brinkerhoff (1988) states that these stages, "show whether and how programs benefit an organization . . . [and] helps to trace any failures to one or more of the six stages" (p. 67). The six stages of this model are:

- Goal setting—Organizational needs, problems, and opportunities are identified. This stage is similar to the performance analysis phase of most PI models.

- Program design—Key questions about what strategies will work are asked and alternative designs are considered.
- Program implementation—Interventions are installed in the organization and evaluated to determine if they are working as intended. This is analogous to the formative evaluation component found in most ID models.
- Immediate outcomes—Tests of knowledge and performance are given to participants to determine if learning is affected.
- Intermediate or usage outcomes—The retention and application of a program or intervention is examined. Questions about how an intervention is adapted are also asked. This stage of the model is similar to summative evaluation.
- Impact and worth—Programs and interventions are evaluated to determine if they address the identified need, close the performance gap, and make a difference. Confirmative evaluation occurs at this stage of the model.

It should be obvious that someone following Brinkerhoff's model is doing more than evaluating a program or intervention after it has been designed and implemented. Like the general model of performance improvement, PI practitioners integrate analysis, design, implementation, and evaluation in a systematic way.

A System for Assessing Performance Results

According to Swanson and Holton (1999):

> The well known four-level evaluation model (Kirkpatrick, 1998) has failed the profession for a number of reasons, but a key failure is its emphasis on reactions versus the fundamental performance results of the host organization. (pp. 4–5)

To address this perceived failure, Swanson and Holton developed the Results Assessment System, a model for measuring the outcomes of performance improvement. This model measures outcomes in three distinct domains: performance, learning, and perception (Swanson & Holton, 1999). Performance results concentrate on the organization and include mission-related outcomes such as the goods and services that customers value. They also relate to the impact of performance improvement strategies to the financial success of the organization. Learning results refer to essential knowledge and expertise. These outcomes relate to individuals within an organization. Perception results focus on participant and stakeholder views. Participants are those with immediate experience with the organization's systems, processes, and products. Stakeholders are the leaders in the organization and other individuals with a vested interest in the desired outcomes and methods of performance improvement.

Swanson and Holton (1999) specify that their system is not an evaluation model because "Assessment of results is a core organizational process. Evaluation is optional" (p. 8). While recognizing the distinction between assessment and evaluation, we think Swanson and Holton's system is evaluative in nature because it fits Scriven's (1991) idea that evaluation can help determine the merit, worth, and value of a product or process. Further, the model is used to make data-driven decisions that may lead to increased performance (Guerra-Lopez, 2007). We also think that evaluation is a critical, required component of systematic models of PI and ID.

THE PHILOSOPHICAL ORIENTATIONS OF PERFORMANCE IMPROVEMENT THEORY

An examination of the models, theories, and foundations of PI suggests three main philosophical orientations of performance improvement: empiricism, pragmatism, and humanism. These approaches are discussed below.

Empiricism relies on observation and verification to examine reality. (See Chapter 3.) Models and theories of performance improvement represent an empirical, scientific orientation. According to Geis (1986) human performance follows specific laws that can often be predicted and controlled. Furthermore, Thiagarajan (1997) indicates that evaluation in PI is mostly based on the scientific method. As Stolovitch and Keeps (1999) state:

> HPT is grounded in scientifically derived theories and the best available empirical evidence. It seeks to achieve desired human performance through means that have been derived from scientific research, when possible, or from documented evidence, when not. (p. 9)

Thus PI, like ID, is a linking science in that it is not only influenced by theory and research, but also by practitioner experience. PI relies on practical experience as well as empirical research (Geis, 1986; Stolovitch & Keeps, 1999). This notion suggests that theories and models of performance improvement are also influenced by the tenets of pragmatism. That is, performance improvement theory reflects the belief that practical findings can be used as the basis for knowledge and meaning. Discussing the role of pragmatism in managing continuous improvement, Emison (2004) writes:

> Pragmatism connects means and ends with the requirements that both be subjected to validation based upon actual rather than theoretical conditions . . . [it] looks to knowledge based on direct, particular experience. (p. 57)

PI also relies on the philosophy of humanism due to the influence of organizational development theory (Dean, 1999; Rosenberg et al., 1999). Alveson (1982) indicates that humanistic organizational improvement focuses on intrinsic motivation, personal growth, and well-being. He writes, "Humanistic organization theory stress[es] the idea of creating organizational structures and leadership doctrines around the self-actualization theory as a universally applicable management strategy" (p. 117).

PERFORMANCE IMPROVEMENT AND INSTRUCTIONAL DESIGN

While PI and ID share many of the same theoretical underpinnings, each area informs and impacts the other. This section discusses some of the influences of performance improvement on ID.

Performance Improvement's Role in Instructional Design Competency Development

A recent competency study conducted by Klein and Fox (2004) shows that academics and practitioners in the ID field think the following PI skills are essential:

- Distinguish between performance problems requiring instructional and noninstructional solutions.
- Conduct a performance analysis for a specific situation to identify how and where performance should change.
- Evaluate performance improvement interventions to determine whether they solve an identified problem.
- Conduct a cause analysis for a specific situation to identify factors that contribute to a performance gap.
- Select a range of possible performance interventions that best meet needs revealed by performance and cause analyses.
- Assess the value of a performance improvement solution in terms of return on investment, attitudes of workers, and client feedback.
- Identify and implement procedures and systems to support and maintain performance improvement interventions.

Furthermore, organizations such as the International Board of Standards for Training, Performance and Instruction have also identified ID competencies that reflect an emphasis on improving job performance and on solving organizational problems (Richey, Fields, & Foxon, 2001). These competencies focus on needs assessment, environmental and cause analysis, noninstructional solutions, and confirmative evaluation as well as applying business skills to managing ID projects. As Richey et al. (2000) note PI serves as a foundation for competence in the ID field today.

Academic programs are ensuring that students obtain proficiency in applying these PI practices (see Dick & Wager, 1998; Klein, 2010; Medsker, Hunter, Stepich, Rowland, & Basnet, 1995). For example, a review of 11 well-established graduate ID programs reveals that all of them offer at least one course focused on performance improvement (Fox & Klein, 2003). These findings suggest that PI practices are becoming more common in the repertoire of instructional designers.

Expansion of Front-End Analysis

An application of PI that impacts ID is the expansion of front-end analysis. While analysis is one of the main components of the generic ID model, designers typically conduct analysis to define what is to be learned from instruction by using techniques such as job, task and content analysis (Seels & Glasgow, 1998). The PI perspective expands this notion of analysis. As Seels and Richey (1994) state: "Performance technology approaches may cause a broadening of the designer's role to include identifying aspects of the problem that are not instructional and working with others to create a multi-faceted solution" (p. 59).

Rossett (1999) distinguishes between training needs assessment (i.e., a process for determining what is in and what is out of an instructional program) and performance analysis (i.e., a process for partnering with clients to figure out what it will take to achieve their goals). She further proposes that training needs assessment identifies the requirements to develop a tangible solution such as classes, job aids, and coaching, while performance analysis identifies opportunities and problems and results in a solution system.

Dick, Carey, and Carey (2009) also make a distinction between needs assessment and performance analysis:

Needs assessment is an indispensible tool for solving problems, but the performance technologist would take a different mind-set into the problem situation and do some analysis before deciding that training should be provided. In common terminology this mind-set is called critical thinking . . . Instructional designers . . . must cultivate this critical thinking mind-set to be effective performance analysts. (p. 18)

In addition, Dick et al. (2009) and Tessmer and Richey (1997) propose that designers should analyze the performance context (i.e., the setting where skills taught during instruction will be transferred) prior to developing instructional solutions. Context analysis examines factors such as the relevance of skills to the workplace, resources, incentives, managerial/supervisor support, and the physical and social aspects of setting where the skills will be used. Performance context analysis is analogous to the environmental analysis and cause analysis components found in the general model of PI.

Strategies to Promote Transfer

Another influence of PI to ID is a focus on instructional strategies for promoting transfer of knowledge and skills to the work environment. Rossett (1997) suggests that preinstructional strategies can strengthen the link between training and performance. These strategies ask participants to screen their work setting before coming to training and to reflect on how prepared their organization is for them to transfer what is learned during training. Garavaglia (1993) notes that instructional designers can increase the likelihood of transfer by using many, varied examples from the setting where knowledge will be applied. Sedlik, Magnus, and Rakow (1980) suggest the use of transfer exercises, drawn from an analysis of the performance objectives of an instructional program, that require learners to apply objectives to real world settings. Finally, Klein, Spector, Grabowski, and de la Teja (2004) indicate that competent instructors in face-to-face, online, and blended settings use instructional strategies to promote transfer. These include using examples relevant to the setting in which skills will be applied, demonstrating how knowledge can be used in a realistic setting, providing opportunities for participants to plan for future application, and exploring with learners the conditions that may impact transfer.

TRENDS IN THE APPLICATION OF PERFORMANCE IMPROVEMENT TO INSTRUCTIONAL DESIGN

There is evidence that many companies and organizations are making the transition from training to PI (Conn & Gitonga, 2004; Rossett & Tobias, 1999). Some organizations are stressing ideas such as performance analysis, solution systems, cross-functionality, customer expectations, and shared knowledge (Rossett & Tobias, 1999). Others are turning toward noninstructional interventions like electronic performance support systems (EPSS) and away from training solutions (Nguyen & Klein, 2008).

Over a decade ago, some authors predicted that PI and ID will converge, especially in corporate settings. For example, Rosenberg (1995) argued that training and education should follow the paradigm shift prompted by PI and suggested that we should pay attention to "solving business, not educational problems" (p. 94). Furthermore, Sherry and Wilson (1996) forecasted that PI and ID will become even more closely aligned.

They stated "the fields of ID and HPT are moving along parallel tracks . . . toward greater reliance on tools and technologies to support learning and performance" (p. 24). More recently, Reiser (2007a) wrote:

> During the 1990's and into the twenty-first century, a variety of developments have had a major impact on instructional design principles and practices. A major development has been the increasing influence of the human performance technology movement . . . This movement, with its emphasis on on-the-job performance (rather than on learning), business results, and noninstructional solutions to performance problems has broadened the scope of the instructional design field. (p. 28)

We think that current trends in the field provide evidence that PI and ID are closer together than ever before. Next, we describe two of these major developments.

Improving Performance with a Range of Interventions

PI includes a range of interventions to improve individual and organizational performance (see Hutchison & Stein, 1998; Langdon et al., 1999; Sanders & Thiagarajan, 2001; Vadivelu & Klein, 2008; Van Tiem et al., 2001). Recent developments in ID "clearly points to the efforts that many professionals in the field are placing on improving human performance in the workplace though a variety of instructional and noninstructional means" (Reiser, 2007b, p. 7).

Some leaders in the field advocate moving away from training as a solution because it is overused and sometimes applied to problems that cannot be solved using instructional interventions. For example, Brethower (2000) asserts:

> The fact is that many HP technologists view training as a last resort, to be employed only when no other means of achieving improved performance will work. Even when instruction is required it is frequently only one among a number of interventions employed to address a problem or realize an opportunity. (p. 319)

However, a recent survey of professionals involved with training, learning, performance improvement, or similar functions within their organization reveals that instructional interventions are used more often than noninstructional interventions (Vadivelu & Klein, 2008). These findings hold constant across respondent groups from the United States and South Asia. However, practitioners from the U.S. are significantly more likely to indicate use of instructional interventions (e.g., training and distance learning), while professionals from South Asia are significantly more likely to report the use of human resource development interventions (e.g., staffing, selection, performance appraisals, and leadership development), work design interventions (e.g., job specifications, quality control, and ergonomics), organizational communication (e.g., information systems and networking), and financial system interventions (e.g., financial forecasting, capital investment, and mergers and acquisitions).

A set of PI interventions that is receiving the attention of many in the field is performance support systems. Depending on the nature of support, these systems can be classified as instructional or noninstructional (McKay & Wager, 2007). They can take many forms including just-in-time training, job aids, and EPSS.

A number of organizations are now using EPSS in order to reduce the cost of developing training and to minimize the time their employees spend away from the job when attending in-class or online training (Clark & Nguyen, 2007; Nguyen & Klein, 2008). For example, Pulchino (2006) reports that 69 percent of online training developers who belong to the eLearning Guild plan to embed performance support directly into software tools and work interfaces.

EPSS provides users with "individualized on-line access to the full range of . . . systems to permit job performance" (Gery, 1991, p. 21). According to Nguyen and Klein (2008) common instances of EPSS include search engines that allow performers to look for information to solve a performance problem, embedded help systems to assist a performer in completing a task, a printed job aid with clearly defined steps to complete an infrequent task, or systems that simplify or automate complex tasks for the performer. EPSS centers on supporting performance while work is being performed rather than beforehand as with training.

Nguyen and Klein (2008) conducted a study to investigate the claim that EPSS is more effective than training to support performance. Findings revealed that users receiving an EPSS only and those receiving an EPSS along with training performed significantly better on a procedural task than users who received training only. These authors call for additional empirical studies of performance support systems due to the increased use of these interventions in work settings.

Changes in Evaluation: Focusing on Organizational Results and Continuous Improvement

Evaluation is one of the main components of the generic ID model. (See Chapter 2.) However, trends in the application of PI to ID are changing the view of evaluation in the field. For example, Dick et al. (2009) expand the concept of formative evaluation by including an examination of the performance context (i.e., the location where learned skills are ultimately required). This type of formative evaluation includes assessing whether skills taught during instruction are retained and used in the performance setting and whether application of the skills has a desired impact on the organization.

Furthermore, PI now moves from formative and summative evaluation to confirmative evaluation. According to Dessinger and Moseley (2004), confirmative evaluation goes beyond formative and summative evaluation to center on transfer of skills taught during training to on-the-job application, organizational impact, and return on investment. These authors point out that evaluation methods in use today such as outcome evaluation, impact evaluation, and "even level four of Kirkpatrick's four levels of evaluation is confirmative evaluation by another name" (p. 9). Shrock and Geis (1999) also indicate that evaluation today focuses on utilization and results. Rothwell (1996) further notes, "Top managers . . . demand accountability. They are also demanding evidence that training produces change that translates into bottom-line results" (p. 283).

A related PI trend is continuous quality improvement. Almost two decades ago, Seels and Richey (1994) wrote, "The quality improvement movement will affect the evaluation domain" (p. 59). More recently, Van Tiem et al. (2004) noted this trend by stating: "Today, with the impact of the quality movement on evaluation, practitioners within the instructional and PT environments are beginning to accept that quality control requires continuous evaluation" (p. 176).

Thus, confirmative evaluation and quality improvement, along with other PI trends such as expanding analysis techniques and utilizing a range of instructional and noninstructional support systems, are impacting the practices of instructional designers. In the next section, we examine the how research influences performance improvement practices.

RESEARCH, PERFORMANCE IMPROVEMENT THEORY, AND INSTRUCTIONAL DESIGN

PI relies on data to improve organizational and individual performance. Research is conducted throughout the entire performance improvement process to identify and analyze opportunities, problems, causes, and solutions, to make decisions while designing and implementing interventions, and to determine if strategies and processes are successful. Stolovitch and Keeps (1999) claim that PI achieves desired results through approaches that have been validated by research. Foshay, Moller, Schwen, Kalman, and Haney (1999) assert that research helps synthesize trends and discover new models, processes, and technologies for improving performance.

However, like the ID field, there is a scarcity of research on PI models and interventions (Klein, 2002; Richey & Klein, 2007). Some leaders in the performance improvement field indicate that research must be better integrated into practice if findings are to add value to PI (Brethower, 2000). Others suggest that the empirical foundations of PI have not kept pace with actual practice and call for increased, targeted research activity (Stolovitch, 2000; Sugrue & Stolovitch, 2000). Still others think PI is in danger of becoming a craft because many professionals identify solutions without collecting empirically-based research data (Kaufman & Clark, 1999).

Empirical Support for Performance Improvement Applications

Recent analyses of the literature suggest that many in the field may be ignoring calls to provide additional empirical evidence. For example, Klein (2002) discovered that only 36 percent of all articles published in *Performance Improvement Quarterly* (*PIQ*) from 1997–2000 included data to draw conclusions. A replication of Klein's study conducted by Marker, Huglin, and Johnsen (2006) revealed that the number of data-based articles published in *PIQ* from 2001–2005 increased to 54 percent. Another replication of Klein's study by Conn and Gitonga (2004) indicated that approximately 20 percent of the articles published in *Educational Technology Research and Development* (*ETR&D*) from 1999–2003 dealt with topics related to workplace learning and performance. However, only five of these *ETR&D* articles reported empirical data. Taken together, these findings are not adequate to address the problem outlined by Clark and Estes (2002):

> The harsh reality is that a significant number of very popular performance products and remedies simply do not work . . . It doesn't have to be that way . . . [if] you adopt the results of solid performance research and turn it into practical and cost-beneficial performance results in your organization. (p. xi)

Of course, the PI field is not completely devoid of research. Klein (2002) reports that the focus of empirical studies published in *PIQ* center on professional practices, strategies for training and instruction, transfer of training and learning, and workplace diversity. He also indicates that less than half of the published studies in *PIQ* center on the implementation of a performance improvement intervention and all of these except one examine instructional solutions such as classroom training. In their replication study, Marker et al. (2006) reports that a mere 22 percent of empirical research in *PIQ* from 2001–2005 examined a PI intervention, with only seven of these studies centering on noninstructional solutions. Furthermore, Conn and Gitonga's (2004) replication study shows that only one article on workplace learning published in *ETR&D* from 1999–2003 focused on a noninstructional intervention.

Recommendations for Continuing Research

According to Foshay et al. (1999), "Research is possible in HPT, but it is likely to employ a variety of alternative paradigms" (p. 895). Dean (1994) further suggests that PI professionals make use of both quantitative and qualitative data, use observation not hearsay to collect facts, and rely on direct, comparative, and economic measures. Studies of the PI literature confirm some of these notions. Both Klein (2002) and Marker et al. (2006) report that PI researchers use surveys, case studies, experiments, evaluation techniques, and naturalistic methods to answer their questions. In addition, PI researchers often use questionnaires to measure participant reaction and performance assessments to evaluate learning outcomes. Application, transfer, and on-the-job performance are considered in some studies, but they are seldom measured through direct observation (Klein, 2002). Finally, almost no studies in the PI literature examine financial outcomes using measures of cost-benefit or return on investment (Guerra, 2001; Klein, 2002; Marker et al., 2006).

These findings suggest areas for future research on performance improvement. First, more studies should center on noninstructional interventions that are valued most by PI practitioners. According to Fox and Klein (2003) these techniques include coaching, communication strategies, EPSS, feedback and information, knowledge management, process improvement, rewards and recognition, and strategic planning.

Future intervention studies should include direct measures of on-the-job performance. Foshay et al. (1999) indicate that the effect of a performance intervention should be judged by cumulative changes in individual behavior. However, examinations of the PI literature discussed above show that researchers mostly rely on self-report to measure transfer. While observation is costly, and often prohibited by organizational constraints, the increased use of direct measures would help inform practitioners about the actual benefits of a particular intervention. Additionally, future research should examine the impact of instructional and noninstructional interventions on organizations and society. As reported above, very few studies currently include data on cost-benefit or return on investment.

In addition, future studies should also attempt to validate PI models and their components. Like ID models, many of the models and processes of performance improvement are based on practitioner experience and hearsay rather than on rigorous empirical study. PI models should be validated using a variety of methods including design and development research (Richey & Klein, 2007).

SUMMARY

This chapter has examined models and theories of performance improvement and how they contribute to the ID knowledge base. The chapter opened with a brief discussion of the theoretical foundations of PI, including the impact of behavioral learning theory and organizational development. Next, a comprehensive model of PI, advocated by the largest professional organization in the field, was discussed. This model includes interrelated components central to improving individual and organizational performance: performance analysis, cause analysis, intervention selection, design and development, implementation and change management, and evaluation. A few specific models and theories of evaluation and organizational planning were also presented to show the relationship between PI and concepts such as transfer of skills, on-the-job application, return on investment, and societal consequences. This explanation was followed by a discussion of the philosophical orientations to PI and the trends in the application of performance improvement to ID. This chapter closes with an examination of PI research literature and suggests ideas for future studies to improve the empirical base of the field.

Table 9.4 provides a summary of key principles, theoretical foundations, philosophical orientations, early contributors, and applications of PI. Furthermore, Table 9.5 offers a synopsis of how the elements of PI theory relates to the domains of ID. We think you will have a firmer grasp of the foundations of ID if you understand and can apply the principles of performance improvement.

Table 9.4 An Overview of Performance Improvement Theory and Instructional Design

1. **Key Principles:**
   - The main elements of generic PI models are performance analysis, cause analysis, intervention selection, design and development, implementation and change management, and evaluation.
   - PI is concerned with measurable outcomes in results-oriented systems.
   - PI can be applied to improve performance of organizations, processes, and individuals.

2. **Philosophical Emphases:** The following generalizations can be made:
   - Human performance follows specific laws that can often be predicted and controlled (i.e., empiricism).
   - PI theory reflects the belief that practical findings can be used as the basis for knowledge and meaning (i.e., pragmatism).
   - Organizational theory emphasizes the use of intrinsic motivation and growth of individual in an organization (i.e., humanism).

3. **Theoretical Foundations:** Behavioral learning theory, communications theory, general systems theory, instructional systems design, and organizational development.

4. **Early Contributors:** William Deterline, Thomas Gilbert, Joe Harless, Roger Kaufman, Donald Kirkpatrick, Robert Mager, and Geary Rummler

5. **Applications to ID:**
   - Evaluation
   - Front-End Analysis
   - Intervention Design and Implementation
   - Strategies for Promoting Transfer

6. **Research Support: Studies of:**
   - Electronic Performance Support Systems (e.g., Nguyen & Klein, 2008)
   - Implementation of Performance Interventions (e.g., Rossett & Tobias, 1999; Vadivelu & Klein, 2008)
   - Review of PI Research (e.g., Clark & Estes, 2002; Klein, 2002; Marker, et al., 2006; Conn & Gitonga, 2002)

7. **Related Concepts:**
   - Human Resource Management
   - Organizational Development
   - Performance Support Systems
   - Strategic Planning

Table 9.5 Instructional Design Domains and Elements Related to Performance Improvement Theory

Learners and Learning Processes
- The three main individual factors that influence performance are knowledge, capacity, and motives.

Learning and Performance Contexts
- Critical Contexts (orienting, transfer, and performance)
- Relevant aspects of the performance context (on-the-job environments, organizational impact, and return on investment)
- Contextual Characteristics (physical resources and materials, managerial and supervisor support, and socio-cultural)

Instructional and Noninstructional Strategies
- Improved Work Environment
- Incentives and Rewards
- Job and Organizational Structure Redesign
- Performance Feedback
- Performance Support Systems
- Resource and Tool Modification
- Training

Designers and Design Processes
- Designer Characteristics (expertise and competence)
- Analysis (cause, cost, environment, gap, job, organization, problem, and performance)
- Change Management
- Assessment and Evaluation (formative, summative, and confirmative)
- Intervention Selection, Design, Development, and Implementation

Chapter 10 synthesizes the ID knowledge base and suggests a taxonomy as a conceptual framework for the field. A summary of the domains and elements of the ID knowledge base is provided, as is a conceptual model of ID.

10

A TAXONOMY OF THE INSTRUCTIONAL
DESIGN KNOWLEDGE BASE

The ultimate goal of this book is to describe the instructional design (ID) knowledge base. This task involves not only providing the details of the field's major theory bases, but it also requires summarizing and synthesizing this vast amount of information. We have addressed the foundational theories of ID in previous chapters. In this final chapter, we will summarize this material through the development of a multifaceted taxonomy of the ID knowledge base.

We are not the first to attempt such a task. Caffarella and Fly (1992) constructed a taxonomy for the entire field of instructional design and technology (IDT). On a smaller scale, Carrier and Sales (1987) devised a taxonomy for the design of computer-based instruction and Knezek, Rachlin, and Scannell (1988) proposed a comprehensive taxonomy for educational computer use. Outside of our field, Greenbaum and Falcione (1980) synthesized the organizational communications research and then used these findings to develop a taxonomy of their discipline's knowledge base. This is closer to our task.

In this chapter we will:

- Explore the nature of taxonomies in general;
- Present a six-part taxonomy of the ID knowledge base; and
- Discuss how such a taxonomy can be used by ID scholars and practitioners alike.

THE CHARACTER OF A TAXONOMY

Taxonomies have long been a staple of science, but they also are used in many other disciplines to define the components of their fields. For example, most educators are familiar with Bloom's taxonomy. (See Chapter 7.) Before presenting a taxonomy for the ID knowledge base, we will examine what taxonomies are and how they can be useful.

The Development of Taxonomies

Greenbaum and Falcione (1980) define taxonomy as "a mode of inquiry into a given subject field, involving the arrangement of objects or concepts into groups on the basis of their relationships . . . a systematic distinguishing, ordering, and naming of type groups within a subject field" (p. 2). This is our sense of the term, although some see taxonomy as being a field in itself, the study of classification (Sokol, 1974).

There are two ways of thinking about taxonomies. The first suggests that the categories of a taxonomy are real and fixed. This is known as essentialism. The second orientation, materialism, views the categories as subject to change since many areas of discussion are constantly evolving (Lyman, O'Brien, & McKern, 2002). ID taxonomies are more likely to fall in the latter category since the knowledge and processes of our field change over time.

Melton (1964) notes that the construction of taxonomies begins by observing the similarities and differences of objects and events. These observations lead to various groups and subgroups. When one examines a final taxonomy, however, it is possible to see overlap among the categories, and they may or not be hierarchical in nature (Sokol, 1974). As understanding of events develop, taxonomies change as well. Thus, "a taxonomy reflects the stages of development of a science" (Melton, 1964, p. 328). This is the materialism point-of-view.

Taxonomy development is not easy. Bloom (1956) recalled that when he and his colleagues first began working on the taxonomy of educational objectives, they were not even sure if objectives could be classified since they "were attempting to classify phenomena which could not be observed or manipulated in the same concrete form as the phenomena of such fields as the physical and biological sciences" (p. 5). Nonetheless, they concluded that since behaviors found in objectives could be observed and described, they could be classified.

There are various ways to establish classes of similar objects or events. It can be done through the scientific study of the objects, such as in biology where the taxonomies identify phylla, families, and species. It can be done statistically using techniques such as cluster analysis. Sokol (1974) refers to this as computer classification and cites examples of this approach being used in many disciplines, including psychiatric diseases, economics, and market research. Both of these approaches result in what has been called empirically constructed taxonomies (Greenbaum & Falcione, 1980).

However, taxonomies can also be theoretically constructed when the initial categories are inferred from collected data. These taxonomies can then be empirically tested by relating them to the existing literature (Greenbaum & Falcione, 1980). Caffarella and Fly's (1992) taxonomy of the IDT field was theoretically constructed and then tested by mapping 1518 dissertations from 46 institutions onto the model to determine if the taxonomy adequately represented the field. Our ID taxonomy is theoretically constructed based upon an analysis of the theories, research, and practical applications that we have described in the previous chapters.

Taxonomies can take many forms. Bloom's (1956) taxonomy is simply an outlined list. Caffarella and Fly's (1992) taxonomy of IDT is a three-dimensional cube with cells highlighting the various parts of the field. Carrier and Sales's (1988) taxonomy of computer-based instruction is a table which identifies general variables, their definitions, and sample elements. Greenbaum and Falcione's (1980) taxonomy consists of major elements, their related major classes, and the related subclasses. Our ID taxonomy is similar to that of Greenbaum and Falcione.

The Purpose of Taxonomies

Taxonomies serve many purposes. Their principle objective is to show the structure of similar objects and the relationships between groups of similar items (Sokol, 1974). For example, Bloom and his colleagues built their taxonomies to facilitate communication among educators. Caffarella and Fly's taxonomy was part of an effort to build a knowledge base of IDT and thereby define the field.

Taxonomies also have important roles in research. Caffarella and Fly (1992) note that taxonomies can "expose gaps in knowledge . . . and holes in research or theory" (p. 98). Greenbaum and Falcione (1980) constructed their disciplinary taxonomy to consolidate research findings of the organizational communications field. Moreover, Sokol (1974) suggests that:

> . . . the principle scientific justification for establishing classifications is that they are heuristic (in the traditional mean of this term as "stimulating interest as a means of furthering investigation") and that they lead to the stating of a hypothesis which can then be tested. (p. 1117)

A class structure itself can lead to a general interpretation of events, and thus the taxonomy can facilitate theory construction in addition to specific research projects. We think our taxonomy of the ID knowledge base could serve many (if not all) of these purposes.

THE TAXONOMIES OF THE INSTRUCTIONAL DESIGN KNOWLEDGE BASE DOMAINS

We view the knowledge base of ID in terms of six domains:

- Learners and Learning Processes;
- Learning and Performance Contexts;
- Content Structure and Sequence;
- Instructional and Noninstructional Strategies;
- Media and Delivery Systems; and
- Designers and Design Processes.

Using the distinctions of Greenbaum and Falcione (1980), these general classes were theoretically constructed based upon our assessment of the literature rather than being empirically devised through scientific study. (See Chapter 1 for a discussion of this structure.) This framework was then expanded as we explored each major theory genre and identified the many elements relating to these six domains. Our task here is to consolidate these elements into six taxonomies, one for each domain.

These six taxonomies include two levels of elements, one which is very general (Level 1) and the second which is more specific (Level 2). Level 2 elements are presented in two ways: as lists of separate items or as behavioral statements. These elements have been derived primarily from the domain and element tables included at the end of Chapters 2 through 9. However, the taxonomies are often devised using more specific terms than were used in the earlier chapters. In some cases, the elements are logical inferences derived from information in the other chapters. In each of these six taxonomies we have identified the theory bases which primarily support the various elements. Therefore, it is possible to fairly quickly identify the key facets of the knowledge base and the source of their validity.

We would like to add one final note. While these taxonomies are very comprehensive and far reaching, they may not be perfectly complete. It is likely that at any given time one could identify other aspects of the ID knowledge base that are not included. This would be expected given not only the complexities of the field, but its changing nature.

Learners and Learning Processes

For most designers the focus of ID is on learners and learning outcomes. This requires an understanding of the complexities of the learning process, as well as an understanding of the many critical human dimensions which come into play. These many complexities are described in the first ID taxonomy: learners and learning processes.

Learners bring a wealth of traits and experiences to an education or training setting that play an important role in determining the success of the instruction. This includes standard profile factors which summarize their backgrounds and capabilities, and the many attitudinal factors that also have a powerful influence on learning. Many of these attitudes impact a person's motivation to learn. Learners also bring a body of prerequisite skills and knowledge to the instructional setting. These entry skills, as they are frequently called, relate not only to the content of that particular instructional experience, but also to the person's skills as a learner. This mixture of cognitive and meta-cognitive skills is critical to being successful in a teaching-learning situation.

Learning has been studied almost since the beginning of formal education and yet there is still little consensus as to what it actually is. These different positions result from differing philosophical and theoretical orientations, and different views of what learning outcomes are most important. As these debates have evolved over the years, other scholars have studied the mind and mental processes, and more recently they are studying the brain itself in an effort to understand learning. In addition, real-life teaching-learning situations have been studied in an effort to identify and understand the many factors which impact how people learn and perform in a variety of environments.

We have synthesized these many elements into the taxonomy of learners and learning processes presented in Table 10.1. This taxonomy consists of six Level 1 elements:

- Learner Profile Characteristics;
- Learner Affective Characteristics;
- Learner Entry Characteristics;
- Views of Learning;
- Cognitive Components of Learning; and
- Factors Impacting Learning.

These seven categories are in turn supported by 46 Level 2 elements which provide the "nuts-and-bolts" detail for the taxonomy. For example, several views of learning are discussed in the foundational literature including strengthening responses with reinforcement, facilitating internal conditions prompted by external events, and supporting individual knowledge construction. These views, along with others, are included as Level 2 elements.

Table 10.1 The Instructional Design Knowledge Base Taxonomy: Learner and Learning Process Domain

Level 1 Element	Level 2 Element	Supporting Theory Bases
Learner Profile Characteristics	Ability	Early Instructional, Performance Improvement
	Aptitude	Early Instructional, Media
	Background Experiences	Communication, Learning, Media
	Culture	Communication
	Demographics	Communication, General Systems, Media
Learner Affective Characteristics	Attitudes	Communication, Early Instructional, Constructivist Design, General Systems, Learning
	Beliefs and Values	Conditions-Based, Constructivist Design, Early Instructional, General Systems
	Desire to Learn	Communication, Early Instructional
	Expectancies	Conditions-Based, Early Instructional, Learning
	Motivation	Conditions-Based, Early Instructional, Learning
	Perseverance and Effort	Conditions-Based, Early Instructional
	Satisfaction	Conditions-Based
	Self-Regulatory System	Constructivist Design, Learning
Learner Entry Characteristics	Existing Mental Models and Schema	Constructivist Design, General Systems, Learning
	Prerequisite Knowledge	Conditions-Based, Constructivist Design, Early Instructional, Performance Improvement
	Prerequisite Learning Strategies	Conditions-Based
	Self-Knowledge	Constructivist Design
	Self-Reflective Skills	Constructivist Design
Views of Learning	Alternative Types of Content Goals	Conditions-Based, Early Instructional
	Behavior Modeling	Learning
	Construction of Schema and Mental Models	Conditions-Based, Constructivist Design, Learning
	Generalization	Conditions-Based, Learning
	Individual Knowledge Construction	Conditions-Based, Constructivist Design
	Integration of Knowledge, Skills, and Attitudes	Conditions-Based
	New Knowledge Distributed Across a Group	Constructivist Design, Media
	Response Strengthening with Reinforcement	Learning
	Series of Internal Conditions Prompted by External Events	Conditions-Based
	Transfer	Conditions-Based, Learning, Performance Improvement
Cognitive Components of Learning	Alternative Types of Memory	Learning
	Attention Mechanisms	Communication, Conditions-Based, Learning
	Memory Traces	Learning
	Mental Schema and Mental Models	Conditions-Based, Constructivist Design, Learning

Table 10.1 *Continued*

Factors Impacting Learning	Consequences	Conditions-Based, Learning, Performance Improvement
	Context	Constructivist Design, Learning, Media
	Guidance	Conditions-Based, Constructivist Design
	Information Load	Communication, Learning
	Motives and Incentives	Performance Improvement
	Organization of Messages	Learning
	Practice	Early Instructional, Learning
	Readiness	Learning
	Reinforcement	Conditions-Based, Early Instructional, Learning
	Retrieval Cues	Learning
	Rewards	Learning, Performance Improvement
	Split Attention	Communication
	Time Devoted to Learning	Early Instructional
	Time Required to Learn	Early Instructional

Learning and Performance Contexts

ID projects occur in a wide array of settings, ranging from preschool education to military training. The breadth of application arenas demands that close attention be given to context. The nature of the teaching-learning environments can greatly influence how instruction is received. This is especially true if the environment is technology based. While the instructional context is important, designers also must attend to the nature of the environment in which performance is expected, whether that be on the job or in a social setting. In addition, learners are often greatly influenced by the environments which shape their attitudes before instruction.

Designers must become adept at recognizing and attending to those contextual factors that have proven to have the most impact on both learning and performance. These factors vary widely. Learning is influenced by internal characteristics such as learner background and socio-cultural effects, but it is also affected by external conditions such as group size or the physical resources and materials available.

Performance, often in the workplace, is frequently shaped by a different array of factors, such as managerial support, rewards, or incentives. However, one's ability to transfer lessons learned depends to a great extent upon the similarity between the learning and the performance context, and factors such as socio-cultural characteristics again play an important role.

Once again we have synthesized the learning and performance context elements into a taxonomy, which is presented in Table 10.2. This taxonomy consists of four Level 1 elements:

- Settings for ID;
- Types of Contexts;
- Contextual Factors Impacting Learning; and
- Contextual Factors Impacting Performance.

These four categories are in turn supported by 26 Level 2 elements.

Table 10.2 The Instructional Design Knowledge Base Taxonomy: The Learning and Performance Context Domain

Level 1 Element	Level 2 Element	Supporting Theory Bases
Settings for ID	Business and Industry Community Agencies Government and Military Health Care Higher Education Pre-K–12 Schools	Constructivist Design, Early Instructional, General Systems, Learning, Performance Improvement
Types of Contexts	Instructional Context	Constructivist Design, Early Instructional, General Systems, Learning
	Orienting Context	General Systems, Learning, Performance Improvement
	Technology-Based Learning Environments	Communication, Constructivist Design
	Transfer and Performance Context	General Systems, Learning, Performance Improvement
Contextual Factors Impacting Learning	Authentic and Complex Activities Group Size	Conditions-Based, Constructivist Design Media
	Interaction and Collaboration	Communication, Constructivist Design, Learning, Media
	Learner Background and Characteristics	Early Instructional, Learning
	Location and Setting	Learning, Media
	Physical Resources and Materials	Communication, General Systems, Media, Performance Improvement
	Socio-cultural Characteristics	Communication, Constructivist Design, General Systems, Learning, Media, Performance Improvement
	Support Available	Conditions-Based, Constructivist Design, Learning, Media
Contextual Factors Impacting Performance	External Influences and Constraints	General Systems, Learning
	Rewards and Incentives	Learning, Performance Improvement
	Managerial and Supervisor Support	General Systems, Performance Improvement
	Physical Resources and Materials	Communication, General Systems, Performance Improvement
	Relevance of Skills to Workplace	General Systems, Performance Improvement
	Return on Investment	Performance Improvement
	Similarity Between Learning and Performance Contexts	Conditions-Based, Media, Learning
	Socio-cultural Characteristics	Communication, Constructivist Design, General Systems, Learning, Media, Performance Improvement

Content Structure and Sequence

Another important component of the ID process is the content. Learners are the "who" in instruction, while the content is the "what" learners should know or be able to do.

Over the years, instructional content has been described in a variety of ways, and classification systems have been developed to organize and explain the breadth of content addressed in teaching and learning situations. For the most part, content has been seen in terms of the type of tasks, skills, and learning goals in the instruction. The types of learning task, however, have been described in many ways. For example, content may be organized and presented differently to the learner when teaching facts, concepts, or principles. At times, a classification system has been developed for one major type of learning task, such as problem solving.

Instructional content can be characterized in terms of its structure as well as the type of information it covers. Language, either verbal or visual, serves as the primary building block of content structure. However, the amount and complexity of the content also impacts the quantity of information a learner can learn and ultimately retain. Therefore, designers must monitor how much content is presented and the form in which it is presented to facilitate successful comprehension of the instruction.

The order in which the content is presented also has a critical role in the instructional process. This sequencing of content is based on numerous factors, including the increasing complexity of the learning tasks, the inherent order of a series of steps, or the recommended order of learning activities. In addition, recent developments in constructivist learning environments allow the sequence of content to be controlled by the learner.

We have synthesized these many elements into the taxonomy of content structure and sequence presented in Table 10.3. This taxonomy consists of three Level 1 elements:

- Content Classification Systems;
- Aspects of Content; and
- Basis of Sequencing.

These three categories are supported by 18 Level 2 elements which provide the detailed components.

Instructional and Noninstructional Strategies

A major part of ID involves selecting or creating the strategies that will be employed to meet goals. Designers use many different types of strategies which serve a wide array of functions. Moreover, the strategies can have unique characteristics. These strategies typically involve instruction of some type. We see instructional strategies as falling into two groups, the first of which involves general delivery approaches (macro-instructional strategies) and the second of which describes more specific tactics incorporated into individual lessons (micro-instructional strategies).

At times designers realize that the problem they are addressing does not lend itself to an instructional solution. Data point to the need for noninstructional interventions, or perhaps to a combination of the two approaches. These interventions are the performance improvement strategies. We feel that the inclusion of these strategies not only reflects the ID knowledge base, but also the day-to-day realities of design practitioners working in organizations with complex and pressing needs.

Table 10.3 The Instructional Design Knowledge Base Taxonomy: The Content Structure and Sequence Domain

Level 1 Element	Level 2 Element	Supporting Theory Base
Content Classification Systems	Cognitive, Affective, Psychomotor Learning Tasks	Conditions-Based, Early Instructional
	Facts, Concepts, Principles, Procedures	Conditions-Based
	Integrated Goals	Conditions-Based
	Remember, Use, Find	Conditions-Based
	Verbal Information, Intellectual Skills, Cognitive Strategies, Motor Skills, Attitudes	Conditions-Based
	Well- and Ill-Structured Problems	Conditions-Based, Constructivist Design
Aspects of Content	Information and Cognitive Load	Communication, Conditions-Based, Learning, Media
	Visual Language	Communication, Learning, Media
	Written Language	Conditions-Based, Communication, Learning
Basis of Sequencing	Content Elaboration	Conditions-Based
	Generality, Example, Practice, and Testing	Conditions-Based
	Hierarchy of Learning Tasks	Conditions-Based, Early Instructional, General Systems
	Job, Task, and Procedure Order	Conditions-Based, General Systems
	Learner-Controlled Sequence	Constructivist Design
	Nine Events of Instruction	Conditions-Based
	Part-Task and Whole-Task Strategies	Conditions-Based, Learning
	Simple to Complex	Conditions-Based, Early Instructional, General Systems
	Spiral Curriculum	Conditions-Based, Early Instructional

Finally, there are other important strategies that aid the instructional process and in turn, learning and performance. We call these facilitation strategies. Facilitation strategies have become increasingly important with the proliferation of e-learning environments and the dominance of the constructivist orientation among designers.

In summary, the instructional and noninstructional strategy taxonomy consists of six first level elements. These are:

- Strategy Functions;
- Strategy Characteristics;
- Macro-instructional Strategies;
- Micro-instructional Strategies;
- Performance Improvement Strategies; and
- Facilitation Strategies.

The taxonomy also includes 48 Level 2 Elements. These provide a more detailed explanation of that part of the knowledge base relating to strategies. The entire taxonomy for instructional and noninstructional strategies is shown in Table 10.4.

Table 10.4 The Instructional Design Knowledge Base Taxonomy: The Instructional and Noninstructional Strategies Domain

Level 1 Element	Level 2 Element	Supporting Theory Bases
Strategy Functions	Acquire Knowledge and Skill	Conditions-Based, Constructivist Design, Learning, Performance Improvement
	Eliminate Noise	Communication
	Improve Job and Organizational Structure and Process	Performance Improvement
	Improve Motivation	Conditions-Based, Performance Improvement
	Improve Work Environment	Performance Improvement
	Increase Learner Control of Instruction	Constructivist Design, Early Instructional
	Provide Instructional Feedback	Communication, Conditions-Based, Learning
	Provide Learner Guidance	Conditions-Based, Constructivist Design
	Provide Performance Feedback	Performance Improvement
	Provide Performance Information	Performance Improvement
	Recall Past Learning	Conditions-Based, Constructivist Design, Learning
	Receive Feedback	Communication
	Secure and Focus Attention	Communication, Conditions-Based, Learning
Strategy Characteristics	Content Represented Through Actions, Pictures and Symbols	Early Instructional
	Matched to Internal Conditions of Learning	Conditions-Based
	Matched to Type of Learning Task	Conditions-Based
Macro-Instructional Strategies	Create Instructor-Led Education and Training	Conditions-Based, Early Instructional, Performance Improvement
	Create Individualized Instruction	Early Instructional, Media
	Create Discovery Learning	Early Instructional
	Create Problem-Based Learning Environments	Constructivist Design, Early Instructional, Learning
	Create Computer-Mediated Instruction	Conditions-Based, Constructivist Design
Micro-Instructional Strategies	Chunk Content	Learning
	Create Advance Organizers	Learning
	Create Cognitive Apprenticeships	Constructivist Design
	Create Mnemonics	Conditions-Based, Learning
	Create Problem-Oriented Instruction	Constructivist Design, Learning

Micro-Instructional Strategies, continued	Create Real-Life Activities and Events	Constructivist Design, Learning, Media
	Individualize Instruction	Early Instructional, Learning, Media
	Model Desired Behaviors	Learning
	Provide Concrete Experiences	Constructivist Design, Media
	Provide Feedback	Conditions-Based, Early Instructional, General Systems, Learning
	Provide for Collaboration	Constructivist Design
	Provide for Learner Motivation	Conditions-Based, Learning
	Provide for Learner Practice and Rehearsal	Conditions-Based, Early Instructional, Learning
	Provide Reinforcement	Learning, Early Instructional
	Provide Direct and Developmental Instruction	Conditions-Based, Early Instructional
	Provide for Retention and Transfer	Conditions-Based, Learning
	Provide Scaffolding Support	Constructivist Design, Early Instructional
	Shape Desired Behavior	Learning
Performance Improvement Strategies	Create Performance Support Systems	Performance Improvement
	Modify Resources and Tools	Performance Improvement
	Provide Incentives	Learning, Performance Improvement
	Redesign Jobs	Performance Improvement
Facilitation Strategies	Facilitate Active Participation	Constructivist Design, Early Instructional, Media
	Facilitate Communication	Communication
	Facilitate Interaction	Communication, Constructivist Design, Media
	Facilitate Learning and Individual Knowledge Construction	Conditions-Based, Constructivist Design
	Facilitate Online Communication	Communication, Constructivist Design, Media

Media and Delivery Systems

While media have always been an important element of instruction, in today's technology-dominated society they play an even more pivotal role in ID. In addition to the traditional print-based instruction and audio-visual aids, the computer's many capabilities provide new avenues for teaching and learning. These include the use of interactive, computer-based materials and many applications of the Internet, computerized simulations, and social networking tools. Good designers are technologically competent.

Media selection, however, is not a simple process. Designers should consider a number of different factors when making media decisions. These include instructional issues such as the nature of the content, the type of interaction expected, and the strategies that the media will complement. There are also environmental considerations, including technology management issues.

Learners, of course, are a major consideration when selecting and using media. Learning with media is facilitated or impeded by one's prior knowledge, abilities, and background experiences. Moreover, affective elements such as attitudes and culture also impact media use.

Media are not stand-alone tools. Rather they are incorporated into broader systems of delivering instruction. Common delivery systems currently employed include online learning and computer-mediated environments, as well as many forms of individualized instruction and instructor-led or facilitated instruction. Designers should consider the interactions between media and these delivery systems when creating instructional interventions. Some of these factors are management issues, such as cost and maintenance and facility requirements. Other factors are basic instructional issues, such as the communication channel required or the capabilities of a particular medium.

Table 10.5 The Instructional Design Knowledge Base Taxonomy: The Media and Delivery Systems Domain

Level 1 Element	Level 2 Element	Supporting Theory Bases
Types of Instructional Media	Computer-Based Materials	Communication, Conditions-Based, Constructivist Design, Learning, Media
	Internet and World-Wide Web	Communication, Constructivist Design, Learning, Media
	Printed Materials	Communication, Media
	Simulation and Virtual Reality	Communication, Conditions-Based, Constructivist Design, Media
	Social Networking Tools	Communication, Constructivist Design, Media
	Television and Film	Communication, Media
Major Elements of Media Selection Models	Content	Media
	Cues	Media
	Environment	Media
	Instructional Strategies	Media
	Interaction	Media
	Learner Characteristics	Media
	Management	Media
	Symbol Systems	Media
Learner Characteristics Related to Media Use	Attitudes	Communication, Learning
	Culture	Communication, Constructivist Design
	Perception	Communication, Constructivist Design, Learning
	Information-Processing Capacity	Communication, Learning
	Prior Knowledge and Experiences	Communication, Constructivist Design, Early Instructional, Learning
	Profile Characteristics and Background	Communication, Conditions-Based, Constructivist Design, Early Instructional, Learning

Types of Delivery Systems	Computer-Mediated	Communication, Conditions-Based, Constructivist Design, Learning, Media
	Individualized	Conditions-Based, Early Instructional, Learning
	Instructor-Led or Facilitated	Communication, Conditions-Based, Early Instructional, Learning, Performance Improvement
	Online	Communication, Conditions-Based, Constructivist Design, Media
Factors Related to Media and Delivery System Use	Media Attributes and Capabilities	Media
	Communication Channel	Communication
	Cost	Media
	Language	Communication
	Maintenance and Technology Support	Media
	Message Design	Communication
	Resources and Facilities	Media

The synthesis of the media and delivery system elements is shown in the taxonomy presented in Table 10.5. This taxonomy consists of five Level 1 elements:

- Types of Instructional Media;
- Major Elements of Media Selection Models;
- Learner Characteristics Related to Media Use;
- Types of Delivery Systems; and
- Factors Related to Media and Delivery System Use.

These five categories are in turn supported by 31 Level 2 elements.

Designers and Design Processes

The last domain of the ID knowledge base relates to designers and design processes. The designers are the second "who" of the ID enterprise and the processes are the "how". Designers orchestrate the ID process, and their background and skills are important to project success. Critical characteristics of the designer include his or her abilities to communicate and interact with all stakeholders involved in the design process, and to reflect on the many aspects of the design task during and upon completion of a project. This expertise is dependent upon the quality and depth of their past design experiences, as well as their formal education in the ID process.

ID itself can be viewed in a variety of ways. While most identify with the general systems approach, others rely upon a recursive approach or an approach that insures the participation of all stakeholders. In addition, there are more specialized design processes such as message design, motivational design, and rapid prototyping. Many of the general orientations to design, however, address the same elements, although often in different manners.

The first of these elements is analysis. This is a phase that addresses a variety of different facets of a design project. It may include an examination of the learning task itself by concentrating on jobs to be taught and how they are completed in a real-life setting. Or the analysis may be of the learning and performance environments, including resources available, costs, or problems of the organization. Or the analysis may be of the learner—the focus of most ID projects.

There are also specific tasks designers must perform. For example, designers typically engage in tasks such as creating performance goals and behavioral objectives, selecting media, and sequencing instruction. However, much of their time is devoted to devising instructional strategies and activities that will facilitate learning. In today's world, designers are also routinely involved in devising noninstructional interventions which will solve organizational performance problems.

The final element in the design process is determining and creating the assessment and evaluation procedure and tools for instruction. This may include the creation of specific criterion-referenced test items, or identifying a process for general goal-free or open-ended assessment. A critical component of the ID process is measuring the effectiveness of the instruction along with learner knowledge and performance. This evaluation may occur during or after the design process.

Multimedia design and production is increasingly important in today's market. This process not only includes the use of computers and the Internet as a delivery method, but also using computer-based design tools and techniques. Often, standard design concerns (such as using visual language and directing student attention) take on new meaning in a technology-enhanced environment.

Table 10.6 The Instructional Design Knowledge Base Taxonomy: The Designer and Design Processes Domain

Level 1 Element	Level 2 Element	Supporting Theory Base
Designer Characteristics	Ability to Communicate	Communication, Constructivist Design
	Ability to Gain Participation	Constructivist Design
	Ability to Reflect	Constructivist Design
	Design Experience	Constructivist Design, Performance Improvement
	Design Expertise and Competence	Constructivist Design, General Systems, Performance Improvement
General Approaches to Design	Instructional Systems Design	Early Instructional, General Systems, Performance Improvement
	Message Design	Communication, Learning, Media
	Motivational Design	Conditions-Based, Learning
	Participatory Design	Constructivist Design
	Rapid Prototyping	General Systems
	Recursive, Reflective Design	Constructivist Design
Objects of Analysis	Authentic Tasks	Constructivist Design
	Cognitive Tasks	Learning
	Content and Concepts	Conditions-Based, Constructivist Design, General Systems, Learning
	Context and Environment	Constructivist Design, General Systems, Learning, Performance Improvement
	Job, Task, and Performance	General Systems, Early Instructional, Performance Improvement

Objects of Analysis, continued	Learner Characteristics	Conditions-Based, Constructivist Design, General Systems, Early Instructional,
	Organization and Cost	General Systems, Performance Improvement
	Performance Gaps	General Systems, Performance Improvement
	Problems and Problem Causes	Constructivist Design, General Systems, Performance Improvement
Design Tasks	Create Behavioral Objectives	General Systems, Early Instructional, Learning
	Create Performance Goals	General Systems, Performance Improvement
	Create or Select Noninstructional Interventions	General Systems, Performance Improvement
	Create or Select Learner Guidance Activities	Conditions-Based, Constructivist Design, Learning
	Create or Select Instructional Strategies	Conditions-Based, Constructivist Design, Learning, Media, Performance Improvement
	Plan for Assessment and Evaluation of Learning and Performance	Conditions-Based, Constructivist Design, General Systems, Performance Improvement
	Select Media to Implement Strategies	Conditions-Based, General Systems, Learning, Media
	Sequence Instruction	Early Instructional, Learning, Conditions-Based
Types of Assessment and Evaluation	Confirmative Evaluation	General Systems, Performance Improvement
	Criterion-Referenced Test Items	General Systems, Learning
	Formative Evaluation	General Systems, Performance Improvement
	Goal-Free and Open-Ended Assessment	Constructivist Design
	Summative Evaluation	General Systems, Performance Improvement
Multimedia Design and Development	Create Learning Objects	General Systems
	Create Online Learning	Media
	Direct Student Attention	Communication, Media
	Use Computer-Based Design Tools	Conditions-Based
	Use Visual Language	Communication, Media

We have synthesized these many elements into the taxonomy of designers and design processes presented in Table 10.6. This taxonomy consists of six Level 1 elements:

- Designer Characteristics;
- General Approaches to Design;
- Objects of Analysis;
- Design Tasks;
- Types of Assessment and Evaluation; and
- Multimedia Design and Development.

These six categories are supported by 38 Level 2 elements which again provide the supporting details of the knowledge base.

USING THE INSTRUCTIONAL DESIGN KNOWLEDGE BASE TAXONOMY

As a whole, these six ID domain taxonomies provide scholars and practitioners alike with a conceptual model of the ID knowledge base. They are a consolidation of research and theory; they also reflect the manner in which this theory has been applied to the design of instruction. These taxonomies present a view of the field that can serve as a guide to designers and researchers as well. We will now explore each of these functions.

Using the Instructional Design Taxonomy to Define Practice

We have defined ID as a very complex process. Not only are there many steps and decisions to be made, but there are many participants, work environments, and resources. Collectively, the six ID domain taxonomies provide a concrete model of the entire design enterprise. While the taxonomies do reduce ID to its essential components, they nonetheless maintain the scope and complexities of the task and reflect the impact of learners, designers, content, context, and available resources.

The Level 2 elements can be seen as presenting arrays of:

- ID tasks and subtasks (e.g., provide practice opportunities, sequence instruction in terms of job, task, or procedure);
- Elements of ID decision making (e.g., learner culture, return on investment)
- ID options (e.g., create computer-mediated learning environments, use visual language); and
- Alternative approaches (e.g., create performance support systems, participatory design, open-ended assessment).

Thus, these knowledge base taxonomies, even though they stem from theory, can also be used as tangible guides to ID practice in many settings.

However, the taxonomies provide another service to practitioners; they provide a succinct rationale for each design decision by means of the supporting theory bases. This is the "know why" part of the knowledge base, and it provides solid ammunition for designers on the firing line who often must justify their decisions to others who typically know little about ID. While all elements of the ID taxonomy have some degree of theoretical support, the amount of support varies. In some instances (such as with retrieval cues or job redesign) a Level 2 element is supported by only one theory base, and this may be logical and fitting.

Using the Instructional Design Taxonomy as a Research Guide

Throughout this book we have emphasized research: the basic research foundations of the various theories that form the knowledge base, research supporting ID applications of the theories, and the additional research necessary to advance the field. The domain taxonomies can help active researchers in a number of ways.

In addition to serving as a definition of the ID field itself, one can view the various taxonomy elements (especially the Level 2 elements) as variables to be addressed in research and theory construction. In an ideal world, each of these variables would be supported by a robust empirical foundation. For some, such a foundation does exist. However, even in these cases, new ID contexts often establish an excellent rationale for additional research. For example, there is a rich research base on the use of feedback, but there might be good reasons for studying the use of feedback in interactive online learning environments. Other variables, such as performance support systems, have only a modicum of related research, and are obvious candidates for rigorous empirical activity. The taxonomies highlight these areas of needed research. What is not always apparent is whether the foundational theories themselves have a solid research base. This problem has been highlighted earlier in our discussions (e.g., with respect to performance improvement models and constructivist design theories). In these situations, additional research is vital.

The variables found in the six ID taxonomies can also facilitate the systematic replication of ID research efforts. Replication of existing research is an often undervalued task in our field, but one which is required to establish a firm empirical foundation for ID theory. The taxonomy structure helps to organize research efforts and could be used to gauge the extent to which a given variable has been replicated.

ID researchers should also direct their attention to gaps in the knowledge base. These are sectors of the domain taxonomies where it appears that legitimate factors affecting ID processes are missing. Such gaps may have materialized because of technological or procedural advancements in the field, or even because of new ways of thinking. Research is then required to empirically verify the role of these missing factors in the teaching-learning process or in organizational improvement.

All of this additional research, of course, could take place without the ID domain taxonomies. However, these taxonomies can facilitate and stimulate the process because they "simplify variation by reducing it to a small, manageable number of kinds more easily discussed" (Lyman et al., 2002, p. 14). This simplified description of what we know about ID makes it much easier to recognize the areas that should be studied further and those topics that have already been empirically validated.

FINAL THOUGHTS

In this book we have summarized eight areas of theory that provide the basis of ID practice as we currently know it. These are:

- General Systems Theory;
- Communication Theory;
- Learning Theory;
- Early Instructional Theory;
- Media Theory;
- Conditions-Based Theory;
- Constructivist Design Theory; and
- Performance Improvement Theory.

These theories encompass a wide range of thinking, much of which comes from other related disciplines. We have explored each theory, its underlying research, and its philosophical orientation. We have also described traditional and emerging ways in which these theories have influenced ID, and have made suggestions for ID research that can further enhance the field.

The ultimate goal of this exploration of theory, research, and practice is to describe the ID knowledge base. This is a knowledge base that is broad enough to encompass the many attitudes and positions represented in the field. It also is comprehensive enough to include factual, scientific, and procedural knowledge. Moreover, the ID knowledge base illustrates the uncompromising link between theory and practice. We think our exploration of the knowledge base meets these criteria. However, we are also making a statement about research and theory and the field of ID in this book. We believe that:

- Theory, validated by empirical research, is the optimal basis for ID decisions.
- The demonstration of ID expertise is dependent upon knowledge of research and theory, as well as technical and procedural skill.
- The future of the ID field depends not only upon our theory, but on the quality of our inquiry, the curiosity and ingenuity of our scholars, and the imagination and creativity of our designers.

GLOSSARY

ADDIE An acronym referring to the major stages in the generic ISD process: Analysis, Design, Development, Implementation, and Evaluation (Morrison, Ross, & Kemp, 2007, p. 13).

Advance Organizer General introductory information used to increase learner understanding of the text by facilitating recall of related prerequisite knowledge.

Affective Domain That area of learning devoted to developing attitudes, values, or appreciations (Morrison et al., 2007, p. 429).

Analogical Picture A visual that portrays a comparison between two entities.

Anchored Instruction A learner-centered instructional strategy in which students become involved in a problem-based case study situated in a real-life setting.

Anti-Individualism A philosophy that emphasizes the role of the physical and social environment in determining individual behavior and beliefs.

Aptitude An innate talent, skill, ability, or specialized previous training that facilitates or impedes learner performance.

Aptitude-Treatment Interaction A research framework for studying the interactions between individual differences and variations in task parameter effects with the ultimate goal of determining "which instructional methods were optimal for different students" (Tobias, 1987, p. 208).

Assessment Instruments Materials developed and used to measure learners' status and progress in both achievement and attitudes (Dick, Carey, & Carey, 2009, p. 379).

Asynchronous Learning Communication between learners and instructors that does not take place simultaneously or in real time (Spector, Merrill, van Merriënboer, & Driscoll, 2008, p. 817).

Attitude Internal states that influence the individual's choices of personal action (Gagné, 1985, p. 219).

Audio-Visual Aids Instructional materials or media that rely on both hearing and vision for their effects, but loosely used to describe virtually all instructional materials and media other than conventional printed materials (Ellington & Harris, 1986, p. 17).

Authentic Activity Coherent, meaningful, and purposeful activities; the ordinary practices of the culture (Brown, Collins, & Duguid, 1989, p. 34).

Behavioral Objectives Descriptions of observable and measurable activities which demonstrate learner achievement following instruction, typically including three components: the intended performance, the conditions related to the demonstration, and the criteria used to evaluate the performance.

Cause Analysis The process of determining the root cause of past, present, and future performance gaps (Van Tiem, Moseley, & Dessinger, 2004, p. 207).

Change Management A process that involves leadership development, problem solving, and process consulting, typically occurring when large, organizational performance issues are being addressed.

Channel A vehicle or medium of message transmission, typically in either audio or visual form.

Chunking The clustering of information into meaningful groups to facilitate long-term memory and recall.

Closed System An organized structure of people, objects, and/or processes that is isolated from its environment.

Cognitive Apprenticeship An instructional strategy that sets learning activities in real-life contexts, endeavors, and interaction.

Cognitive Domain That area of learning devoted to acquiring information, knowledge, and intellectual abilities relative to a subject or topic (Morrison et al., 2007, p. 429).

Cognitive Entry Behavior The knowledge and meta-cognitive skills students bring to a teaching-learning situation.

Cognitive Load The impact of message structure on cognitive processing, including the difficulty of the material (intrinsic load), the way the instruction is designed and organized (extrinsic load), and the effort learners must exert to take the material and construct a mental schema (germane load).

Cognitive Strategies The learned capabilities that enable us to manage our own thinking and learning processes (Gagné & Medsker, 1996, p. 73).

Cognitive Task Analysis A method of identifying nonobservable instructional content, typically focusing on knowledge and thinking processes that accompany observable performance.

Collaborative Learning A situation in which large or small groups of learners "develop, compare, and understand multiple perspectives on an issue" (Karagiori & Symeou, 2005, p. 21) through activities such as sharing, discussion, peer teaching, or involvement in learning communities.

Collaborative Technology Tools that facilitate interactions between learners and between instructors and learners.

Competency A knowledge, skill, or attitude that enables one to effectively perform the activities of a given occupation or function to the standards expected in employment (Richey, Fields, & Foxon, 2001, p. 180).

Complex Learning The integration of knowledge, skills, and attitudes; the coordination of qualitatively different constituent skills, and often the transfer of what is learned in the school or training setting to daily life and work settings (van Merriënboer & Kirschner, 2007, p. 4).

Computer-Based Instruction   A type of instructional material typically based upon small discrete units of linked content; encompasses tutorials, guided practice, simulations, and testing.

Computer-Mediated Instruction   An instructional delivery system utilizing a variety of computer technologies and resources and typically involving learner interaction.

Concept   A name or expression given to a class of facts, objects, or events, all of which have common features (Morrison et al., 2007, p. 430).

Conceptual Model   A general, verbal description of a particular view of reality that is typically supported by experience, deductive logic, or inferences from observations.

Confirmative Evaluation   A type of evaluation that "goes beyond formative and summative evaluation to judge the continued merit, value, or worth of a long-term training program" (Dessinger & Moseley, 2004, p. 204).

Constructivism   A philosophical orientation viewing knowledge as being individually constructed and unique to each person; also a school of thought which holds that learning occurs because personal knowledge is constructed by active learners who derive meaning from their experience and its context.

Content Scaffold   A mechanism used to support students' understanding of the subject matter, such as a tool directing students' attention to key terms and principles.

Context Data   Information pertaining to the setting and environment in which design and development occurs, or in which the intervention is implemented, or in which the skills and knowledge are applied (Richey & Klein, 2007, p. 155).

Contextual Analysis   A systematic process of identifying the critical elements of a design and development setting or environment (Richey & Klein, 2007, p. 155).

Cooperative Learning   A process in which group members work together to accomplish shared goals.

Criterion-Referenced Assessment   Techniques for determining learner mastery of prespecified content (Seels & Richey, 1994, p. 127).

Cues   Audio, visual, or nonvisual details that direct attention to relevant aspects of print and nonprint messages.

Curriculum Continuity   The proposition that instruction and practice should continually recur so that students can learn important concepts and objectives.

Curriculum Integration   A process of relating objectives and experiences in a particular subject matter to other content areas.

Delivery System   Macro-level instructional strategies; teaching methods.

Design and Development Research   The systematic study of design, development, and evaluation processes with the aim of establishing an empirical basis for the creation of instructional and noninstructional products and tools and new or enhanced models that govern their development (Richey & Klein, 2007, p. 156).

Designer Characteristics   Those facets of the designer's profile and experiential background that may impact the design and development process (Richey & Klein, 2007, p. 156).

Designer Decision-Making Research   Investigations of designer activities including designer problem solving, designer thinking, and designer use of models; commonly includes explorations of the differences between novice and expert designers (Richey & Klein, 2007, p. 156).

Development   The process of translating the design specifications into physical form (Seels & Richey, 1994, p. 127).

Discovery Learning   A method of instruction in which a series of planned activities lead students to prescribed content conclusions without the formal presentation of that information; often involves problem-solving situations.

Display   A sequence of learning activities that combines the type of presentation with the targeted level of performance and the targeted content; prominent in component display theory.

Distance Education   An educational program characterized by the separation, in time or place, between instructor and student and in which communication media are used to allow interchange (Spector et al., 2008, p. 820).

Distributed Cognition   A situation in which the information learned is allocated across the members of a group rather than being confined to a single person.

Elaboration Strategies   A sequencing process in which general ideas are followed with various levels of content expansion, each of which provides additional content detail or complexity.

Electronic Performance Support System (EPSS)   An enabler of work tasks delivered by electronic technology provided to individuals or teams at the time of need on the job; typical support includes procedural guidance or references to factual information needed to complete tasks (Spector et al., 2008, p. 820).

Empiricism   A philosophical orientation that views knowledge as being derived from experience and acquired through the senses and observation.

Encoding   The process of converting an idea to be communicated into language, typically written or visual language.

Enterprise   Multiple types of learning tasks directed toward a common, integrated goal.

Enterprise Scenario   An activity or project that relates various knowledge and skill objectives to a final goal, and often to a larger project that encompasses this goal.

Environment   The setting which provides the persons and objects which enter a system, establishes the constraints upon a system, and receives the products of a system; also seen as a general learning or work context.

Epitome   A general overview of a section of content; a component of elaboration theory.

Equifinality   The process by which a system reaches its final goals through interaction with its surroundings.

Evaluation   A process to determine the adequacy, effectiveness, worth, and value of an instructional or noninstructional intervention.

Expository Presentation Strategy   Instruction that centers on telling students the information to be learned.

External Conditions of Learning   The manner in which instruction is arranged; the steps and activities involved in learning.

Extinction   The elimination of a previously learned response through the systematic removal of reinforcement.

Feedback   Information about the outcomes of a system which has been collected from the environment and used to stabilize a system; also "information on goal attainment designed to help workers, teams, or functional units monitor and evaluate their progress in achievement of desired accomplishments" (Spector et al., 2008, p. 820).

Formative Evaluation   Gathering information on the adequacy of an instructional product or program and using this information as a basis for further development (Seels & Richey, 1994, p. 128); may also apply to noninstructional products.

Four-Component Instructional Design (4C-ID)   An ID model developed by Jeroen van Merriënboer that focuses on the integration and coordination of skills that make up complex learning.

Four-Level Model of Evaluation   An approach developed by Donald Kirkpatrick to assist managers determine the impact of training programs, includes the examination of reactions, learning, behavior, and results.

Front-End Analysis   A process used to identify the needs of an organization and to examine plausible alternatives to meet those needs.

Gap Analysis   A technique used to identify and prioritize the difference between desired optimal performance and current actual performance.

Generalization   A process of transferring a given response to new stimuli that are similar to those used in the original training; also a process of developing abstract principles from particular instances.

Generative Instructional Strategies   Those activities which allow learners with extensive prior knowledge and well-developed learning strategies to control their own learning.

Globalized Instruction   Teaching and learning materials which are culture-free and applicable to any group of learners.

Hard Scaffold   Static learner supports which are planned in advance and based on anticipated student difficulties.

Hermeneutics   The art and science of interpreting verbal and nonverbal meaning from the perspective of an individual's culture and mindset.

Hierarchical Sequencing   An arrangement of instruction in which "each learning task becomes a prerequisite for the next task in the series and is, in turn, dependent on the achievement of certain prerequisites in the previous tasks" (Bloom, 1976, p. 27).

Humanism   A philosophical orientation which emphasizes human welfare, emotions, and feelings.

Idealism   A philosophical orientation suggesting that reality is based upon the mind or one's ideas; it is typically contrasted to realism.

Ill-Structured Problem   A dilemma that has multiple solutions, unknown elements, and inconsistent relationships among its related concepts, rules, and principles.

Immersive Technologies   Devices that replicate real-world experiences such as simulations, games, virtual reality, and online worlds.

Individual Constructivism   A belief that learning is the "result of a personal interpretation of knowledge" (Smith & Ragan, 2005, p. 19) and cognitive reorganization.

Individualized Instruction   A general teaching strategy in which content, instructional materials, or pace of learning may vary for learners to accommodate individual differences.

Information Feedback   See *Feedback*.

Information Gatekeepers   Individuals, groups, or materials that control access to or distribution of new ideas, processes, and techniques.

Information Load   The burden placed upon working memory by a message's structure and meaning, especially the number of words or amount of detail, redundancy, presentation rate, and sentence structure.

Inquisitory Presentation Strategy   Instruction that centers on questioning students rather than presenting information.

Instructional Context   The setting and environment in which teaching and learning occurs.

Instructional Design   The science and art of creating detailed specifications for the development, evaluation, and maintenance of situations which facilitate learning and performance.

Instructional Strategy   A sequence of planned activities designed to lead to achieving a given learning goal.

Instructional Systems Design   An organized procedure for developing instructional materials or programs that includes the steps of analyzing (defining what is to be learned), designing (specifying how the learning should occur), developing (authoring or producing the material), implementing (using the materials or strategies in context), and evaluating (determining the adequacy of instruction) (Seels & Richey, 1994, p. 129).

Instructional Transaction   A mutual, dynamic, real-time give-and-take between the instructional system and the student in which there is an exchange of information (Merrill, Li, & Jones, 1990, p. 9); typically consisting of multiple displays and multiple interactions with the learners.

Integrative Goal   A combination of several individual objectives that are to be integrated into a comprehensive purposeful activity (Gagné & Merrill, 1990, p. 23).

Intellectual Skills   Organizing and structuring facts for learning to form concepts, principles, rules, attitudes, and interactions (Morrison et al., 2007, p. 431).

Internal Conditions of Learning   The mental processes which occur during an instructional situation, includes "previously learned capabilities" (Gagné, Briggs, & Wager, 1992, p. 9).

Internal Summarizer   A series of activities at the end of a lesson that provide a review of the lesson's content, specific examples of the ideas presented, and self-test practice situations; a component of elaboration theory.

Internal Synthesizer   The part of a lesson which shows the relationships among the various ideas that have been presented; a component of elaboration theory.

Intervention   A planned instructional or noninstructional solution that facilitates a change in performance.

Intrinsic Cognitive Load   The impact of the message structure on cognitive processing due to the basic nature and difficulty of the material.

ISD   See *Instructional Systems Design.*

Job Analysis   See *Task Analysis.*

Just-in-Time Information   Content that is made available to workers without formal instruction that enables them to complete the particular task at hand, typically in electronic form.

Learner Analysis   A process of gathering and studying learner characteristic data, including factors related to general background and attitudes, prerequisite knowledge and skills, and learning style.

Learner Characteristics   Those facets of the learner's experiential background that impact the effectiveness of a learning process (Seels & Richey, 1994, p. 130).

Learning   The relatively permanent change in a person's knowledge or behavior due to experience (Mayer, 1982, p. 1040).

Learning Community   A group of people who share common values and beliefs and are actively engaged in learning together and from each other.

Learning Hierarchy   A diagram which shows "descriptions of successively achievable intellectual skills, each of which is stated as a performance class" (Gagné, 1973, p. 21).

Learning Objects   A representation designed to afford uses in different educational contexts (Churchill, 2007, p. 484).

Learning Path   The sequence of activities that a learner selects and follows through an instructional product; commonly pertains to computer-mediated instruction (Richey & Klein, 2007, p. 158).

Linking Science   A discipline which connects theory to practice.

Localized Instruction   Teaching and learning materials that are culture-specific and meet the needs of a particular group of learners.

Logical Picture   A visual that presents factual information (e.g., a map).

Logical Positivism   A philosophy that emphasizes the use of sensory data as a means of determining truth.

Long-Term Memory   The ability to permanently store, manage, and retrieve information for later use.

Macro-Level Planning   A tactical examination of organizational results and what the organization delivers to its clients.

Mastery Learning   An individualized approach to instruction in which students work at their own pace until they fully achieve the stated objectives with corrective instruction provided to those with learning difficulties.

Mathematical Model   An equation or formula describing relationships between the elements of a situation; typically accompanied with a narrative explanation.

Media   The physical means via which instruction is presented to learners (Reiser, 2007a, p. 18).

Media Ecology   A philosophical and theoretical position that views media not as tools, but rather as an environment that shapes perception, interaction, and social behavior.

Mega-Level Planning   The strategic examination of an organization and its impact on external clients and society.

Memory   The mental faculty of retaining and recalling past experiences (Seel, 2008, p. 40).

Memory Trace   A current representation of past events resulting from perception and encoding of information; also a hypothesized biochemical change in the brain resulting from responses to past stimuli.

Mental Model   An internal representation of the world that shapes subsequent behavior, based upon an individual's experience.

Mental Schema   See *Schema.*

Message Design   Planning for the manipulation of the physical form of the message (Grabowski, 1995, p. 226).

Meta-Analysis   The statistical analysis of a large collection of analysis results of individual studies for the purpose of integrating the findings (Glass, 1976, p. 3).

Meta-Cognitive Scaffold   A mechanism designed to facilitate learners as they plan and monitor learning activities and evaluate and reflect on their own learning.

Micro-Level Planning   An operational examination of organizational results and their consequences for individuals and small groups within the organization.

Mnemonics   A meaningful, often self-generated cue for retrieving information from long-term memory.

Models   Representation of idealized and simplified views of reality presented with a degree of structure and order; also demonstrations of desired behavior.

Motor Skill   An area of learning devoted to developing body movements.

Multi-channel Instruction   Teaching-learning activities that deliver messages through more than one vehicle or medium, typically both audio and visual.

Multimedia   Instructional materials that utilize several different delivery resources and tools, typically employing computer technologies.

Needs Assessment   A systematic process for determining goals, identifying discrepancies between goals and the status quo, and establishing priorities for action (Briggs, 1977, p. xxiv).

Negative Feedback   Information which allows a system to function in a stable fashion by keeping the system on course and maintaining a constant product.

Negative Reinforcement   A process of increasing the likelihood of a desired response by removing an unpleasant stimulus.

Noise   Factors that interfere with the accurate reception of a message; may be physical, cultural, or visual.

Nonrecurrent Skill   A novel aspect of a complex task performance which is unique to a given problem situation.

Objectivism   A philosophical orientation that maintains that reality exists independent of individual interpretation.

Online Learning   Instruction delivered using the Web, Internet, or other distance technologies (Klein, Spector, Grabowski, & de la Teja, 2004, p. 127).

Open-Ended Assessment   A testing situation which has a variety of correct answers often used to determine if learners understand and can use knowledge they have constructed for themselves.

Open System   An organized structure of people, objects, and processes that "receives inputs from the environment, transforms them through operations within the system, submits outputs to the environment, and receives feedback indicating how well these functions are carried out" (Rothwell & Kazanas, 2004, p. 11).

Operational Planning   See *Micro-Level Planning*.

Organizational Development   A process that "facilitates needed changes in an effort to improve efficiency and competitiveness" (Van Tiem et al., 2004, p. 209).

Organizational Elements Model   A systematic approach developed by Roger Kaufman that is used to identify and align organizational results and their consequences.

Orienting Context   The setting or environment that influences learner knowledge, attitudes, and skills related to an instructional event.

Part-Task Sequencing Strategy   An instructional sequence that breaks a complex task into component parts, each of which are taught separately, and then combined into the whole task.

Performance Analysis   A process of partnering "with clients to identify and respond to problems and opportunities, and to study individuals and the organization to determine an appropriate cross-functional solution system" (Rossett, 1999b, p. 227).

Performance Feedback   See *Feedback*.

Performance Gap   The differences between optimal and actual knowledge and skills.

Performance Improvement   A focus on improving individual, group, and organizational behavior and accomplishment through the use of a variety of interventions (Richey & Klein, 2007, p. 159).

Performance Objectives   See *Behavioral Objectives*.

Phenomenology   A philosophical orientation that suggests that reality is comprised of objects and events as they are perceived by the individual and is not independent of human consciousness.

Positive Feedback   Information from the environment which allows a system to reorganize itself.

Positive Reinforcement   A process of increasing the likelihood of a response by providing a pleasant stimulus.

Practical Knowledge   Information and understandings that are directed towards useful ends, such as in the workplace or in everyday life.

Practice Science   A discipline that has elements that are both theoretical and practical.

Pragmatism   A philosophical orientation that reflects the belief that practical findings can be used as the basis for knowledge and meaning.

Prerequisite Skills   Knowledge and skills subordinate to the intended outcome of instruction that are expected to have been mastered prior to the given instructional event.

Primary Presentation Form   Learning activities that focus on either generalities or instances of the content and are conveyed either through direct presentation of the content or questioning techniques; an element of component display theory.

Problem-Based Learning   A student-centered pedagogical strategy that poses significant contextualized, real-world, ill-structured situations while providing resources, guidance, instruction, and opportunities for reflection to learners as they develop content knowledge and problem-solving skills (Hoffman & Ritchie, 1997, p. 97).

Problem Solving   A high-level learning outcome building upon learned rules and schema and resulting in the resolution of a dilemma as well as new knowledge and possibly new cognitive strategies.

Procedural Analysis   See *Task Analysis*.

Procedural Information   A sequence of steps followed to complete a given task.

Procedural Models   Verbal or visual descriptions of how to perform a task; derived from experience or theory and often used as problem-solving guides.

Process Consulting   A method of seeking and giving advice which "results in revising processes and often involves reengineering or restructuring an organization" (Van Tiem et al., 2004, p. 210).

Programmed Instruction   A type of individualized instruction in which the content has been divided into small hierarchically sequenced units and learners are required to correctly respond to each unit at their own pace before progressing through the material.

Psychomotor Domain   That area of learning devoted to becoming proficient in performing a physical action involving muscles of the body (Morrison et al., 2007, p. 432).

Rapid Prototyping   An instructional design methodology that "involves the development of a working model of an instructional product that is used early in a project to assist in the analysis, design, development and evaluation of an instructional innovation" (Jones & Richey, 2000, p. 63).

Rationalism   A philosophical orientation that emphasizes the role of reasoning in the creation of new knowledge.

Realism   A philosophical orientation that views sensed objects as representing those actually existing in nature and are independent of the mind; the opposite of idealism.

Receiver Theories   Explanations of the communication process that emphasize the message being sensed and interpreted by the recipient as intended by the sender.

Recurrent Skill   A routine aspect of a complex task performance that can be applied in similar situations.

Reflective Feedback   A process of elaboration which requires learners to justify their responses after the receipt of corrective information.

Reinforcement   A stimulus event that increases the probability of a previous response.

Representational Technology   Devices, such as printed materials or film, that present information and require only one-way interaction.

Rich Learning Environment   An instructional setting which "encourages multiple learning styles and multiple representations of knowledge from different conceptual and case perspectives" (Karagiori & Symeou, 2005, p. 20).

Rich Media   Advanced technologies that are capable of enhancing the communication process by providing immediate feedback, multiple channel cues, language variety, and a personal focus.

Scaffold   A mechanism that provides learners with the support needed to extend their capabilities into a new domain simultaneously allowing independent thinking.

Schema   Organized knowledge structures in long-term memory representing generic concepts.

Secondary Presentation Form   An instructional event that elaborates upon the initial presentation of information, including items such as prerequisite knowledge, mnemonic aids, feedback, or additional examples; an element of component display theory.

Self-Efficacy   A belief in one's ability to complete a desired task.

Self-Knowledge   A combination of one's personal learning history and the common knowledge of society.

Self-Regulating System   An organized structure that includes processes allowing it to control its own outcomes usually through performance evaluation and modification.

Sensory Memory   The brief retention of information initially perceived; typically in visual or auditory form.

Sequencing   A process of ordering instructional content and activities.

Shaping   The gradual training of organisms to perform a desired behavior by reinforcing successive approximations of that behavior.

Short-Term Memory   See *Working Memory*.

Situated Cognition   A general approach to instruction that views concept acquisition and development as a type of enculturation achieved by involvement in authentic activities as opposed to an abstract presentation of information.

Social Constructivism   The belief that "effective learning occurs via interaction with and support from people and objects in the world" (Hickey, 1997, p. 175); also a belief that meaning is negotiated from multiple perspectives.

Social Networking Technology   Tools that facilitate collective intelligence through social negotiation when participants are engaged in a common goal or a shared practice (Gunawardena et al., 2009, p. 6); includes media such as weblogs, podcasting, audio blogs, and wikis.

Social Presence   The extent to which people are felt to be physically present during distance learning interactions.

Soft Scaffold   A dynamic and situational support mechanism that requires teachers to continuously diagnose learners so that the support is appropriate and timely.

Spiral Curriculum   An instructional program that addresses and builds on basic ideas repeatedly until students fully grasp the content.

Split Attention   A phenomena occurring during the learning process when instructional information is presented in audio and visual modalities.

Strategic Planning   See *Mega-Level Planning.*

Structural Knowledge   Knowledge of how concepts within a domain are interrelated (Jonassen, Beissener, & Yacci, 1993, p. 4).

Subsumptive Sequencing   The ordering of instructional tasks based upon their prerequisite relationships; often guided by a learning hierarchy.

Subsystem   Organized component structures of a target system with identifiable, but more limited purposes and functions.

Summative Evaluation   Gathering information on the effectiveness of an instructional or noninstructional intervention to make determinations of the worth of the intervention or make recommendations about its retention (Richey & Klein, 2007, p. 159).

Supplantive Instructional Strategies   Those techniques which provide support for students with low prior knowledge and few learning strategies.

Suprasystem   An overarching, organized structure of people, objects, and processes that includes a target system.

Symbol System   The manner in which information is structured and presented; may include physical, cultural, or psychological representations.

Symbolic Models   A graphical representation of an object used as a mathematical representation of a process used for analysis and planning.

Synchronous Learning   A form of communication where interaction occurs in real time, using tools such as video-conferencing and chat (Klein et al., 2004, p. 129).

System   A set of objects together with relationships between the objects and between their attributes (Hall & Fagen, 1975, p. 52).

System Analysis   A two-phased process which includes the identification of component system parts, and the relationships among the parts and with the whole system.

System Synthesis   A process that creates new systems by either establishing new relationships among existing objects or processes, or identifying new objects or processes and their relationships.

Systems Approach   A scientific, systematic, and rational procedure for optimizing outcomes of an organization or structure by implementing a set of related operations to study an existing system, solve problems, and develop new or modify existing systems (Ryan, 1975, p. 121).

Tactical Planning   See *Macro-Level Planning.*

Task Analysis   A process used to determine how a job or procedure is performed; typically used as a method of content identification.

Taxonomy   The classification of data into a hierarchy to indicate their relationships (Russ-eft, Bober, de la Teja, Foxon, & Koszalka, 2008, p. 171).

Teaching Machine   A mechanical device that delivers instruction, tests knowledge, and provides immediate feedback; often involves programmed instruction.

Technology-Enhanced Learning Environment   A learner-centered and learner-controlled instructional setting in which "students acquire skills or knowledge, usually with the help of teachers or facilitators, learning support tools, and technological resources" (Wang & Hannafin, 2005, p. 5).

Think-Aloud Methods   A research strategy in which participants describe out loud what they are thinking while carrying out a task (Richey & Klein, 2007, p. 160).

Transfer   The application of knowledge and skills acquired through instruction, often in a work environment.

Transfer Context   The setting and environment in which information learned is applied and used.

Transfer of Training   See *Transfer*.

Verification Feedback   Information that confirms whether a response was right or wrong.

Virtual Reality   A computer-based environment that simulates real or imaginary worlds and provides visual, auditory, or tactile experiences.

Visual Language   A vehicle for presenting ideas through the use of pictures, graphics, icons, or other nonverbal means; based upon principles of perception.

Web-Based Instruction   See *Online Learning*.

Well-Structured Problem   A puzzling situation that has a known solution that requires the application of a fixed number of concepts, rules, and principles.

Whole-Task Sequencing Strategy   An approach to sequencing in which the training immediately starts with learning tasks based on the simplest version of real-life tasks (van Merriënboer & Kirschner, 2007, p. 292).

Working Memory   The short-term storage of a limited amount of information for immediate use, rehearsal or encoding.

REFERENCES

Adelskold, G., Alklett, K., Axelsson, R., & Blomgren, G. (1999). Problem-based distance learning of energy issues via computer network. *Distance Education, 20*(1), 129–143.

Albanese, M. A., & Mitchell, S. (1993). Problem-based learning: A review of literature on its outcomes and implementation issues. *Academic Medicine, 68*(1), 52–81.

Albion, P., & Maddux, C. (2007). Editorial: Networked knowledge: Challenges for teacher education. *Journal of Technology and Teacher Education, 15*(3), 303–310.

Allen, W. H. (1956). Audio-visual materials. *Review of Educational Research, 26*(2), 125–156.

Allen, W. H. (1959). Research on new educational media: Summary and problems. *Audio Visual Communication Review, 7*(2), 83–96.

Allen, W. H. (1971). Instructional media research: Past, present, and future. *Audio Visual Communication Review, 19*(21), 5–18.

Allen, W. H. (1975). Intellectual abilities and instructional media design. *Audio Visual Communication Review, 23*(2), 139–170.

Alvesson, M. (1982). The limits and shortcomings of humanistic organization theory. *Acta Sociologica, 25*(2), 117–131.

Andrews, D. H., & Goodson, L. A. (1980). A comparative analysis of models of instructional design. *Journal of Instructional Development, 3*(4), 2–16.

Angeli, C. (2008). Distributed cognition: A framework for understanding the role of computers in classroom teaching and learning. *Journal of Research on Technology in Education, 40*(3), 271–279.

Arts, J. A. R., Gijselaers, W. H., & Segers, M. S. R. (2002). Cognitive effects of an authentic computer-supported, problem-based learning environment. *Instructional Science, 30*, 465–495.

Atkinson, J. W. (1966). Motivational determinants of risk-taking behavior. In J. W. Atkinson & N. T. Feather (Eds.), *A theory of achievement motivation* (pp. 11–29). New York: Robert E. Krieger Publishing Company, Inc.

Atkinson, J. W., & Raynor, J. O. (1974). *Motivation and achievement.* New York: V.H. Winston & Sons Publishers.

Atkinson, R. C., & Shiffrin, R. M. (1968). Human memory: A proposed system and its control processes. In K. W. Spence & J. T. Spence (Eds.), *The psychology of learning and motivation. Advances in research and theory* (Vol. 2) (pp. 89–195). New York: Academic Press.

Ausubel, D. P. (1978). In defense of advance organizers: A reply to the critics. *Review of Educational Research, 48*(2), 251–257.

Baker, R., & Dwyer, F. (2000). A meta-analytic assessment of the effect of visualized instruction. *International Journal of Instructional Media, 27*(4), 417–426.

Banathy, B. H. (1968). *Instructional systems.* Palo Alto, CA: Fearon Publishers.

Banathy, B. H. (1996). Systems inquiry and its application in education. In D. H. Jonasssen (Ed.), *Handbook of research for educational communications and technology* (pp. 74–92). New York: Simon & Schuster Macmillan.

Bandura, A. (1973). *Aggression: A social learning process.* Englewood Cliffs, NJ: Prentice-Hall.

Bandura, A. (1977a). *Social learning theory.* Englewood Cliffs, NJ: Prentice-Hall.

Bandura, A. (1977b). Self-efficacy: Toward a unifying theory of behavioral change. *Psychological Review, 84,* 191–215.

Bandura, A. (1978). The self-esteem in reciprocal determinism. *American Psychologist, 37,* 122–147.

Bandura, A. (1986). *Social foundations of thought and action: A social cognitive theory.* Englewood Cliffs, NJ: Prentice-Hall.

Bandura, A. (1997). *Self-efficacy: The exercise of control.* New York: Freeman.

Barritt, C., & Alderman, F. L. (2004). *Creating a reusable learning objects strategy: Leveraging information and learning in a knowledge economy.* San Francisco: Pfeiffer, A Wiley Imprint.

Barry, A. M. S. (1997). *Visual intelligence: Perception, image, and manipulation in visual communication.* Albany, NY: State University of New York Press.

Bednar, A. K., Cunningham, D., Duffy, T. M., & Perry, J. D. (1992). Theory into practice: How do we link? In T. M. Duffy & D. H. Jonassen (Eds.), *Constructivism and the technology of instruction: A conversation* (pp. 17–34). Hillsdale, NJ: Lawrence Erlbaum Associates, Publishers.

Beldarrain, Y. (2006). Distance education trends: Integrating new technologies to foster student interaction and collaboration. *Distance Education, 27*(2), 139–153.

Bennett, F. (1999). *Computers as tutors solving the crisis in education.* Sarasota, FL: Faben.

Berlo, D. (1960). *The process of communication.* New York: Holt, Rinehart and Winston.

Bertalanffy, L. von (1968). *General system theory: Foundations, development, applications.* New York: George Braziller.

Binder, C. (1993). Behavioral fluency: A new paradigm. *Educational Technology, 33*(10), 8–14.

Binder, C. (1996). Behavioral fluency: Evolution of a new paradigm. *Behavioral Analyst, 19*(2), 163–197.

Bittle, C. N. (1936). *Reality and the mind: Epistemology.* Milwaukee, WI: The Bruce Publishing Company.

Blalock, H. M. (1969). *Theory construction: From verbal to mathematical formulations.* Englewood Cliffs, NJ: Prentice-Hall, Inc.

Block, J. H., & Burns, R. B. (1976). Mastery learning. *Review of Research in Education, 4*(1), 3–49.

Bloom, B. S. (Ed.) (1956). *Taxonomy of educational objectives: The classification of educational goals, Handbook I: Cognitive domain.* New York: David McKay Company, Inc.

Bloom, B. S. (1971). Learning for mastery. In B. S. Bloom, J. T. Hasting, & G. F. Madaus (Eds.), *Handbook on formative and summative evaluation of student learning* (pp. 43–57). New York: McGraw-Hill.

Bloom, B. S. (1976). *Human characteristics and school learning.* New York: McGraw-Hill.

Boulding, K. (1964). General systems as a point of view. In M. C. Mesarović (Ed.), *Views on general systems theory: Proceedings of the Second Systems Symposium at Case Institute of Technology* (pp. 25–38). New York: John Wiley & Sons, Inc.

Bower, G. H., & Hilgard, E. R. (1981). *Theories of Learning* (5th ed.). Englewood Cliffs, NJ: Prentice-Hall.

Branson, R. K. (1975). *Inter-service procedures for instructional systems development: Executive summary and model.* Tallahassee, FL: Center for Educational Technology, Florida State University. (ERIC Document Reproduction Service No. ED 122022).

Brethower, D. (1999). Human performance interventions of a noninstructional nature. In H. Stolovitch & E. Keeps (Eds.), *Handbook of human performance technology* (2nd ed.) (pp. 319–320). San Francisco: Jossey-Bass.

Brethower, D. (2000). Integration theory, research and practice in human performance technology. *Performance Improvement, 39*(4), 33–43.

Briggs, L. J. (1970). *Handbook of procedures for the design of instruction.* Pittsburgh, PA: American Institutes for Research.

Briggs, L. J. (1977). *Instructional design: Principles and applications.* Englewood Cliffs, NJ: Educational Technology Publications.

Briggs, L. J., Gagné, R. M., & May, M. A. (1967). A procedure for choosing media for instruction. In L. J. Briggs, P. L. Campeau, R. M. Gagné, & M. A. May (Eds.), *Instructional media: A procedure for the design of multimedia instruction, a critical review of research and suggestions for future research* (pp. 28–52). Pittsburgh, PA: American Institutes for Research.

Brinkerhoff, R. O. (1988). An integrated evaluation model for HRD. *Training and Development Journal, 42*(2), 66–68.

Brown, A., & Green, T. D. (2006). *The essentials of instructional design: Connecting fundamental principles with process and practice.* Upper Saddle River, NJ: Pearson Education, Inc.

Brown, H. I. (2005). Empiricism. In T. Honderich (Ed.), *The Oxford guide to philosophy* (pp. 242–245). New York: Oxford University Press, Inc.

Brown, J. S., Collins, A., & Duguid, P. (1989). Situated cognition and the culture of learning. *Educational Researcher, 18*(1), 32–42.

Bruner, J. S. (1960). *The process of education.* Cambridge, MA: Harvard University Press.

Bruner, J. S. (1966). *Toward a theory of instruction.* Cambridge, MA: Harvard University Press.

Bruner, J. S. (1990). *Acts of meaning.* Cambridge, MA: Harvard University Press.

Bruner, J. S. (2006). *In search of pedagogy.* New York: Routledge.

Brush, T., & Saye, J. (2000). Design, implementation, and evaluation of student-centered learning: A case study. *Educational Technology Research and Development, 48*(2), 79–100.

Burge, T. (1979). Individualism and the mental. *Midwest Studies in Philosophy, 4,* 73–121.

Burton, J. K., Moore, D. M., & Magliaro, S. G. (2004). Behaviorism and instructional technology. In D. Jonassen (Ed.), *Handbook of research for educational communications and technology* (2nd ed.) (pp. 3–36). New York: Simon & Schuster Macmillan.

Caffarella, E. P., & Fly, K. (1992). Developing a knowledge base and taxonomy in instructional technology. In M. R. Simonson & K. Jurasek (Eds.), *14th Annual Proceedings of Selected Research and Development Presentations at the 1992 National Convention of the Association for Educational Communications and Technology* (pp. 95–102). Ames, IA: Iowa State University. (ERIC Document Reproduction Service No. ED 347977).

Caladine, R. (2008). *Enhancing e-learning with media-rich content and interactions.* Hershey, PA: Information Sciences Publishing.

Campbell, J. (1982). *Grammatical man.* New York: Simon and Schuster.

Campeau, P. L. (1967). Selective review of literature on audiovisual media of instruction. In L. J. Briggs, P. L. Campeau, R. M. Gagné, & M. A. May (Eds.), *Instructional media: A procedure for the design of multi-media instruction, a critical review of research and suggestions for future research* (pp. 99–142). Pittsburgh, PA: American Institutes for Research.

Campos, M. N. (2007). Ecology of meanings: A critical constructivist communication model. *Communication Theory, 17*(4), 386–410.

Carlson, P., & Davis, B. (1998). An investigation of media selection among directors and managers: From "self" to other orientation. *MIS Quarterly, 22*(3), 335–363.

Carrier, C. A., & Sales, G. C. (1987). A taxonomy for the design of computer-based instruction. *Educational Technology, 27*(10), 15–17.

Carroll, J. B. (1963). A model of school learning. *Teacher's College Record, 64,* 723–733.

Carroll, J. B. (1989). The Carroll model: A 25-year retrospective and prospective review. *Educational Researcher, 18*(1), 26–31.

Carroll, W., & Bandura, A. (1982). The role of visual monitoring in observation learning of action patterns: Making the unobservable observable. *Journal of Motor Behavior, 14,* 153–167.

Cennamo, K. (2003). Design as knowledge construction: Constructing knowledge of design. *Computers in the Schools, 20*(4), 13–35.

Cennamo, K. S., Abell, S. K., & Chung, M. (1996). Designing constructivist materials: A layers of negotiation model. *Educational Technology, 36*(7), 39–48.

Cennamo, K., & Kalk, D. (2005). *Real world instructional design.* Belmont, CA: Thomson/Wadsworth.

Cervero, R. M., & Wilson, A. L. (1994). *Planning responsibly for adult education: A guide to negotiating power and interests.* San Francisco: Jossey-Bass.

Chen, C.-I., Calinger, M., Howard, B. C., & Oskorus, A. (2008). Design principles for 21st century educational technology: Connecting theory and practice. *International Journal of Information and Communication Technology Education, 4*(4), 19–30.

Cho, K., & Jonassen, D. H. (2002). The effects of argumentation scaffolds on argumentation and problem solving. *Educational Technology Research and Development, 50*(2), 5–22.

Chou, C.-T. (2001). *Student interaction in a collaborative distance-learning environment: A model of learner-centered computer-mediated interaction* (University of Hawaii). Retrieved from Dissertations & Theses: Full Text (Publication No. AAT 3005200).

Churchill, D. (2007). Towards a useful classification of learning objects. *Educational Technology Research and Development, 55*(5), 479–497.

Churchman, C. W. (1964). An approach to general systems theory. In M. C. Mesarović (Ed.), *Views on general systems theory: Proceedings of the Second Systems Symposium at Case Institute of Technology* (pp. 173–175). New York: John Wiley & Sons, Inc.

Churchman, C. W. (1965/1996). On the design of educational systems. *Audiovisual Instruction, 10*(5), 361–365. (Reprinted in D. P. Ely & T. Plomp [Eds.] [1996] *Classic Writings on Instructional Technology* [pp. 39–46]. Englewood, CO: Libraries, Unlimited, Inc.).

Clariana, R. B., Wagner, D., & Murphy, L. C. (2000). Applying a connectionist description of feedback timing. *Educational Technology Research and Development, 48*(3), 5–21.

Clark, R. E. (1983). Reconsidering research on learning from media. *Review of Educational Research, 53*(4), 445–459.

Clark, R. E., & Estes, F. (2002). *Turning research into results: A guide to selecting the right performance solutions.* Atlanta, GA: Center for Effective Performance.

Clark, R. C., & Nguyen, F. (2008). Behavioral, cognitive and technological models for performance improvement. In J. M. Spector, M. D. Merrill, J. van Merriënboer, & M. P. Driscoll (Eds.), *Handbook of research on educational communications and technology* (3rd ed.) (pp. 507–524). New York: Lawrence Erlbaum Associates, Publishers.

Clark, R. E., & Salomon, G. (1986) Media in teaching. In M. C. Wittrock (Ed.), *Handbook of research on teaching* (3rd ed.) (pp. 464–478). New York: Macmillan Publishing Company.

Coats, L. (1985). *The effect of Gagne's nine instructional events on posttest and retention test scores among high school students* (University of North Carolina at Chapel Hill). Retrieved from Dissertations & Theses: Full Text (Publication No. AAT 8605585).

Cobb, P. (1994). Where is the mind? Constructivist and sociocultural perspectives on mathematical development. *Educational Researcher, 23,* 13–20.

Cobb, T. (1997). Cognitive efficiency: Toward a revised theory of media. *Educational Technology Research and Development, 45*(4), 21–35.

Conn, C. A., & Gitonga, J. (2004). The status of training and performance research in the AECT journals. *TechTrends, 48*(2), 16–21.

Connolly, P. E. (2005). Virtual reality & immersive technology in education. *International Journal of Information and Communication Technology Education, 1*(1), 12–18.

Cortes, F., Przeworski, A., & Sprague, J. (1974). *Systems analysis for social scientists.* New York: John Wiley & Sons.

Czaja, S. J., Charness, M., Fisk, A. D., Hertzog, C., Nair, S. N., Rogers, W. A., et al. (2006). Factors predicting the use of technology: Findings from the Center for Research and Education on Aging and Technology Enhancement (CREATE). *Psychology and Aging, 21*(2), 333–352.

Daft, R. L., Lengel, R. H., & Trevino, L. K. (1987). Message equivocality, media selection, and manager performance: Implications for information systems. *MIS Quarterly, 11*(3), 355–366.

Dale, E. (1946). *Audio-visual methods in teaching.* New York: The Dryden Press.

Davis, E. A., & Linn, M. C. (2000). Scaffolding students' knowledge integration: Prompts for reflection in KIE. *International Journal of Science Education, 22,* 819–837.

Dean, P. (1999). Designing better organization with human performance technology and organizational development. In H. Stolovitch & E. Keeps (Eds.), *Handbook of human performance technology* (2nd ed.) (pp. 321–323). San Francisco: Jossey-Bass.

Dean, P., & Ripley, D. E. (1997). *Performance improvement pathfinders: Models for organizational learning.* Washington, DC: International Society for Performance Improvement.

DeGennaro, D. (2008). Learning designs: An analysis of youth-initiated technology use. *Journal of Research on Technology in Education, 41*(1), 1–20.

Dempsey, J. V., & Sales, G. C. (1993). *Interactive instruction and feedback.* Englewood Cliffs, NJ: Educational Technology Publications.

Dennen, V. P. (2004). Cognitive apprenticeships in educational practice. In D. Jonassen (Ed.), *Handbook of research for educational communications and technology* (2nd ed.) (pp. 813–828). New York: Simon & Schuster Macmillan.

Department of the Air Force. (1979). *Instructional system development AF manual 50-2.* Washington, D.C.: U.S. Government Printing Office.

Department of the Navy, Chief of Naval Education and Training. (1980). *User manual, Author training course,* NAVEDTRA 10003. Washington, D.C.: Author.

Design-Based Research Collective. (2003). Design-based research: An emerging paradigm for educational inquiry. *Educational Researcher, 32*(1), 5–8.

Dessinger, J. C., & Moseley, J. L. (2004). *Confirmative evaluation: Practical strategies for valuing continuous improvement.* San Francisco: Pfeiffer.

Deterline, W. A., & Rosenberg, M. J. (1992). *Workplace productivity: Performance technology success stories.* Washington, DC: International Society for Performance Improvement.

Diamond, R. M. (1989). *Designing and improving courses and curricula in higher education.* San Francisco: Jossey-Bass. (ERIC Document Reproduction Service No. ED 304 056).

Dick, W. (1987). A history of instructional design and its impact on educational psychology. In J. A. Glover & R. R. Ronning (Eds.), *Historical foundations of educational psychology* (pp. 183–202). New York: Plenum Press.

Dick, W., & Carey, L. (1978). *The systematic design of instruction.* Glenview, IL: Scott, Foresman and Company.

Dick, W., Carey, L., & Carey, J. O. (2009). *The systematic design of instruction* (7th ed.). Upper Saddle River, NJ: Merrill.

Dick, W., & Johnson, R. B. (2007). Evaluation in instructional design: The impact of Kirkpatrick's four-level model. In R. A. Reiser & J. V. Dempsey (Eds.), *Trends and Issues in Instructional Design and Technology* (2nd ed.) (pp. 94–103). Upper Saddle River, NJ: Merrill/Prentice-Hall.

Dick, W., & Wager, W. (1998). Preparing performance technologists: The role of a university. In P. J. Dean & D. E. Ripley (Eds.), *Performance improvement interventions: Performance technologies in the workplace* (pp. 239–251).Washington, DC: International Society for Performance Improvement.

Diesing, P. (1991). *How does social science work? Reflections on practice.* Pittsburgh, PA: University of Pittsburgh Press.

Doty, C. R. (1969). *The effect of practice and prior knowledge of educational objectives on performance* (Ohio State University). Retrieved from Dissertations & Theses: Full Text (Publication No. AAT 6904876).

Drack, M., & Apfalter, W. (2007). Is Paul A. Weiss' and Ludwig von Bertalanffy's system thinking still valid today? *Systems Research and Behavioral Science, 24,* 537–546.

Dresang, E. T., Gross, M., & Holt, L. (2007). New perspectives: An analysis of gender, net-generation children, and computers. *Library Trends, 56*(2), 360–386.

Driscoll, M. P. (2005). *Psychology of learning for instruction* (3rd ed.). Boston, MA: Pearson Education, Inc.

Driscoll, M. P. (2007). Psychological foundations of instructional design. In R. A. Reiser & J. V. Dempsey (Eds.), *Trends and Issues in Instructional Design and Technology* (2nd ed.) (pp. 36–44). Upper Saddle River, NJ: Pearson Education.

Dubin, R. (1969). *Theory building.* New York: The Free Press.

Duchastel, P. C. (1980). Research on illustrations in text: Issues and perspectives. *Educational Communication and Technology Journal, 28*(4), 283–287.

Duchastel, P. C. (1982). Textual display techniques. In D. H. Jonassen (Ed.), *The technology of text: Principles for structuring, designing, and displaying text, Volume One* (pp. 167–192). Englewood Cliffs, NJ: Educational Technology Publications.

Duffy, T. M., & Cunningham, D. J. (1996). Constructivism: Implications for the design and delivery of instruction. In D. H. Jonassen (Ed.), *Handbook of research for educational communications and technology* (pp. 170–198). New York: Simon & Schuster Macmillan.

Duffy, T. M., & Jonassen, D. H. (1992). Constructivism: New implications for instructional technology. In T. M. Duffy & D. H. Jonassen (Eds.), *Constructivism and the technology of instruction: A conversation* (pp. 1–16). Hillsdale, NJ: Lawrence Erlbaum Associates, Publishers.

Eastmond, D. (1995). *Alone but together: Adult distance study through computer conferencing.* Cresskill, NJ: Hampton Press.

Edelson, D. C., Gordin, D. N., & Pea, R. D. (1999). Addressing the challenges of inquiry-based learning through technology and curriculum design. *The Journal of the Learning Sciences, 8*(3&4), 391–450.

Edwards, L. (1982). Delivering health education programs. *Health Values: Achieving High Level Wellness, 6*(6), 13–19.

Ellington, H., & Harris, D. (1986). *Dictionary of instructional technology.* London: Kogan Page.

Emison, G. A. (2004). Pragmatism, adaptation, and total quality management: Philosophy and science in the service of managing continuous improvement. *Journal of Management in Engineering, 20*(2), 56–61.

Ericsson, K. A., & Chase, W. C. (1982). Exceptional memory. *American Scientist, 70,* 607–615.

Ertmer, P. A., Evenbeck, E., Cennamo, K. S., & Lehman, J. D. (1994). Enhancing self-efficacy for computer technologies through the use of positive classroom experiences. *Educational Technology Research and Development, 42*(3), 45–62.

Fawcett, J. (1989). Analysis and evaluation of conceptual models of nursing (2nd ed.). Philadelphia, PA: F. A. Davis Company.

Finn, J. D. (1957a). Automation and education: I: General Aspects. *Audio Visual Communication Review, 5*(1), 343–360.

Finn, J. D. (1957b). Automation and education: II: Automatizing the classroom – Background of the effort. *Audio Visual Communication Review, 5*(2), 451–467.

Finn, J. D. (1960). Automation and education: III: Technology and the instructional process. *Audio Visual Communication Review, 8*(1), 5–26.

Fleming, M. L. (1987). Displays and communication. In R. M. Gagné (Ed.), *Instructional technology: Foundations* (pp. 233–260). Hillsdale, NJ: Lawrence Erlbaum Associates, Publishers.

Foshay, W. R., & Moller, L. (1992). Advancing the field through research. In H. Stolovitch & E. Keeps (Eds.), *Handbook of human performance technology* (pp. 701–714). San Francisco: Jossey-Bass.

Foshay, W., Moller, L., Schwen, T., Kalman, H., & Haney, D. (1999). Research in human performance technology. In H. Stolovitch & E. Keeps (Eds.), *Handbook of human performance technology* (2nd ed.) (pp. 895–914). San Francisco: Jossey-Bass.

Fox, E. J. (2008). Contextualistic perspectives. In J. M. Spector, M. D. Merrill, J. van Merriënboer, & M. P. Driscoll (Eds.), *Handbook of research on educational communications and technology* (3rd ed.) (pp. 55–66). New York: Lawrence Erlbaum Associates, Publishers.

Fox, E. J., & Klein, J. D. (2003). What should instructional designers and technologists know about human performance technology? *Performance Improvement Quarterly, 16*(3), 87–98.

Fox, R. (2001). Constructivism examined. *Oxford Review of Education, 27*(1), 23–35.

Gage, N. L. (1978). *The scientific basis of the art of teaching.* New York: Teachers College Press.

Gagné, R. M. (1964). Problem solving. In A. W. Melton (Ed.), *Categories of human learning* (pp. 293–317). New York: Academic Press.

Gagné, R. M. (1965). *The conditions of learning.* New York: Holt, Rinehart and Winston, Inc.

Gagné, R. M. (1968/2000a). Contributions of learning to human development. *Psychological Review, 75,* 177–191. (Reprinted in R. C. Richey (Ed.), *The Legacy of Robert M. Gagné.* Syracuse, NY: ERIC Clearinghouse on Information & Technology).

Gagné, R. M. (1968/2000b). Learning hierarchies. *Educational Psychologist, 6,* 1–9. (Reprinted in R. C. Richey (Ed.), *The Legacy of Robert M. Gagné.* Syracuse, NY: ERIC Clearinghouse on Information & Technology).

Gagné, R. M. (1972/2000). Domains of learning. *Interchange, 3,* 1–8. (Reprinted in R. C. Richey (Ed.), *The Legacy of Robert M. Gagné.* Syracuse, NY: ERIC Clearinghouse on Information & Technology).

Gagné, R. M. (1973). Learning and instructional sequence. In F. N. Kerlinger (Ed.), *Review of research in education, Vol. 1* (pp. 3–33). Itasca, NY: Peacock.

Gagné, R. M. (1984). Learning outcomes and their effects: Useful categories of human performance. *American Psychologist, 39,* 377–385.

Gagné, R. M. (1985). *The conditions of learning* (4th ed.). New York: Holt, Rinehart and Winston.

Gagné, R. M., Briggs, L .J., & Wager, W. W. (1992). *Principles of instructional design* (4th ed.). Fort Worth, TX: Harcourt Brace Jovanovich College Publishers.

Gagné, R., & Medsker, K. (1996). *The conditions of learning: Training applications.* Fort Worth, TX: Harcourt Brace.

Gagné, R. M., & Merrill, M. D. (1990). Integrative goals for instructional design. *Educational Technology Research and Development, 38*(1), 23–30.

Gagné, R. M., Wager, W. W., Golas, K. C., & Keller, J. M. (2005). *Principles of instructional design* (5th ed.). Belmont, CA: Wadsworth/Thomson Learning.

Garavaglia, P. L. (1980). How to ensure transfer of training. *Training & Development, 47*(10), 63–68.

Garner, R., Gillingham, M., & White, C. (1989). Effects of "seductive details" on macroprocessing and microprocessing in adults and children. *Cognition and Instruction, 6*(1), 41–57.

Geiger, S., & Reeves, B. (1993). The effects of scene changes and semantic relationships on attention to television. *Communication Research, 20*(2), 155–175.

Geis, G. L. (1986). Human performance technology. In M. E. Smith (Ed.), *Introduction to performance technology (Volume 1).* Washington, DC: National Society for Performance and Instruction, 1–20.

Geis, G. L., & Smith, M. E. (1992). The function of evaluation. In H. Stolovitch & E. Keeps (Eds.), *Handbook of human performance technology* (pp. 130–150). San Francisco: Jossey-Bass.

Gerber, M., Grundt, S., & Grote, G. (2008). Distributed collaboration activities in a blended learning scenario and the effects on learning performance. *Journal of Computer-Assisted Learning, 24*(3), 232–244.

Gery, G. (1991). *Electronic performance support systems.* Tolland, MA: Gery Associates.

Gijbels, D., Dochy, F., Van den Bossche, P., & Segers, M. (2005). Effects of problem-based learning: A meta-analysis from the angle of assessment. *Review of Educational Research, 75*(1), 27–61.

Gilbert, N. J., & Driscoll, M. P. (2002). Collaborative knowledge building: A case study. *Educational Technology Research and Development, 50*(1), 59–79.

Gilbert, T. F. (1996). *Engineering worthy performance.* Amherst, MA: HRD Press.

Ginsburg, H., & Opper, S. (1979). *Piaget's theory of intellectual development* (2nd ed.). Englewood Cliffs, N.J.: Prentice-Hall, Inc.

Glass, G. (1976). Primary, secondary, and meta-analysis of research. *Educational Researcher, 5*(10), 3–8.

Glynn, S. M., Britton, B. K., & Tillman, M. H. (1985). Typographical cues in text: Management of the reader's attention. In D. H. Jonassen (Ed.), *The technology of text: Principles for structuring, designing, and displaying text, Volume Two* (pp. 192–209). Englewood Cliffs, NJ: Educational Technology Publications.

Gordon, M. (2009). Between constructivism and connectedness. *Journal of Teacher Education, 59*(4), 322–332.

Gordon, S. E. (1994). *Systematic training program design: Maximizing effectiveness and minimizing liability.* Englewood Cliffs, NJ: PTR Prentice Hall.

Grabowski, B. L. (1995). Message design: Issues and trends. In G. J. Anglin (Ed.), *Instructional technology: Past, present, and future* (2nd ed.) (pp. 222–232). Englewood, CO: Libraries Unlimited, Inc.

Grabowski, B. L. (2004). Generative learning contributions to the design on instruction and learning. In D. H. Jonassen (Ed.), *Handbook of research for educational communications and technology* (2nd ed.) (pp. 719–743). Mahwah, NJ: Lawrence Erlbaum Associates, Publishers.

Graesser, A. C., Chipman, P., & King, B. G. (2008). Computer-mediated technologies. In J. M. Spector, M. D. Merrill, J. van Merriënboer, & M. P. Driscoll (Eds.), *Handbook of research on educational communications and technology* (3rd ed.) (pp. 211–224). New York: Lawrence Erlbaum Associates, Publishers.

Gredler, M. E. (2001). *Learning and instruction: Theory to practice* (4th ed.). Upper Saddle River: NJ: Merrill Prentice Hall.

Gredler, M. E. (2004). Games and simulations and their relationship to learning. In D. Jonassen (Ed.), *Handbook of research on educational communications and technology* (2nd ed.) (pp. 571–581). Mahwah, NJ: Lawrence Erlbaum Associates, Publishers.

Greenbaum, H. H., & Falcione, R. L. (1980). Organizational communication research: An exploratory application of a conceptual model for an organized knowledge base. A paper presented at the 40th annual meeting of The Academy of Management. (ERIC Document Reproduction Service No. ED 199919).

Gropper, G. L. (1976). A behavioral perspective of media selection. *Audio-Visual Communication Review, 24*(2), 157–186.

Guerra, I. (2001). Performance improvement based on results: Is our field adding value? *Performance Improvement Quarterly, 40*(1), 6–10.

Guerra-Lopez, I. (2007). *Evaluating impact: Evaluation and continual improvement for performance improvement practitioners.* Amherst, MA: HRD Press.

Gunawardena, C. N., Hermans, M. B., Sanchez, D., Richmond, C., Bohley, M., & Tuttle, R. (2009). A theoretical framework for building online communities of practice with social networking tools. *Educational Media International, 46*(1), 3–16.

Gustafson, K. L., & Branch, R. M. (2002). *Survey of instructional development models* (4th ed.). Syracuse University, Syracuse, NY: ERIC Clearinghouse on Information & Technology.

Gustafson, K. L., & Branch, R. M. (2007). What is instructional design? In R. A. Reiser & J. V. Dempsey (Eds.), *Trends and issues in instructional design and technology* (pp. 10–16). Upper Saddle River, NJ: Pearson/Merrill Prentice Hall.

Guthrie, E. R. (1960). *The psychology of learning.* Gloucester, MA: Peter Smith.

Hakkinen, P. (2002). Challenges for design of computer-based learning environments. *British Journal of Educational Technology, 33*(4), 461–469.

Hall, A. D., & Fagen, R. E. (1975). Definition of system. In B. D. Ruben & J. Y. Kin (Eds.), *General systems theory and human communication* (pp. 52–65). Rochelle Park, NJ: Hayden Book Company, Inc.

Hamlyn, D. W. (2005). Idealism, philosophical. In T. Honderich (Ed.), *The Oxford guide to philosophy.* Oxford, UK: Oxford University Press.

Hammond, D. (2002). Exploring the genealogy of systems thinking. *Systems Research and Behavioral Science, 19,* 429–439.

Hannafin, M. J. (1987). The effects of orienting activities, cueing and practice on learning of computer based instruction. *Journal of Educational Research, 81*(1), 48–53.

Hannafin, M. J., Hannafin, K. M., Hooper, S. R., Rieber, L. P., & Kini, A. S. (1996). Research on and research with emerging technologies. In D. H. Jonassen (Ed.), *Handbook of research on educational communications and technology* (pp. 378–402). Mahwah, NJ: Lawrence Erlbaum Associates, Publishers.

Hannafin, M. J., Hannafin, K. M., Land, S. M., & Oliver, K. (1997). Grounded practice and the design of constructivist learning environments. *Educational Technology Research and Development, 45*(3), 101–117.

Hannifin, M. J., & Hill, J. R. (2007). Epistemology and the design of learning environments. In R. A. Reisier & J. V. Dempsey (Eds.), *Trends and Issues in Instructional Design and Technology* (pp. 53–71). Upper Saddle River, NJ: Pearson Education.

Hannafin, M. J., Phillips, T., Rieber, L. P., & Garhart, C. (1987). The effects of orienting activities and cognitive processing time on factual and inferential learning. *Educational Communications and Technology Journal, 35*(2), 75–84.

Harless, J. H. (1970). *An ounce of analysis is worth a pound of objectives.* Newnan, GA: Harless Performance Guild.

Harless, J. H. (1994). *Performance quality improvement system.* Newnan, GA: Harless Performance Guild.

Harre, R. (1960). *An introduction to the logic of the sciences.* London: Macmillan and Co. Ltd.

Hartley, J. (1996). Text design. In D. H. Jonassen (Ed.), *Handbook of research on educational communications and technology* (pp. 795–820). Mahwah, NJ: Lawrence Erlbaum Associates, Publishers.

Hartley, J. (2004). Designing instructional and informational text. In D. H. Jonassen (Ed.), *Handbook of research on educational communications and technology* (2nd ed.) (pp. 917–948). Mahwah, NJ: Lawrence Erlbaum Associates, Publishers.

Haughton, E. C. (1972). Aims: Growing and sharing. In J. B. Jordan & L. S. Robbins (Eds.), *Let's try doing something else kind of thing* (pp. 20–29). Arlington, VA: Council on Exceptional Children.

Hay, K. E., & Barab, S. A. (2001). Constructivism in practice: A comparison and contrast of apprenticeship and constructionist learning environments. *The Journal of the Learning Sciences, 10*(3), 281–322.

Heath, R. L., & Bryant, J. (2000). *Human communication theory and research: Concepts, contexts, and challenges* (2nd ed.). Mahwah, NJ: Lawrence Erlbaum Associates, Publishers.

Heinich, R. (1970). *Technology and the management of instruction* (AECT Monograph No. 4). Washington, DC: Association of Educational Communications and Technology.

Heise, U. K. (2002). Unnatural ecologies: The metaphor of the environment in media theory. *Configurations, 10*(1), 149–200.

Hickey, D. T. (1997). Motivation and contemporary socio-constructivist instructional perspectives. *Educational Psychologist, 32*(3), 175–193.

Higgins, N., & Reiser, R. (1985). Selecting media for instruction: An exploratory study. *Journal of Instructional Development, 8*(2), 6–10.

Hilgard, E. R. (1956). *Theories of learning* (2nd ed.). New York: Appleton-Century Crofts.

Hill, J. R., Wiley, D., Nelson, L. M., & Han, S. (2004). Exploring research on internet-based learning: From infrastructure to interactions. In D. H. Jonassen (Ed.), *Handbook of research on educational communications and technology* (2nd ed.) (pp. 433–460). Mahwah, NJ: Lawrence Erlbaum Associates, Publishers.

Hmelo, C. E., & Evensen, D. H. (2000). Problem-based learning: Gaining insights on learning interactions through multiple methods of inquiry. In D. Evensen & C. Hmelo (Eds.), *Problem-based learning: a research perspective on learning interactions* (pp. 1–16). Mahwah, NJ: Lawrence Erlbaum Associates, Publishers.

Hoban, C. F., Hoban, C. F., Jr., & Zisman, S. B. (1937). *Visualizing the curriculum.* New York: The Dryden Press, Inc.

Hoffman, B., & Ritchie, D. (1997). Using multimedia to overcome the problems with problem based learning. *Instructional Science, 25,* 97–115.

Hogan, K., & Pressley, M. (1997). Scaffolding scientific competencies within classroom communities of inquiry. In K. Hogan & M. Pressley (Eds.), *Scaffolding student learning* (pp. 74–107). Cambridge, MA: Brookline Books.

Hollan, J., Hustchins, E., & Kirsh, D. (2000). Distributed cognition: Toward a new foundation for human-computer interaction research. *ACM Transactions on Computer-Human Interaction, 7*(2), 174–196.

Hong, N. S., Jonassen, D. H., & McGee, S. (2003). Predictors of well-structured and ill-structured problem solving in an astronomy simulation. *Journal of Research in Science Teaching, 40*(1), 6–33.

Hoover, K. R., & Donovan, T. (1995). *The elements of social scientific thinking* (6th ed.). Belmont, CA: Thompson/Wadsworth.

Huddlestone, J., & Pike, J. (2008). Seven key decision factors for selecting e-learning. *Cognition, Technology & Work, 10*(3), 237–247.

Huglin, L. M. (2009). HPT roots and branches: Analyzing over 45 years of the field's own citations. *Performance Improvement Quarterly, 21*(4), 95–115.

Hung, W., & Jonassen, D. H. (2006). Conceptual understanding of causal reasoning in physics. *International Journal of Science Education, 28*(5), 1–21.

Hutchison, C. S., & Stein, F. (1998). A whole new world of interventions: The performance technologist as integrating generalist. *Performance Improvement, 37*(5), 18–25.

Januszewski, A. (2001). *Educational technology: The development of a concept.* Englewood, CO: Libraries Unlimited, Inc.

Johnson, C. (2008). Learning, animated. *Training and Development, 62*(11), 28–31.

Johnson, D. W., & Johnson, R. T. (2004). Cooperation and the use of technology. In D. Jonassen (Ed.), *Handbook of research for educational communications and technology* (2nd ed.) (pp. 785–811). New York: Simon & Schuster Macmillan.

Jonassen, D. H. (1992). Evaluating constructivist learning: Do they make a marriage? In T. M. Duffy & D. H. Jonassen (Eds.), *Constructivism and the technology of instruction: A conversation* (pp. 137–148). Hillsdale, NJ: Lawrence Erlbaum Associates, Publishers.

Jonassen, D. H. (1997). Instructional design model for well-structured and ill-structured problem-solving learning outcomes. *Educational Technology Research and Development, 45*(1), 65–95.

Jonassen, D. H. (2000). Toward a design theory of problem-solving. *Educational Technology Research and Development, 48*(4), 63–85.

Jonassen, D. H. (2003). Designing research-based instruction for story problems. *Educational Psychology Review, 15*(3), 267–269.

Jonassen, D. H. (2011). *Learning to solve problems: A handbook for designing problem-solving learning environments.* New York: Routledge.

Jonassen, D. H., Beissner, K., & Yacci, M. (1993). *Structural knowledge: Techniques for representing, conveying, and acquiring structural knowledge.* Hillsdale, NJ: Lawrence Erlbaum Associates, Publishers.

Jonassen, D. H., & Hannum, W. H. (1986). Analysis of task analysis procedures. *Journal of Instructional Development, 9*(2), 2–12.

Jonassen, D. H., & Henning, P. (1999). Mental models: Knowledge in the head and knowledge in the world. *Educational Technology, 39*(3), 37–42.

Jonassen, D. H., Hennon, R. J., Ondrusek, A., Samouilova, M., Spaulding, K. L., Yueh, H.-P. et al. (1997). Certainty, determinism, and predictability in theories of instructional design: Lessons from science. *Educational Technology, 37*(1), 27–34.

Jonassen, D. H., & Kwon, H. I. (2001). Communication patterns in computer-mediated vs. face-to-face group problem solving. *Educational Technology: Research and Development, 49*(10), 35–52.

Jonassen, D. H., Peck, K. L., & Wilson, B. G. (1999). *Learning with technology: A constructivist perspective.* Upper Saddle River, NJ: Merrill/Prentice Hall.

Jonassen, D., Prevish, T., Christy, D., & Stavulaki, E. (1999). Learning to solve problems on the Web: Aggregate planning in a business management course. *Distance Education, 20*(1), 49–63.

Jones, T. S., & Richey, R. C. (2000). Rapid prototyping in action: A developmental study. *Educational Technology Research and Development, 48*(2), 63–80.

Joo, Y.-J., Bong, M., & Choi, H.-J., (2000). Self-efficacy for self-regulated learning, academic self-efficacy, and internet self-efficacy in web-based instruction. *Educational Technology Research and Development, 48*(2), 5–17.

Joyce, B., & Weil, M. (1986). *Models of Teaching* (3rd ed.). Englewood Cliffs, NJ: Prentice-Hall.

Kanuka, H., & Anderson, T. (1998). On-line interchange, discord, and knowledge construction. *Journal of Distance Education, 13*(1), 57–74.

Kaplan, A. (1964). *The conduct of inquiry.* San Francisco: Chandler Publishing Company.

Karagiorgi, Y., & Symeou, L. (2005). Translating constructivism into instructional design: Potential and limitations. *Educational Technology & Society, 8*(91), 17–27.

Kaufman, R. A. (1970). Systems approaches to education: Discussion and attempted integration. In *Social and technological change: Implications for education.* Eugene, OR: Center for Advanced Study of Educational Administration, University of Oregon.

Kaufman, R. (2006). *Change, choices, and consequences: A guide to mega thinking and planning.* Amherst, MA: HRD Press.

Kaufman, R. (2009). Mega thinking and planning: An introduction to defining and delivering individual and organizational success. *Performance Improvement Quarterly, 22*(2), 5–15.

Kaufman, R., & Clark, R. (1999). Reestablishing performance improvement as a legitimate area of inquiry, activity, and contribution: Rules of the road. *Performance Improvement, 38*(9), 13–18.

Kaufman, R., Keller, J., Watkins, R. (1994). What works and what doesn't: Evaluation beyond Kirkpatrick. *Performance and Instruction, 35*(2), 8–12.

Kaufman, R., Rojas, A. M., & Mayer, H. (1993). *Needs assessment: A user's guide.* Englewood Cliffs, NJ: Educational Technology Publications.

Kaufman, R., Thiagarajan, S., & MacGillis, P. (1997). The changing realities of human and organizational performance improvement. In R. Kaufman, S. Thiagarajan, & P. MacGillis (Eds.), *The guidebook of performance improvement* (pp. 1–17). San Francisco: Jossey-Bass/Pfeiffer.

Keller, J. M. (1979). Motivation and instructional design: A theoretical perspective. *Journal of Instructional Development, 2*(4), 26–34.

Keller, J. M. (1983). Motivational design of instruction. In C. M. Reigeluth (Ed.), *Instructional-design theories and models: An overview of their current status.* (pp. 383–434). Hillsdale, NJ: Lawrence Erlbaum Associates, Publishers.

Keller, J. M. (1987a). The systematic process of motivational design. *Performance & Instruction, 26*(9–10), 1–8.

Keller, J. M. (1987b). Strategies for stimulating the motivation to learn. *Performance & Instruction, 26*(8), 1–7.

Keller, J. M. (2010). *Motivational design for learning and performance: The ARCS model approach.* New York: Springer.

Kemp, J. E. (1985). *The instructional design process.* New York: Harper & Row, Publishers.

Kevinen, O., & Ristelä, P. (2003). From constructivism to a pragmatist conception of learning. *Oxford Review of Education, 29*(3), 363–375.

Kilbourn, R. W. (1961). Midwest airborne television and the technology of education. *Audio Visual Communication Review, 9*(4), 201–205.

Kim, B., & Reeves, T .C. (2007). Reframing research on learning with technology: In search of the meaning of cognitive tools. *Instructional Science, 35,* 207–256.

Kim, C. M., & Keller, J. M. (2008). Effects of motivational and volitional email messages with personal messages on undergraduate students' motivation, study habits and achievement. *British Journal of Educational Technology, 39*(1), 36–51.

Kim, H., & Hannafin, M. J. (2008). Grounded design of web-enhanced case-based activity. *Educational Technology Research and Development, 56*(2), 161–179.

Kirkpatrick, D. L. (1996) Great ideas revisited. *Training and Development, 50*(1), 54–59.

Kirkpatrick, D. L. (1998). *Evaluating training programs: The four levels.* San Francisco: Berrett-Koehler.

Kirschner, P. (2004). Design, development, and implementation of electronic learning environments for collaborative learning. *Educational Technology Research and Development, 52*(3), 39–46.

Kirschner, P., Strijibos, J., Krejins, K., & Beers, P. J. (2004). Designing electronic collaborative learning environments. *Educational Technology Research and Development, 52*(3), 47–66.

Klein, J. D. (1990). An analysis of the motivational characteristics of college re-entry students. *College Student Journal, 24,* 281–286.

Klein, J. D. (2002). Empirical research on performance improvement. *Performance Improvement Quarterly, 15*(1), 99–110.

Klein, J. D. (2010). Trends in performance improvement: Expanding the reach of instructional design and technology. In M. Orey, S. A. Jones, & R. M. Branch (Eds.), *Educational Media and Technology and Yearbook: Volume 35* (pp. 135–147). New York: Springer.

Klein, J. D., & Fox, E. J. (2004). Performance improvement competencies for instructional technologists. *TechTrends, 48*(2), 22–25.

Klein, J. D., & Freitag, E. T. (1992). Training students to utilize self-motivational strategies. *Educational Technology, 32*(3), 44–48.

Klein, J. D., & Schnackenberg, H. L. (2000). Effects of informal cooperative learning and the affiliation motive on achievement, attitude, and student interactions. *Contemporary Educational Psychology, 25,* 332–341.

Klein, J. D., Spector, J. M., Grabowski, B., & de la Teja, I. (2004). *Instructor competencies: Standards for face-to-face, online, and blended settings.* Greenwich, CT: Information Age Publishing.

Kliebard, H. M. (1970). The Tyler rationale. *The School Review, 78*(2), 259–272.

Knezek, G. A., Rachlin, S. L., & Scannell, P. (1988). A taxonomy for educational computing. *Educational Technology, 28*(3), 15–19.

Knowlton, J. Q. (1966). On the definition of "picture". *Audio Visual Communication Review, 14*(2), 157–183.

Kozma, R. B. (1991). Learning with media. *Review of Educational Research, 61*(2), 179–211.

Krathwohl, D., Bloom, B., & Masia, B. (1964). *Taxonomy of educational objectives, Handbook II: Affective domain.* New York: Longman.

Krippendorf, K. (1975). The systems approach to communication. In B. D. Ruben & J. Y. Kin (Eds.), *General systems theory and human communication* (pp. 138–163). Rochelle Park, NJ: Hayden Book Company, Inc.

Kulhavy, R. W., & Stock, W. A. (1989). Feedback in written instruction: The place of response certitude. *Educational Psychology Review, 1*(4), 279–308.

Kulhavy, R. W., & Wager, W. (1993). Feedback in programmed instruction: Historical context and implications for practice. In J. V. Dempsey & G. C. Sales (Eds.), *Interactive instruction and feedback* (pp. 3–20). Englewood Cliffs, NJ: Educational Technology Publications.

Kulik, C.-L. C., Kulik, J. A., & Bangert-Drowns, R. L. (1990). Effectiveness of mastery learning programs: A meta-analysis. *Review of Educational Research, 60*(2), 265–299.

Kuo, M. A., & Hooper, S. (2004). The effects of visual and verbal coding mnemonics on learning Chinese characters in computer-based instruction. *Educational Technology Research and Development, 52*(3) 23–34.

Lacey, A. R. (2005). Humanism. In T. Honderich (Ed.), *The Oxford guide to philosophy* (pp. 401–402). New York: Oxford University Press, Inc.

Lamont, C. (1984). Humanism. In D. D. Runes (Ed.), *Dictionary of philosophy* (p. 147). Totowas, NJ: Rowman & Allanheld.

Lancaster, F. W., & Warner, A. (1985). Electronic publication and its impact on the presentation of information. In D. H. Jonassen (Ed.), *The technology of text: Principles for structuring, designing, and displaying text, Volume Two* (pp. 292–309). Englewood Cliffs, NJ: Educational Technology Publications.

Land, S. M., & Hannafin, M. J. (1997). Patterns of understanding with open-ended learning environments: A qualitative study. *Educational Technology Research and Development, 45*(2), 47–73.

Langdon, D. G., Whiteside, K. S., & McKenna, M. M. (1999). *Intervention resource guide: 50 performance improvement tools.* San Francisco: Jossey-Bass/Pfeiffer.

Larson, M. B., & Lockee, B. B. (2004). Instructional design practice: Career environments, job roles, and a climate of change. *Performance Improvement Quarterly, 17*(1), 22–40.

Laszlo, E. (1972). *Introduction to systems philosophy.* New York: Harper & Row Publishers.

Laverde, A. C., Cifuentes, Y. S., & Rodríguez, H. Y. R. (2007). Toward an instructional design model based upon learning objects. *Educational Technology Research and Development, 55*(6), 671–681.

Leshin, C. B., Pollock, J., & Reigeluth, C. M. (1992). *Instructional design strategies and tactics.* Englewood Cliffs, NJ: Educational Technology Publications.

Levie, H. W., & Dickie, K. E. (1973). The analysis and application of media. In R. N. W. Travers (Ed.), *Second handbook of research on teaching* (pp. 858–882). Chicago: Rand McNally.

Liaw, S., (2002). Understanding user perceptions of world-wide web environments. *Journal of Computer Assisted Learning, 18,* 137–148.

Lin, H., & Chen, T. (2007). Reading authentic EFL text using visualization and advanced organizers in a multimedia learning environment. *Language Learning & Technology, 11*(3), 83–106.

Littlejohn, S. W. (1989). *Theories of human communication* (3rd ed.). Belmont, CA: Wadsworth Publishing Company.

Liu, C. H., & Matthews, R. (2005). Vygotsky's philosophy: Constructivism and its criticisms examined. *International Education Journal, 6*(3), 386–389.

Loh, E. L. (1972). *The effect of behavioral objectives on measures of learning and forgetting on high school algebra* (University of Maryland). Retrieved from Dissertations & Theses: Full Text (Publication No. AAT 7227259).

Lumsdaine, A. A. (1963). Instruments and media of instruction. In N. L. Gage (Ed.), *Handbook of research on teaching* (pp. 583–682). Chicago: Rand McNally.

Lumsdaine, A. A. (1964). Educational technology, programmed learning, and instructional science. In E. R. Hilgard (Ed.), *Theories of learning and instruction* (pp. 371–401). Chicago: University of Chicago Press.

Lundvall, B., & Johnson, B. (1994). The learning economy. *Journal of Industry Studies, 1*(2), 23–42.

Lyman, R. L., O'Brien, M. J., & McKern, W. C. (2002). *W.C. McKern and the Midwest Taxonomic Method.* Tuscaloosa, AL: The University of Alabama Press.

Mager, R. (1962). *Preparing instructional objectives.* Palo Alto, CA, Fearon Publishing.

Mager R. E., & McCann, J. (1961). *Learner-controlled instruction.* Palo Alto, CA: Varian Publishing.

Mager, R., & Pipe, P. (1997). *Analyzing performance problems or you really oughta wanna* (3rd ed.). Atlanta, GA: Center for Effective Performance.

Main, R. G. (1993). Integrating motivation into the instructional design process. *Educational Technology, 33*(12), 37–41.

Marker, A., Huglin, L., & Johnsen, L. (2006). Empirical research on performance improvement: An update. *Performance Improvement Quarterly, 19*(4), 7–22.

Marsh, P. O. (1979). The instructional message: A theoretical approach. *Educational Communications and Technology Journal, 27*(4), 303–318.

Martin, B. L., & Briggs, L. J. (1986). *The affective and cognitive domains: Integration for instruction and research.* Englewood Cliffs, NJ: Educational Technology Publications.

Martin, F., & Klein, J. D. (2008). Effects of objectives, practice and review in multimedia instruction. *Journal of Educational Multimedia and Hypermedia, 17*(2), 178–189

Martin, F., Klein, J. D., Sullivan, H. (2007). The impact of instructional elements in computer-based instruction. *British Journal of Educational Technology, 38*(4), 623–636.

Mayer, R. E. (1982). Learning. In H. Mitzel (Ed.), *Encyclopedia of educational research* (pp. 1040–1058). New York: The Free Press.

Mayer, R. E. (2008). Applying the science of learning: Evidence-based principles for the design of multimedia instruction. *American Psychologist, 63*(8), 760–769.

Mayer, R. E., & Anderson, R. B. (1992). The instructive animation: Helping students build connections between words and pictures in multimedia learning. *Journal of Educational Psychology, 84*(4), 444–452.

Mayer, R. E., Griffith, E., Jurkowitz, I. T. N., & Rothman, D. (2008). Increased interestingness of extraneous details in a multimedia science presentation leads to decreased learning. *Journal of Experimental Psychology: Applied, 14*(4), 329–339.

Mayer, R. E., Heiser, J., & Lonn, S. (2001). Cognitive constraints on multimedia learning: When presenting more material results in less learning. *Journal of Educational Psychology, 93*(1), 187–198.

Mayer, R. E., & Moreno, R. (1998). A split-attention effect in multimedia learning: Evidence for dual processing systems in working memory. *Journal of Educational Psychology, 90*(2), 312–320.

McDonald, F. J., & Allen, D. W. (1967). *Training effects of feedback and modeling procedures on teaching.* Palo Alto, CA: School of Education, Stanford University.

McIntyre, J. J. (2003). Participatory democracy: Drawing on C. West Churchman's thinking when making public policy. *Systems Research and Behavioral Science, 20,* 489–498.

McKay, J., & Wager, W. W. (2007). Electronic performance support systems: Visions and viewpoints. In R. A. Reiser & J. V. Dempsey (Eds.), *Trends and issues in instructional design and technology* (2nd ed.) (pp. 147–155). Upper Saddle River, NJ: Merrill/Prentice-Hall.

McLellan, H. (2004). Virtual realities. In D. H. Jonassen (Ed.), *Handbook of research on educational communications and technology* (2nd ed.) (pp. 461–497). Mahwah, NJ: Lawrence Erlbaum Associates, Publishers.

McNeil, J. D. (1969). Forces influencing curriculum. *Review of Educational Research, 39*(3), 293–318.

Means, T. B., Jonassen, D. H., & Dwyer, F. M. (1997). Enhancing relevance: Embedded ARCS strategies vs. purpose. *Educational Technology Research and Development, 45*(1), 5–17.

Medsker, K., Hunter, P., Stepich, D., Rowland, G., & Basnet, K. (1995). HPT in academic curricula: Survey results. *Performance Improvement Quarterly, 8*(4), 6–21.

Melton, A. W. (1964). The taxonomy of human learning: Overview. In A.W. Melton (Ed.), *Categories of human learning* (pp. 325–339). New York: Academic Press.

Merrill, M. D. (1983). Component display theory. In C. M. Reigeluth (Ed.), *Instructional-design theories and models: An overview of their current status* (pp. 279–333). Hillsdale, NJ: Lawrence Erlbaum Associates, Publishers.

Merrill, M. D. (1999). Instructional transaction theory. In C. M. Reigeluth (Ed.), *Instructional-design theories and models, Volume II: A new paradigm of instructional theory* (pp. 397–424). Mahwah, NJ: Lawrence Erlbaum Associates, Publishers.

Merrill, M. D. (2002). First principles of instruction. *Educational Technology Research and Development, 50*(3), 43–59.

Merrill, M. D., & Boutwell, R. C. (1973). Instructional development: Methodology and research. In F. N. Kerlinger (Ed.), *Review of research in education, Vol.1* (pp. 95–131). Itasca, NY: Peacock.

Merrill, M. D., Jones, M. K., & Li, Z. (1992). Instructional transaction theory: Classes of transactions. *Educational Technology, 32*(6), 12–26.

Merrill, M. D., Li, Z., & Jones, M. K. (1990). Second generation instructional design (ID$_2$). *Educational Technology, 30*(2), 7–14.

Merrill, M. D., Li, Z., & Jones, M. K. (1991). Instructional transaction theory: An introduction. *Educational Technology, 31*(6), 7–12.

Merrill, M. D., & Wilson, B. A. (2007). The future of instructional design. In R. A. Reisier & J. V. Dempsey (Eds.), *Trends and Issues in Instructional Design and Technology* (pp. 335–351). Upper Saddle River, NJ: Pearson Education.

Meyrowitz, J. (1993). Images of media: Hidden ferment—and harmony—in the field. *Journal of Communication, 43*(3), 55–66.

Miller, G. A. (1951). *Language and communication.* New York: McGraw Hill Book Company, Inc.

Miller, G. A. (1956). The magical number seven, plus or minus two. *Psychological Review, 63,* 81–97.

Miller, J. G. (1978). *Living systems.* New York: McGraw Hill Book Company, Inc.

Misanchuk, E. R. (1978). Descriptors of evaluation in instructional development: Beyond the formative-summative distinction. *Journal of Instructional Development, 2*(1), 15–19.

Molenda, M., & Boling, E. (2008). Creating. In A. Januszewski & M. Molenda (Eds.), *Educational technology: A definition with commentary* (pp. 81–139). New York: Lawrence Erlbaum Associates, Publishers.

Moore, D. M., Burton, J. K., & Myers, R. J. (1996). Multiple-channel communication: The theoretical and research foundations of multimedia. In D. H. Jonassen (Ed.), *Handbook of research on educational communications and technology* (pp. 851–875). Mahwah, NJ: Lawrence Erlbaum Associates, Publishers.

Moore, D. M., Burton, J. K., & Myers, R. J. (2004). Multiple-channel communication: The theoretical and research foundations of multimedia. In D. H. Jonassen (Ed.), *Handbook of research on educational communications and technology* (2nd ed.) (pp. 979–1005). Mahwah, NJ: Lawrence Erlbaum Associates, Publishers.

Morrison, G. R., Ross, S. M., & Kemp, J. E. (2007). *Designing effective instruction* (5th ed.). Hoboken, NJ: John Wiley & Sons, Inc.

Mory, E. H. (1996). Feedback research. In D. H. Jonassen (Ed.), *Handbook of research on educational communications and technology* (pp. 919–956). New York: Simon & Schuster Macmillan.

Mousavi, S. Y., Low, R., & Sweller, J. (1995). Reducing cognitive load by mixing auditory and visual presentation models. *Journal of Educational Psychology, 87*(2), 319–334.

Mowrer, O. H. (1960). *Learning theory and behavior.* New York: John Wiley and Sons.

Murphy, K. L., & Collins, M. P. (1997). Development of communication conventions in instructional electronic chats. *Journal of Distance Education, 12*(1), 177–200.

Naidu, S. (1997). Collaborative reflective practice: An instructional design architecture for the Internet. *Distance Education, 18,* 259–271.

Nguyen, F., & Klein, J. D. (2008). The effect of performance support and training as performance interventions. *Performance Improvement Quarterly, 21*(1), 95–114.

Ni, X., & Branch, R. (2008). Complexity theory. In J. Spector, M. Merrill, J. van Merrienboer, & M. Driscoll (Eds.), *Handbook of research on educational communications and technology* (3rd ed.) (pp. 29–32). New York: Lawrence Erlbaum Associates, Publishers.

Norman, G. R., & Schmidt, H. G. (1992). The psychological basis of problem-based learning: A review of the evidence. *Academic Medicine, 67*(9), 557–565.

Nurmi, S., & Jaakkola, T. (2006). Effectiveness of learning objects in various instructional settings. *Learning, Media and Technology, 31*(3), 233–247.

Oettinger, A. G. (1969). *Run, computer, run: The mythology of educational innovation.* Cambridge, MA: Harvard University Press.

Oh, S-Y. (2006). *The effects of reusable motivational objects in designing reusable learning object-based instruction* (Florida State University). Retrieved from Dissertations & Theses: Full Text (Publication No. AAT 3216527).

Okey, J. R., & Santiago, R. S. (1991). Integrating instructional and motivational design. *Performance Improvement Quarterly, 4*(2), 11–21.

Oliver, K., & Hannafin, M. J. (2000). Student management of web-based hypermedia resources during open-ended problem solving. *Journal of Educational Research, 94*(2), 75–92.

Oliver, R., & Omari, A. (2001). Student responses to collaborating and learning in a web-based environment. *Journal of Computer Assisted Learning, 17,* 34–47.

Olsen, C. R. (1972). *A comparative study of the effect of behavioral objectives on class performance and retention in physical science* (University of Maryland). Retrieved from Dissertations & Theses: Full Text (Publication No. AAT 7218957).

Olson, D. R. (1974). Preface. In D. R. Olson (Ed.), *Media and symbols, the forms of expression, communication and education. The seventy-third yearbook of the National Society for the Study of Education, Part I* (pp. xi–xii). Chicago: The University of Chicago Press.

Paivio, A. (1991). Dual coding theory: Retrospect and current status. *Canadian Journal of Psychology, 45,* 255–287.

Paivio, A. (2007). *Mind and its evolution: A dual coding theoretical approach.* Mahwah, NJ: Lawrence Erlbaum Associates, Publishers.

Parkhurst, P. E. (1975). Generating meaningful hypotheses with aptitude-treatment interactions. *Audio Visual Communication Review, 23*(2), 171–183.

Pea, R. D. (1993). Practices of distributed intelligence and designs for education. In G. Salomon (Ed.), *Distributed cognitions: Psychological and educational considerations* (pp. 47–87). Cambridge, England: Cambridge University Press.

Pedaste, M., & Sarapuu, T. (2006). Developing an effective support system for inquiry learning in a Web-based environment. *Journal of Computer Assisted Learning, 22,* 47–62.

Perkins, D. N. (1992). Technology meets constructivism: Do they make a marriage? In T. M. Duffy & D. H. Jonassen (Eds.), *Constructivism and the technology of instruction: A conversation* (pp. 45–55). Mahwah: NJ: Lawrence Erlbaum Associates Publishers, Inc.

Perkins, D. N. (1993). Person-plus: A distributed view of thinking and learning. In G. Salomon (Ed.), *Distributed cognitions: Psychological and educational considerations* (pp. 88–110). Cambridge, England: Cambridge University Press.

Petrie, H. G. (1972). Theories are tested by observing the facts: Or are they? In L. G. Thomas (Ed.), *Philosophical redirection of educational research: The seventy-first yearbook of the National Society for the Study of Education, Part I* (pp. 47–73). Chicago: The National Society for the Study of Education.

Petrina, S. (2004). Sidney Pressey and the automation of education, 1924–1934. *Technology and Culture, 45*(2), 305–330.

Pettersson, R. (1989). *Visuals for information: Research and practice.* Englewood Cliffs, NJ: Educational Technology Publications.

Phillips, D. C. (1995). The good, the bad, and the ugly: The many faces of constructivism. *Educational Researcher, 24*(7), 5–12.

Phillips, T., Hannafin, M., & Tripp, S. (1988). The effects of practice and orienting activities on learning from interactive video. *Educational Communications and Technology Journal, 36*(2), 93–102.

Pintrich, P. R., & Schunk, D. H. (2002). *Motivation in education: Theory, research, and applications* (2nd ed.). Upper Saddle River, NJ: Merrill Prentice Hall.

Piskurich, G. M. (2006). *Rapid instructional design: Learning ID fast and right* (2nd ed.). San Francisco: Pfeiffer.

Posiak, F. D., & Morrison, G. R. (2008). Controlling split attention and redundancy in physical therapy instruction. *Educational Technology Research and Development, 56*(4), 379–399.

Pulchino, J. (2006, April 3). *Future direction in e-learning 2006 report.* Retrieved March 29, 2006, from the eLearning Guild database http://www.elearningguild.org.

Putnam, H. (1964). The compleat conversationalist: A "systems approach" to the philosophy of language. In M. C. Mesarović (Ed.), *Views on general systems theory: Proceedings of the Second Systems Symposium at Case Institute of Technology* (pp. 89–105). New York: John Wiley & Sons, Inc.

Quan-Haase, A. (2007). University students' local and distant social ties: Using and integrating modes of communication on campus. *Information, Communication & Society, 10*(5), 671–693.

Quiñones, M. A., Ford, J. K., Sego, D. J., & Smith, E. M. (1995/1996) The effects of individual and transfer environment characteristics on the opportunity to perform trained tasks. *Training Research Journal, 1*(1), 29–49.

Ragan, T. J., & Smith, P. L. (2004). Conditions theory and models for designing instruction. In D. H. Jonassen (Ed.), *Handbook of research for educational communications and technology* (2nd ed.) (pp. 623–649). Mahwah, NJ: Lawrence Erlbaum Associates, Publishers.

Ragan, T. J., Smith, P. L., & Curda, L. K. (2008). Objective-referenced, conditions-based theories and models. In J. M. Spector, M. D. Merrill, J. van Merriënboer, & M. P. Driscoll (Eds.), *Handbook of research on educational communications and technology* (3rd ed.) (pp. 383–399). New York: Lawrence Erlbaum Associates, Publishers.

Ravits, J. (1997). An ISD model for building online communities: Furthering the dialog. In M. Simonson (Ed.), *19th Annual Proceedings: Selected Research and Development Presentations at the 1997 National Convention of the Association for Educational Communications and Technology* (pp. 297–307). Ames, IA.: Iowa State University. (ERIC Document Reproduction Service No. ED 409832).

Reed, G. (1988). *The psychology of anomalous experience: A cognitive approach* (Rev. ed.). Buffalo, NY: Prometheus Books.

Reeves, T. C. (1997). A model of the effective dimensions of interactive learning on the World Wide Web. In J. Veteli (Ed.), *Proceedings of Interaktiivinen Teknologia Koulutuksessa* (pp. 86–93). Hameenlinna, Finland.

Reid, D. J., Zhang, J., & Chen, Q. (2003). Supporting scientific discovery learning in a simulation environment. *Journal of Computer Assisted Learning, 19,* 9–20.

Reigeluth, C. M. (1983). Instructional design: What is it and why is it? In C. M. Reigeluth (Ed.), *Instructional-design theories and models: An overview of their current status* (pp. 3–36). Hillsdale, NJ: Lawrence Erlbaum Associates, Publishers.

Reigeluth, C. M. (1997). Instructional theory, practitioner needs, and new directions: Some reflections. *Educational Technology, 37*(1), 42–47.

Reigeluth, C. M. (1999). The elaboration theory: Guidance for scope and sequence decisions. In C. M. Reigeluth (Ed.), *Instructional-design theories and models, Volume II: A new paradigm of instructional theory* (pp. 425–453). Mahwah, NJ: Lawrence Erlbaum Associates, Publishers.

Reigeluth, C. M., & Darwazeh, A. (1982). The elaboration theory's procedure for designing instruction: A conceptual approach. *Journal of Instructional Development, 5*(3), 22–32.

Reigeluth, C. M., & Frick, T. W. (1999). Formative research: A methodology for creating and improving design theories. In C. M. Reigeluth (Ed.), *Instructional-design theories and models, Volume II: A new paradigm of instructional theory* (pp. 633–651). Mahwah, NJ: Lawrence Erlbaum Associates, Publishers.

Reigeluth, C. M., & Stein, F. S. (1983). The elaboration theory of instruction. In C. M. Reigeluth (Ed.), *Instructional-design theories and models: An overview of their current status* (pp. 335–381). Hillsdale, NJ: Lawrence Erlbaum Associates, Publishers.

Reiser, R. A. (1994). Examining the planning practices of teachers: Reflections on three years of research. *Educational Technology, 34*(3), 11–16.

Reiser, R. A. (2007a). A history of instructional design and technology. In R. A. Reiser & J. V. Dempsey (Eds.), *Trends and issues in instructional design and technology* (2nd ed.)(pp. 17–34). Upper Saddle River, NJ: Pearson/Merrill Prentice Hall.

Reiser, R. A, (2007b). What field did you say you were in? In R. A. Reiser & J. V. Dempsey (Eds.), *Trends and issues in instructional design and technology* (2nd ed.) (pp. 2–9). Upper Saddle River, NJ: Merrill/Prentice-Hall.

Reiser, R. A., & Gagné, R. M. (1983). *Selecting media for instruction.* Englewood Cliffs, NJ: Educational Technology Publications.

Resta, P., & Lafferriere, T. (2007). Technology in support of collaborative learning. *Educational Psychology Review, 19*(1), 65–83.

Richey, R. (1986). *The theoretical and conceptual bases of instructional design.* London: Kogan Page, Ltd.

Richey, R. C. (1992). *Designing instruction for the adult learner: Systemic training theory and practice.* London: Kogan Page, Ltd.

Richey, R. C. (1995). Trends in instructional design: Emerging theory-based models. *Performance Improvement Quarterly, 8*(3), 97–111.

Richey, R. C., & Klein, J. D. (2007). *Design and development research: Methods, strategies, and issues.* Mahwah, NJ: Lawrence Erlbaum Associates, Publishers.

Richey, R. C., Fields, D. C., & Foxon, M. (2001). *Instructional design competencies: The standards* (3rd ed.). Syracuse, NY: ERIC Clearinghouse on Information & Technology.

Roehler, L. R., & Cantlon, D. J. (1997). Scaffolding: A powerful tool in social constructivist classrooms. In K. Hogan and M. Pressley (Eds.), *Scaffolding student learning: Instructional approaches and issues* (pp. 6–42). Cambridge, MA: Brookline.

Romiszowski, A. J. (1981). *Designing instructional systems: Decision making in course planning and curriculum design.* London: Kogan Page, Ltd.

Romiszowski, A. J., & Mason, R. (2004). Computer-mediated communication. In D. H. Jonassen (Ed.), *Handbook of research on educational communications and technology* (2nd ed.) (pp. 397–431). Mahwah, NJ: Lawrence Erlbaum Associates, Publishers.

Rommetveit, R. (1974). *On message structure: A framework for the study of language and communication.* London: John Wiley.

Rosenberg, M. J. (1995). Performance technology, performance support, and the future of training: A commentary. *Performance Improvement Quarterly, 8*(1), 94–99.

Rosenberg, M. J., Coscarelli, W. C., & Hutchison, C. S. (1999). The origins and evolution of the field. In H. Stolovitch & E. Keeps (Eds.), *Handbook of human performance technology* (2nd ed.) (pp. 24–46). San Francisco: Jossey-Bass.

Rossett, A. (1997). That was a great class, but … *Training & Development, 51*(7) 18–24.

Rossett, A. (1999a). Analysis for human performance technology. In H. Stolovitch & E. Keeps (Eds.), *Handbook of human performance technology* (2nd ed.) (pp. 139–162). San Francisco: Jossey-Bass.

Rossett, A. (1999b). *First things fast: A handbook for performance analysis.* San Francisco: Jossey-Bass.

Rossett, A., & Tobias, C. (1999). A study of the journey from training to performance. *Performance Improvement Quarterly, 12*(3), 31–43.

Rothwell, W. J., & Kazanas, H. C. (2004). *Mastering the instructional design process: A systematic approach* (3rd ed.). San Francisco: Pfeiffer.

Rotter, J. B. (1954). *Social learning and clinical psychology.* New York: Prentice-Hall.

Rotter, J. B., Chance, J. E., & Phares, E. J. (1972). *Applications of social learning theory of personality.* New York: Holt, Rinehart & Winston.

Rumelhart, D. E., & Norman, D. A. (1978). Accretion, tuning, and restructuring: Three modes of learning. In J. W. Cotton & R. L. Klatzky (Eds.), *Semantic factors in cognition* (pp. 37–53). Hillsdale, NJ: Lawrence Erlbaum Associates, Publishers.

Rummler, G. A., & Brache, A. P. (1995). *Improving performance: How to manage the white space on the organization chart* (2nd ed.). San Francisco: Jossey-Bass.

Russ-Eft, D. E., Bober, M. J., de la Teja, I., Foxon, M., & Koszalka, T. A. (2008). *Evaluator competencies: Standards for the practice of evaluation in organizations.* San Francisco: Jossey-Bass.

Ryan, T. A. (1975). Analysis of the systems approach. In S. D. Zalatimo & P.J. Sleeman (Eds.), *A systems approach to learning environments* (pp. 118–129). Pleasantville, NY: Docent Corporation.

Saettler, P. (1968). Design and selection factors. *Review of Educational Research, 38*(2), 115–128.

Saettler, P. (1990). *The evolution of American educational technology.* Englewood, CO: Libraries Unlimited, Inc.

Salomon, G. (1974). What is learned and how it is taught. The interaction between media, message, task, and learner. In D. R. Olson (Ed.), *NSSE Yearbook: Media and symbols, the forms of expression, communication and education* (pp. 383–406). Chicago: The University of Chicago Press.

Salomon, G. (1994). *Interaction of media, cognition, and learning: An exploration of how symbolic forms cultivate mental skills and affect knowledge acquisition.* Hillsdale, NJ: Lawrence Erlbaum Associates, Publishers.

Sanders, E. S., & Thiagarajan, S. (2001). *Performance intervention maps.* Alexandria, VA: American Society for Training and Development.

Sasayama, G. M. D. (1984). *Effects of rules, examples and practice on learning concept-classification, principle-using and procedure-using tasks: A cross cultural study* (Brigham Young University). Retrieved from Dissertations & Theses: Full Text (Publication No. AAT 8505584).

Satwicz, T., & Stevens, R. (2008). A distributed perspective on collaborative activity. In J. Spector, M. Merrill, J. van Merrienboer, & M. Driscoll (Eds.), *Handbook of research on educational communications and technology* (3rd ed.) (pp. 163–171). New York: Lawrence Erlbaum Associates, Publishers.

Saye, J. W., & Brush, T. (2002). Scaffolding critical reasoning about history and social issues in multimedia-supported learning environments. *Educational Technology Research and Development, 50*(3), 77–96.

Scardamalia, M., & Bereiter, C. (1996). Computer support for knowledge-building communities. In T. Kotchman (Ed.), *CSCL: Theory and practice of an emerging paradigm* (pp. 14–37). Mahwah, NJ: Lawrence Erlbaum Associates, Publishers.

Schank, R. C., Berman, T. R., & Macpherson, K. A. (1999) Learning by doing. In C. M. Reigeluth (Ed.), *Instructional-design theories and models: A new paradigm of instructional theory, Volume II* (pp. 161–182). Mahwah, NJ: Lawrence Erlbaum Publishers, Inc.

Schraagen, J. M., Chipman, S. F., & Shalin, V. L. (2000). *Cognitive task analysis.* Mahwah, NJ: Lawrence Erlbaum Associates, Publishers.

Schramm, W. (1954). How communication works. In W. Schramm (Ed.), *The process and effects of mass communication* (pp. 3–26). Urbana, IL: University of Illinois Press.

Schramm, W. (1971). The nature of communication between humans. In W. Schramm & D. F. Roberts (Eds.), *The process and effects of mass communication* (pp. 3–53). Urbana, IL: University of Illinois Press.

Schwaninger, M. (2006). System dynamics and the evolution of the systems movement. *Systems Research and Behavioral Science, 23,* 583–594.

Schwartz, N. H. (2008). Exploiting the use of technology to teach: The value of distributed cognition. *Journal of Research on Technology in Education, 40*(3), 389–404.

Schwen, T. M., Kalman, H. K., & Evans, M. A. (2006). A framework for new scholarship in human performance technology. *Performance Improvement Quarterly, 19*(2), 5–26.

Scriven, M. (1991). *Evaluation thesaurus* (4th ed.). Newberry Park, CA: Sage.

Sedlik, J. M., Magnus, A. K., & Rakow, J. (1980). Key elements to an effective training system. *Training & Development Journal, 34*(7), 10–12.

Seel, N. M. (2008). Empirical perspectives on memory and motivation. In J. M. Spector, M. D. Merrill, J. van Merriënboer, & M. P. Driscoll (Eds.), *Handbook of research on educational communications and technology* (3rd ed.) (pp. 39–54). New York: Lawrence Erlbaum Associates, Publishers.

Seels, B. (1994). Visual literacy: The definition problem. In D. M. Moore & F. M. Dwyer (Eds.), *Visual literacy: A spectrum of visual learning* (pp. 97–112). Englewood Cliffs, NJ: Educational Technology Publications.

Seels, B., Fullerton, K., Berry, L., & Horn, L. J. (2004). Research on learning from television. In D. H. Jonassen (Ed.), *Handbook of research on educational communications and technology* (2nd ed.) (pp. 249–334). Mahwah, NJ: Lawrence Erlbaum Associates, Publishers.

Seels, B., & Glasgow, Z. (1998). *Making instructional design decisions* (2nd ed.). Columbus, OH: Merrill Publishing Company.

Seels, B. B., & Richey, R. C. (1994). *Instructional technology: The definition and domains of the field.* Washington, DC: Association for Educational Communications and Technology.

Severin, W. (1967). Another look at cue summation. *Audio Visual Communication Review, 15*(3), 233–245.

Shannon, C. E., & Weaver, W. (1949). *The mathematical theory of communication.* Urbana, IL: The University of Illinois Press.

Sharma, P., & Hannafin, M. J. (2007). Scaffolding in technology-enhanced learning environments. *Interactive Learning Environments, 15*(1), 27–46.

Shellnut, B., Knowlton, A., & Savage, T. (1999). Applying the ARCS model to the design and development of computer-based modules for manufacturing engineering courses. *Educational Technology Research and Development, 47*(2), 100–110.

Sherry, L., & Wilson, B. (1996). Supporting human performance across disciplines: A converging of roles and tools. *Performance Improvement Quarterly, 9*(4), 19–36.

Shin, N., Jonassen, D. H., & McGee, S. (2003) Predictors of well-structured and ill-structured problem solving in an astronomy simulation. *Journal of Research in Science Teaching, 40*(1), 6–33.

Shirvani, H. (2009). Does your elementary mathematics methodology class conform to constructivist epistemology? *Journal of Instructional Psychology, 36*(3), 245–259.

Shrock, S. A., & Geis, G. L. (1999). Evaluation. In H. Stolovitch & E. Keeps (Eds.), *Handbook of human performance technology* (2nd ed.) (pp. 185–209). San Francisco: Jossey-Bass.

Silvern, L. C. (1972). *Systems engineering applied to training.* Houston, TX: Gulf Publishing Company.

Simons, K. D., & Klein, J. D. (2007). The impact of scaffolding and student achievement levels in a problem-based learning environment. *Instructional Science, 35*(1), 41–72.

Skinner, B. F. (1958). Teaching machines. *Science, 128,* 969–977.

Slavin, R. E. (1987). Mastery learning reconsidered. *Review of Educational Research, 57*(2), 175–213.

Smaldino, S. E., Lowther, D. L., & Russell, J. D. (2008). *Instructional media and technologies for learning* (9th ed.). Englewood Cliffs, NJ: Prentice Hall.

Smith, J. M. (1971). *Relations among behavioral objectives, time of acquisition, and retention* (University of Maryland). Retrieved from Dissertations & Theses: Full Text (Publication No. AAT 7104526).

Smith, P. L., & Ragan, T. J. (2005). *Instructional design* (3rd ed.). Hoboken, NJ: John Wiley & Sons, Inc.

Snellbecker, G. E. (1974). *Learning theory, instructional theory, and psychoeducational design.* New York: McGraw-Hill Book Company.

Snow, R. E. (1973). Theory construction for research on teaching. In R. M. W. Travers (Ed.), *Second handbook of research on teaching* (pp. 77–112). Chicago: Rand McNally & Company.

Snow, R. E., & Salomon, G. (1968). Aptitudes and instructional media. *Audio Visual Communication Review, 16*(4), 341–357.

Snyder, M. M. (2009) Instructional-design theory to guide the creation of online learning communities for adults. *Tech Trends, 53*(1), 48–56.

Sokol, R. R. (1974). Classification: Purposes, principles, progress, prospects. *Science, 185*(4157), 1115–1123.

Song, S. H., & Keller, J. M. (2001). Effectiveness of motivationally adaptive computer-assisted instruction on the dynamic aspects of motivation. *Educational Technology Research and Development, 49*(2), 5–22.

Spector, J. M. (2008). Theoretical foundations. In J. M. Spector, M. D. Merrill, J. van Merriënboer, & M. P. Driscoll (Eds.), *Handbook of research on educational communications and technology* (3rd ed.) (pp. 21–28). New York: Lawrence Erlbaum Associates, Publishers.

Spector, J. M., Merrill, M. D., van Merriënboer, J., & Driscoll, M. P. (Eds.) (2008). *Handbook of research on educational communications and technology* (3rd ed.). New York: Lawrence Erlbaum Associates, Publishers.

Spitzer, D. R. (1999). The design & development of high-impact interventions. In H. Stolovitch & E. Keeps (Eds.), *Handbook of human performance technology* (pp. 136–154). San Francisco: Jossey-Bass.

Stolovitch, H. (2000). Human performance technology: Research and theory to practice. *Performance Improvement, 39*(4), 7–16.

Stolovitch, H. (2007). The development and evolution of human performance improvement. In R. A. Reiser & J. V. Dempsey (Eds.), *Trends and issues in instructional design and technology* (2nd ed.) (pp. 134–146). Upper Saddle River, NJ: Merrill/Prentice-Hall.

Stolovitch, H. D., & Keeps, E. J. (1999). What is human performance technology? In H. Stolovitch & E. Keeps (Eds.), *Handbook of human performance technology* (2nd ed.) (pp. 3–23). San Francisco: Jossey-Bass.

Strang, H. R., Badt, K. S., Kauffman, J. M., & Maggio, M. L. (1988). The use of computer-generated speech in training basic teaching skills. *Educational Technology, 28*(7), 37–40.

Strike, K. A. (1972). Explaining and understanding: The impact of science on our concept of man. In L. G. Thomas (Ed.), *Philosophical redirection of educational research: The seventy-first yearbook of the National Society for the Study of Education, Part I* (pp. 26–46). Chicago: The National Society for the Study of Education.

Strike, K. A. (1979). An epistemology of practical research. *Educational Researcher, 9*(1), 10–16.

Sugrue, B., & Stolovitch, H. (2000). Appropriate inquiry in performance technology. *Performance Improvement, 39*(1), 33–36.

Su, Y. (2007). *The impact of scaffolding type and prior knowledge in a hypermedia, problem-based environment* (Arizona State University). Retrieved from Dissertations & Theses: Full Text (Publication No. AAT 3288016).

Sui, P. K., (1986). Understanding Chinese prose: Effects of number of ideas, metaphor, and advance organizer on comprehension. *Journal of Educational Psychology, 78*(6), 417–423.

Summers, C., Reiff, P., & Weber, W. (2008). Learning in an immersive digital theater. *Advances in Space Research, 42*, 1848–1854.

Sun, P.-C., & Cheng, H. K. (2007). The design of instructional multimedia in e-learning: A media richness theory-based approach. *Computers & Education, 49*(3), 662–676.

Sussman, E. B. (1998). Cooperative learning: A review of factors that increase the effectiveness of cooperative computer-based instruction. *Journal of Educational Computing Research, 18*(4), 303–322.

Swanson, R. A. (1999). The foundations of performance improvement and implications for practice. In R. J. Torraco (Ed.), *Performance improvement: Theory and practice* (pp. 1–25). Baton Rouge, LA: Academy of Human Resource Development.

Swanson, R. A., & Holton R. F. (1999). *Results: How to assess performance, learning, and perceptions in organizations.* San Francisco: Berrett-Koehler.

Sweller, J., van Merrienboer, J. J. G., & Paas, F. G. W. C. (1998). Cognitive architecture and instructional design. *Educational Psychology Review, 10*(3), 251–296.

Taylor, B., & Ellis, J. (1991). An evaluation of instructional systems development in the Navy. *Educational Technology Research and Development, 39*(1), 93–103.

Taylor, W. D., & Johnsen, J. B. (1986). Resisting technological momentum. In J. A. Culbertson & L. L. Cunningham (Eds.), *Microcomputers and education. Eighty-fifth yearbook of the National Society for the Study of Education, Part I* (pp. 216–233). Chicago: The University of Chicago Press.

Tessmer, M., & Richey, R. C. (1997). The role of context in learning and instructional design. *Educational Technology Research and Development, 45*(2), 85–115.

Thiagarajan, S. (1997). Evaluation: Seven dimensions, six steps, five phases, and four guidelines. In R. Kaufman, S. Thiagarajan, & P. MacGillis (Eds.), *The guidebook of performance improvement* (pp. 489–517). San Francisco: Jossey-Bass/Pfeiffer.

Tilaro, A., & Rossett, A. (1993). Creating motivating job aids. *Performance and Instruction, 32*(9), 13–20.

Tobias, S. (1987). Learner characteristics. In R. M. Gagné (Ed.), *Instructional technology: Foundations* (pp. 207–231). Hillsdale, NJ: Lawrence Erlbaum Associates, Inc., Publishers.

Tomasulo, F. P. (1990) Phenomenology: Philosophy and media theory – an introduction. *Quarterly Review of Film and Video, 12*(3), 1–8.

Torkelson, G. M. (1977). AVCR – One quarter century: Evolution of theory and research. *Audio Visual Communication Review, 25*(4), 317–358.

Tracey, M. W. (2009). Design and development research: A model validation case. *Educational Technology Research and Development, 57*(4), 553–571.

Travers, R. M. W. (1970). *Man's information system: A primer for media specialist and educational technologists.* Scranton, PA: Chandler Publishing Company.

Tulving E., & Watkins, M. J. (1975). Structure of memory traces. *Psychological Review, 82*(4), 261–275.

Tyler, R. W. (1949). *Basic principles of curriculum and instruction* (originally published as *Syllabus for Education 305*). Chicago: The University of Chicago Press.

Tyler, R. W. (1967). A talk with Ralph Tyler. *Phi Delta Kappan, 49,* 75–77.

Tyler, R. W. (1980). *Landmarks in the literature: What was learned from the eight-year study.* New York University Education Quarterly, *11*(2), 29–32 (ERIC document reproduction #EJ224722).

Uribe, D., Klein, J. D., & Sullivan, H. (2003). The effect of computer-mediated collaborative learning on solving ill-defined problems. *Educational Technology Research and Development, 51*(1), 5–19.

Vadivelu, R., & Klein, J. D. (2008). A cross-cultural analysis of HPT. *Performance Improvement Quarterly, 20*(3/4), 147–165.

Van Gerven, P. W. M., Paas, F., & Tabbers, H. K. (2006). Cognitive aging and computer-based instructional design: Where do we go from here? *Educational Psychology Review, 18*(2), 141–157.

van Merriënboer, J. J. G. (1997). *Training complex cognitive skills: A four-component instructional design model for technical training.* Englewood Cliffs, NJ: Educational Technology Publications.

van Merriënboer, J. J. G. (2007). Alternate models of instructional design: Holistic design approaches. In R. A. Reiser & J. V. Dempsey (Eds.), *Trends and issues in instructional design and technology* (2nd ed.) (pp. 72–81). Upper Saddle River, NJ: Merrill/Prentice-Hall.

van Merriënboer, J. J. G., Clark, R. E., & de Crook, M. B. M. (2002). Blueprints for complex learning: The 4C/ID model. *Educational Technology Research and Development 50*(2), 39–64.

van Merriënboer, J. J. G., & Kester, L. (2008). Whole task models in education. In J. M. Spector, M. D. Merrill, J. van Merrienboer, & M. P. Driscoll (Eds.), *Handbook of research for educational communications and technology* (3rd ed.) (pp. 441–456). Mahwah, NJ: Lawrence Erlbaum.

van Merriënboer, J. J. G., & Kirschner, P. A. (2007). *Ten steps to complex learning: A systematic approach to four-component instructional design.* Mahwah, NJ: Lawrence Erlbaum Associates, Publishers.

Van Tiem, D. M., Moseley, J. L., & Dessinger, J. C. (2001). *Performance improvement interventions: Enhancing people, process, and organizations through performance technology.* Silver Springs, MD: International Society for Performance Improvement.

Van Tiem, D. M., Moseley, J. L., & Dessinger, J. C. (2004). *Fundamentals of performance technology: A guide to improving people, process, and performance* (2nd ed.). Silver Springs, MD: International Society for Performance Improvement (http://www.ispi.org).

Vernon, D. T. A., & Blake, R. L. (1993). Does problem-based learning work? A meta-analysis of evaluative research. *Academic Medicine, 68*(7), 550–563.

Visscher-Voerman, I., & Gustafson, K. L. (2004). Paradigms in the theory and practice of education and training design. *Educational Technology Research and Development, 52*(2), 69–89.

Visser, J., & Keller, J. M. (1990). The clinical use of motivational messages: An inquiry into the validity of the ARCS model of motivational design. *Instructional Science, 19,* 467–500.

Visser, L., Plomp, T., Amirault, R. J., & Kuiper, W. (2002). Motivating students at a distance: The case of an international audience. *Educational Technology Research and Development, 50*(2), 94–110.

Voss, D. R. (2008). *The development of a model for nonverbal factors impacting the design of visual information* (Wayne State University). Retrieved from Dissertations & Theses: Full Text (Publication No. AAT 3310879).

Vygotsky, L. S. (1978). *Mind in society.* Cambridge, MA: Harvard University Press.

Wallace, W. A. (1979). *From a realist point of view: Essays on the philosophy of science.* Washington, D.C.: University Press of American.

Wang, F., & Hannafin, M. J. (2005). Design-based research and technology-enhanced learning environments. *Educational Technology Research and Development, 53*(4), 5–23.

Wang, Y.-S., Wu, M.-C., & Wang, H.-Y. (2009). Investigating the determinants and age and gender differences in the acceptance of mobile learning. *British Journal of Educational Technology, 40*(1), 92–118.

Webb, N. M., & Palincsar, A. S. (1996). Group processes in the classroom. In D. Berliner & R. Calfee (Eds.), *Handbook of educational psychology* (pp. 841–873). New York: Macmillan.

Weber, J. J. (1922). *Comparative effectiveness of some visual aids in seventh grade instruction.* Chicago: The Educational Screen, Inc.

Weinberg, H. (1971). *Effects of presenting varying specificity of course objectives to students on learning motor skills and associated cognitive material* (Temple University). Retrieved from Dissertations & Theses: Full Text (Publication No. AAT 7110839).

Weiner, B. (1966). Effects of motivation on the availability and retrieval of memory traces. *Psychological Bulletin, 65*(1), 24–37.

Weinstein, G., & Fantini, M. (1970). *Toward humanistic education: A curriculum affect.* New York: Praeger Publishers.

West, E. K., Farmer, J. A., & Wolff, P. M. (1991). *Instructional design: Implications from cognitive science.* Englewood Cliffs, NJ: Prentice Hall.

Westley, B. H., & MacLean, M. S. (1955). A conceptual model for communications research. *Audio Visual Communications Review, 3*(1), 3–12.

Wijekumar, K., & Jonassen, D. H. (2007). The role of computer tools in experts solving ill-structured problems. *Computers in Human Behavior, 23*(1), 664–704.

Wild, M., & Henderson, L. (1997). Contextualizing learning in the World Wide Web: Accounting for the impact of culture. *Education and Information Technologies, 2*(3), 179–192.

Wilkinson, G. L. (1980). *Media in instruction: 60 years of research.* Washington, D.C.: Association for Educational Communications and Technology.

Willis, J. (2000). The maturing of constructivist instructional design: Some basic principles that can guide practice. *Educational Technology, 40*(1), 5–16.

Willis, J. (2009a). Three trends in instructional design. In J. Willis (Ed.), *Constructivist instructional design (C-ID): Foundations, models, and examples* (pp. 11–45). Charlotte, NC: Information Age Publishing, Inc.

Willis, J. (2009b). Basic principles of a recursive, reflective instructional design model: R2D2. In J. Willis (Ed.), *Constructivist instructional design (C-ID): Foundations, models, and examples* (pp. 283–312). Charlotte, NC: Information Age Publishing, Inc.

Willis, J. (2009c). A general set of procedures for C-ID: R2D2. In J. Willis (Ed.), *Constructivist instructional design (C-ID): Foundations, models, and examples* (pp. 313–355). Charlotte, NC: Information Age Publishing, Inc.

Wilson, B., & Cole, P. (1991). A review of cognitive teaching models. *Educational Technology Research and Development, 39*(4), 47–67.

Winn, W. (1984). Why media? *Instructional Innovator, 27*(2), 31–32.

Winn, W. (2004). Cognitive perspectives in psychology. In D. Jonassen (Ed.), *Handbook of research for educational communications and technology* (2nd ed.) (pp. 79–112). New York: Simon & Schuster Macmillan.

Winn, W., & Holliday, W. (1982). Designing principles for diagrams and charts. In D. H. Jonassen (Ed.), *The technology of text: Principles for structuring, designing, and displaying text, Volume One* (pp. 277–300). Englewood Cliffs, NJ: Educational Technology Publications.

Wood, D., Bruner, J., & Ross, G. (1976). The role of tutoring in problem solving. *Journal of Child Psychology and Psychiatry, 17*(2), 89–100.

Woolfolk, A. E. (1998). *Educational psychology* (7th ed.). Needham Heights, MA: Allyn and Bacon.

Wu, Y.-T., & Tsai, C.-C. (2005). Development of elementary school students' cognitive structures and information-processing strategies under long-term constructivist-oriented science instruction. *Science Education, 89*(5), 822–846.

Young, A. C., Reiser, R. A., & Dick, W. (1998). Do superior teachers employ systematic instructional planning procedures? A descriptive study. *Educational Technology Research and Development, 46*(2), 65–78.

Young, M. F. (1993). Instructional design for situated learning. *Educational Technology Research and Development, 41*(1), 43–58.

Young, P. A. (2008). Integrating culture into the design of ICTs. *British Journal of Educational Technology, 39*(1), 6–17.

Young, P. A. (2009). *Instructional design frameworks and intercultural models.* Hershey, PA: Information Science Reference.

Zahorik, J. A. (1976). A task for curriculum research. *Educational Leadership, 33*(7), 487–489.

Zhao, S. (1996). The beginning of the end or the end of the beginning? The theory construction movement revisited. *Sociological Forum, 11*(2), 305–318.

Zimmerman, C. L. (1972). *An experimental study of the effects of learning and forgetting when students are informed of behavioral objectives before or after a unit of study* (University of Maryland). Retrieved from Dissertations & Theses: Full Text (Publication No. AAT 7221140).

INDEX